BEAR

BEAR

MYTH, ANIMAL, ICON

WOLF D. STORL

North Atlantic Books
Berkeley, California

Published by   Cover design by Jasmine Hromjak
North Atlantic Books   Book design by Happenstance Type-O-Rama
Berkeley, California   Printed in the United States of America

Originally published as *Der Bar* by AT Verlag. Translated from the original German by Christine Storl.

Bear: Myth, Animal, Icon is sponsored and published by the Society for the Study of Native Arts and Sciences (dba North Atlantic Books), an educational nonprofit based in Berkeley, California, that collaborates with partners to develop cross-cultural perspectives, nurture holistic views of art, science, the humanities, and healing, and seed personal and global transformation by publishing work on the relationship of body, spirit, and nature.

North Atlantic Books' publications are available through most bookstores. For further information, visit our website at www.northatlanticbooks.com or call 800-733-3000.

Library of Congress Cataloguing-in-Publication data is available
from the publisher upon request.

ISBN: 9781623171636 (print) | ISBN: 9781623171643 (ebook)

1 2 3 4 5 6 7 8 9 Sheridan 22 21 20 19 18

Printed on recycled paper

North Atlantic Books is committed to the protection of our environment. We partner with FSC-certified printers using soy-based inks and print on recycled paper whenever possible.

CONTENTS

Poppies are blooming in the fields,

mountains are filled with song;

the blossom of our hearts,

dear bear, come and visit!

RUSSIAN FOLK SONG

Bear sketch from a Stone Age cave (Combarelles, Dordogne; Aurignacien culture)

INTRODUCTION

*The more we get engrossed in time and hurry along with it, the far-
ther away it takes us from the everlasting. This also applies as far
as animals are concerned; never have we known more and (at the
same time) less about them, never more regarding their anatomy and
behavior, and never less regarding their divine nature, their pristine
radiance of the creation. Fairy tales and myths reveal them to be
miraculous and ancient; cults understand them to be divine beings.*

ERNST JUENGER, AUTHOR'S TRANSLATION
FROM *HUND UND KATZ*, 1974

I lived in bear country, in the Rocky Mountains and on the northwestern
Pacific Coast, for about five years at various times, where bears, especially
black bears, are still very present. In 1963, I spent about six months in the
wilderness in Yellowstone where I met up with Bruin[1] on a daily basis. The
kitchen smells attracted bears; they sniffed curiously around doorframes
and garbage cans. I met up with them on secluded hiking paths and *always*
yielded them the right of way while admiring them from a respectful distance. While dozing near a campfire at night, I occasionally heard one sniffing and grumbling out in the darkness. I saw them with playful little bears
splashing in the lake, swimming or fishing, saw them smacking their lips with
pleasure in the berry bushes, saw their blue droppings full of digested blue-
berries and their paw tracks here and there on the muddy banks of streams.
If one spends enough time in the wilderness, one begins to see bears as most
Native Americans or other peoples who live close to nature in bear country do—as magical beings, as "humans" in animal shape, possibly even as
a teacher who can appear in dreams and somehow remind us of our own

primeval, innocent, wild nature. It goes without saying that, in this way, one gets to know bears quite differently than in biology classes, at the zoo, or during a safari vacation.

Now I live near the Alps in southern Germany, near Switzerland. Here, there are beautiful mountains, lakes, and forests. It is wonderful to hike here, but something is missing, something that actually belongs to the country—the howling of wolves that sends a chill up the spine on a full moon night, circling vultures above a dead wild animal, and the occasional bear ambling along the forest path. In our over-civilized world, too little takes our breath away, stirs up our archaic Neanderthal soul, or is able to awaken our awe for the creation. The virtual images of the ever-present entertainment industry can never replace genuine nature or wilderness without which our souls become impoverished. Everything is safe—too safe! Everything is controlled, scientifically documented, and schoolmasterly explained. Even the mountains and forests are becoming increasingly tamed. The old Squamish Chief See Yahtlh (a.k.a. Seattle) was right when he warned the white intruders: "What is man without the beasts? If all the beasts were gone, man would die from a great loneliness of the spirit. For whatever happens to the beasts, soon happens to man" (Seattle 1854).

Now let us ponder our brother and sister bear who have accompanied us along our pathway since the Stone Age, who send dreams and inspirations to medicine people and shamans, who give berserkers strength and courage, and who communicate knowledge to healers. I write as an anthropologist and touch upon not only the biological and ecological aspects of the bear's being but also, and primarily, the ethnological and mythological ones. However, my concern is not simply one of information. I want to focus the bear into our consciousness so that we can dream him back into our hearts. And as far as Western Europe is concerned, we must even dream him back into existence.

CHAPTER 1
Bear Shamans and Plant Healers

The souls! They are not in the bodies.
The bodies are in the souls!

CHRISTIAN SIRY,
DIE MUSCHEL UND DIE FEDER

We have almost forgotten: animals are our helpers and companions. All too often we see them only in a utilitarian way. Cats are useful because they hunt mice, dogs protect property, cows produce milk, and horses are here for us to ride. But when we see animals with the eyes of the heart, we realize that their value cannot be expressed in merely economic and utilitarian terms. While studies have shown that children who grow up with pets are psychologically more well-balanced and that old people also fare better, especially if they are alone, with even just a goldfish or a bird, psychological well-being is not the aspect I want to emphasize. My area of interest goes into a much wider perspective, into the archetype of the animals, and, in this particular case, the mythological bear archetype.

Animals have very subtle senses and often sense what is approaching the people, or even other animals, they live with long before the people themselves become aware of something. It seems they can see into energetic, astral dimensions that are invisible to us. I believe that they even sometimes deflect the karmic suffering, or a similar serious illness meant for their owner, by taking it on themselves, even to the point of dying from it.

Animal allies can help us understand and comply with our own fates better by communicating to us telepathically. Pets can do this, but wild animals are even more powerful because they haven't been through the process of domestication. Some of us have close contact with wild animals and may have the opportunity to experience the phenomenon with deer, wild rabbits, coyotes, birds, snakes, and even tiny animals such as ants and bugs. For people who go far enough into the wilderness, contact with mountain lions, big game, and bears is possible.

In our schools, we do not learn about this connection to animal souls. Our attention is focused on other "more important" things, on lifeless mechanisms and abstract data, which makes it possible for us to function in "the system." But the soul needs something else in order to be happy. Some of us are lucky enough to learn in childhood from relatives or friends how to connect with animals. But even beginner adults can connect with animals simply by opening their souls more when out in nature. Animal spirits tend to appear when we are open to them. Maybe a certain kind of animal has always interested you, or someone in your family knows about an animal that your ancestors were connected to or has always had a special friendship with your family.

UNDERSTANDING THE NATURE OF ANIMALS

Animals are very much closer to our souls than inanimate and completely mute plants or rocks are. They are embodied souls, just like we are. Just like us, they live within a wide realm of likes and dislikes, pain and pleasure. I believe that plants and minerals also actually possess something like a sentient soul and a wise spirit—but these are not directly connected to their physical bodies, as is the case with animated, breathing human beings and animals. Plant and mineral "souls" and "spirits" are definitely much more distant; they exist far beyond their physical bodies, effused in macrocosmic nature. For this reason, logic and material rationality cannot help us behold "soul" and "spirit"—and that is why science, which focuses only on what is logical and can be measured and weighed, cannot show us this aspect of our existence. But shamans have the ability to step outside of ordinary daily consciousness. A strong shaman, who may even have a bear as a totem, can also communicate with these even more remote kinds of spirits.

Animals are *living* beings. Every animal breathes. Its soul flows along with the rhythm of each breath. Feelings, moods, and emotions are closely connected to the rhythm of breathing in and out. The old English word *deor*, related to our word "deer," comes from Indo-Germanic *dheusóm* (Old English *deor*, Dutch *dier*, Swedish *djor*) and means "breathing, animated being." The English word *animal*, which is from Latin *animal*, *animalis*, is related to the concept *anima*, *animus* (soul, breath, wind, spirit, living being). When an animal or a human being stops breathing, the anima, or soul, leaves the body and goes back to another dimension; the warmth of life disperses, and the body stiffens and begins to dissolve into its material components.

As any shaman or anyone who knows animals will tell us, animal souls are pure and cannot be false like human souls can be. No abstract thoughts, no "creative intellect," no "cultural constructs of reality," and no lies split animals from their direct natural environment. Animals are directly and undividedly involved in their environment and surroundings. Smells, sounds, and moods of the environment; sun and moon rhythms; and the seasons determine their activities. They are very much unlike humans who have complicated and abstract symbol systems, who communicate with words, and whose thoughts are linked to a complex and huge physical brain. Nature itself "thinks" for animals. They partake in the orderly intelligence of the macrocosmic spirit.

Seen in this light, it is not really all that clear that the cerebral-cognitive abilities of animals are less developed or less evolved than those of humans. An animal's spirit is not an individually incarnated one; rather, it is part of a "group spirit"—as most indigenous peoples describe it—or part of the spirit of the "lord of the animals" or "in the otherworld," with the "mother of the animals" in a cave, inside a mountain, or "on green pastures in the otherworld." As anthropologists hear from native peoples, this "group spirit" is a spiritual being, a deity, a deva. It is that which guides the wild geese to the sunny south in late fall, guides the birds as to how to build their nests, warns the animals about tidal waves or earthquakes, and lets them know which plants are edible, which are healing, and which are poisonous. In modern times, this is called "instinct," a word that was introduced into science in the seventeenth century and simply means "drive" (from Latin *instinguere* = to prod on, to drive on as a shepherd drives sheep with a stick). But what is it that drives the behavior of the animals? Today, we believe we know: "genetic programming" guides hereditary, stereotypical behavior that has not been learned and can barely be changed by learning processes. Exogenous forces (warmth, light, smells, etc.) trigger endogenous, genetically fixed reactions—this is the present materialistic-positivistic doctrine based on analyses and measurements in laboratories.

Native peoples are not known to have laboratories occupied by busy scientists wearing white jackets, nor have they developed an exclusively rationalistic method to achieve knowledge. Their knowledge of animals is based on living near the wild feathered or furry animals of their surroundings. These human-animal communities stretch over many generations. Humans and animals know each other. They have always had relations with each other—positive and negative—and live in a symbiosis. Native peoples know every sound in their wild natural surroundings. They can also read the finest traces of other beings exactly, such as when leaves have been nibbled on, fresh tracks have been made on moist ground, fur has been snagged by bushes, or feathers are found in unusual places. They have observed animals closely and intensively and over many generations.

But they not only observe externally; they also go beyond the ordinary senses. Dreams and visions as well as shamanic techniques such as deep meditation, long fasts and vigils, trances, dances and drumming for some tribes, and mind-altering plants for some others connect them to the specific animal spirit, with the lord, or the mother, of the animals. They dress in the fur of the animal of a bison, an elk, or a bear, move and dance the way the animal moves, and sing age-old songs about that animal until they are in unison with it and the border between human and animal disappears. Their soul flies then as a raven, owl, or eagle, swims like a dolphin, lopes as a wolf with the pack through the tundra or prairie, or moves as an elk through the forests. Unlike scientists, who only observe animals externally and measure their external reactions, they experience the animals, so to say, from the inside.[1]

According to Cheyenne medicine man Bill Tallbull, humans are not even necessarily the initiators in this intensive interaction. He explained to me that the animals themselves usually seek contact with certain people rather than the other way around. The animals want to give humans inspiration, dreams, helpful instructions, or warnings. Shamans do not look for their totemic animals. Instead, the animals reach out to the humans that they are willing to protect. Anthroposophist Karl Koenig (2013, 90) writes in a similar vein:

> Animals intervene in human lives and humans intervene radically into animals' existence. They interpenetrate each other's lives, and it is not only fear and superstition that determine the different taboos, festivities and magical rites. The inner world of the animals, their actions, their behavior, their imaginations and extrasensory experiences have, in fact, a definite impact on the imagination, feelings, and actions of the native people who live in the same environment.

Animals' telepathic communication with people can be experienced sometimes even from pets or other domesticated animals: One night a cow on the pasture near my house fell into a big, abandoned cement pit full of water that had not been fenced off, and it could not get back out. In the form of the Egyptian cow god Hathor, the cow appeared to me in a dream telling of her distress and where to find her. Authorities arrived just in time to heave her out and save her life. If we are open for it, the connection is there. I also remember how the ants taught me to write when I was a young, slow pupil. I had observed them for hours on end and wrote about what I saw. It was the first time I was really able to write a story. And, once a cormorant's wing was frozen to the ice in a canal behind our house in northern Freesia because a drastic temperature drop had frozen the ice so suddenly. I felt drawn to go out even into the extremely bitter cold, found the bird, and was able to get its wing free. I felt like the bird had literally called me out to gain my attention and help.

For people who still live as hunters and gatherers or as simple tillers, the lord of the animals—the archetypal animal spirit or the primordial animal deity—is not some abstract idea or merely a matter of belief. It is a direct experience. Shamans do not imagine they can talk to animals; they *do* talk to them. The shaman gets answers and acts accordingly, and this communication has concrete effects in the "real" world. What he or she finds out from the animals is not a product of subjective fantasy. Likewise, a young Native American man talks to the animal teacher that appears to him in a vision quest and learns from it what duties he is to fulfill in this life. Siberian shamans speak with the lord of the animals who tells them the location of the wild animals gifted to the humans to hunt and satisfy their hunger. The Inuit *Angakkok* seeks out *Sedna,* the mother of the sea mammals, to find out where the seals are and ask permission to hunt some of them. Animal spirits also show healers which healing plants to use. Animal spirits who have befriended people warn them of approaching danger.[2] Animals also impose rules of conduct and taboos on people that must be adhered to. The gods will also often temporarily take on an animal form.

Our own human ancestors were generally much more connected to nature before industrial times demanded their constant attention, and they also had access to the magical side of animals. Fairy tales, myths, and supposed superstition, all of which have a very long pagan history, demonstrate it definitively. Helpful animals that speak appear again and again to the heroes in these tales, next to fairies, dwarves, and numerous otherworldly beings (Meyer 1988, 114). According to the original Grimms' *Cinderella* tale, doves and birds help Cinderella with the nearly impossible task of separating the bad peas from the good ones in time to go to the ball, and two doves in a hazelnut bush (growing over Cinderella's mother's grave) tell the young prince which of the young women are the false brides—as he rides on his horse with his presumed bride, the doves coo, "Blood in the shoe, blood in the shoe, the wrong bride are you!" (In the original version, the first stepsister cut her toe off to fit into the shoe and the other cut her heel off, thus fooling the prince until the birds told him as they were on their way to his castle). In another Grimms' tale, *The Goose Girl,* Falada the talking horse tells the princess what the imposter, formerly her servant, is hiding from her. Ants also help the dumbest and youngest of three brothers find hidden pearls, ducks help him find a key that was sunk in a lake, and bees show him who the true princess is by landing on her lips because she is the sweetest.

They help him, whose brothers are always shaking their heads over his stupidity, because he is good and kind to the animals. Fairy tales are full of such examples. Even Christian tales are full of stories about animals that have befriended people. A dog and a raven bring Saint Roch bread every day so that he will not starve as he struggles with pestilence. Bears bring wood for Saint Gall so he can build chapels.

We modern, educated people may smile condescendingly and comment, "Yes, but those are just fairy tales." Yes, those are fairy tales, in the literal sense of the word "tales." The German word *maer* (Old High German *mari,* from which comes the German word *Maerchen* = fairy tale) means "lore, narration from an otherworldly dimension." Everyone knows that fairy tales are not based on empirical, scientific facts, but they are still true—an older name in English is actually "wonder tales." They allude to the more essential, transcendent nature of reality. The pure spirit of the different animals, which is filled with wisdom, can only be grasped with shamanic abilities. True tales and legends can tell us about these things.

ANIMAL ALLIES

Indigenous peoples tell us that each person has his or her animal or animal helpers that are connected to the person for better or for worse. The Aztecs called a person's doppelganger *nagual,* that is, the animal that mirrors the person's wild nature. The *nagual* often shows itself during pregnancy. During the night of a birth, Central American Indios watch to see and hear which animals appear. If a jaguar, a boar, or another strong animal appears, then the newborn will surely have a strong personality and will possibly become a shaman. Often the child will be named after his or her animal doppelganger. For European peoples of ancient times, such thoughts were not at all strange either. In Scandinavia, animal doppelgangers were called "accompanying souls," or *fylgia* (related to "follow"). The souls of strong men or women roam the woods as bears, wild pigs, stags, or wolves. They fly through the skies as eagles, ravens, and swans, and as salmon or otters they swim through the waters (Meyer 1988, 262). The warrior Bjarki (described in a story in Chapter 13) fought as a bear on the battlefield while his body lay rigidly in a deep trance.

The connection to powerful animals is shown in such names as Rudolf (Old High German *hrod* and *wolf* = glorious wolf), Bernhard (Old High German *bero* and *harti* = powerful, persevering bear), Bjoern (Swedish for "bear"), Bertram (Old High German *behrat* and *hraban* = shining raven), Arnold (Old High German *arn* and *walt* = he who rules like an eagle), Falko (Old High German *falkho* = hawk, falcon), Art and Arthur (Old Celtic *arto* = bear), and Urs or Ursula (Latin *ursus* = bear). Such names are echoes of totemic name-giving in the realm of European culture.

A shaman without an animal familiar would be weak and helpless, while any animal can be this kind of friend. Ravens can fly out for the shaman and find things that remain otherwise hidden, as was the case for the Old Nordic god, Odin. While his body is lying rigid and in a trance, a South American shaman can send his spirit out in the shape of a jaguar to roam the jungle. With the help of a wild boar spirit helper, a *jhankrie*, a Nepalese shaman, can sleuth out the disease or the magic arrow that is in the patient's body making him sick. Native American shamans, or dream dancers, fly in the form of an eagle while doing the sun dance and return with messages from high spirits to help guide the tribe. "Changed into were-wolves," Lithuanian peasants used to comb through forests and wilderness in the full moon night of May, fighting the winter spirits that bring the last harmful frosts of the year.

A shaman on a magical journey, riding a bear. The drawing on the shaman's costume is that of a Samojedic shaman from Siberia.

Legends are also full of prophetic swans, talking horses, magical stags, and other animals that interact with shamanistic personalities. Albeit our long-forgotten heritage, shamanism is also even relevant for modern people. Shamans, who were once rivals to Christian missionaries, were discredited and bedeviled in the course of Christian conversion in Europe. But, for a long time, many not-quite-converted people remained and would send their animal familiars, *spiritus familiaris*, to roam the forests at night as wolves or bears, moving stealthily as black cats through the villages, or flying as wide-eyed owls.

Although brutally abolished during the Inquisition of the late Middle Ages, witchcraft is one of the last vestiges of old European pagan shamanism (Mueller-Ebeling, Raetsch, and Storl 2003, 48). However, animal alliances did not die with the ascendance of Christianity; Christian traditions, too, include animal companions. Examples include the donkey at the crib, Joseph's riding animal, cows, and sheep at the holy infant's manger, Luke as a steer, John as an eagle, and the Holy Spirit as a dove. Konrad von Wuerzburg even saw Christ as a weasel: "Christ the high weasel in all of his power, slipped down into the depths of hell and bit the murderously poisonous worm to death" (Zerling and Bauer 2003, 333).

The tradition of shamanism and its acquaintance with protective animal spirits is still very much alive for native peoples around the world. For Native Americans, every medicine man or woman has an animal helper that gives them strength, sends dreams, and accompanies them on trips into the spirit world. The animal spirit can adopt the medicine man or woman as a child or even marry him or her—even if the person concerned already has a human spouse. "Eagle dreamers," "bison dreamers," and other medicine people who are bonded with the coyote, the ants, or the badger usually show characteristics of their animal familiars in their own personalities. A shaman who has a stag familiar, the "stag dreamer," will be robust, very healthy, and, like a stag with his harem, enjoy many women. He will be able to heal sick women and possess love magic to bring young men and women together (Lame Deer and Erdoes 1972, 155). A buffalo shaman is a great visionary who can lead his tribe safely, like a buffalo bull would. A snake shaman, who is usually summoned to this role by the bite of a poisonous snake, is connected to these reptiles and knows the herbs and songs that can cure snake bites. The soul of the wolf shaman is pure like freshly fallen snow and can roam far into the spirit world. A rabbit medicine man is very clever, but, like a rabbit, he can also die of shock (Garrett 2003, 29).

Of all the medicine people, the bear shaman, or bear dreamer, has a very special status because bears are, in fact, almost like humans. The Quechua people in the Andes call bears *ukuku*, which means half-human. Those who know bears well tell us that each bear has a very individual personality. However, unlike humans, its ego is not capsuled off and caught up in a net of culturally specified verbal and symbolic constructs. Despite the bear's particular individuality, it remains intimately connected to the macrocosmic group soul, to the bear spirit, to nature. In this way, the bear is a mediator between the worlds, and this is exactly how many indigenous people have experienced the bear. For them, a bear is not simply an animal; a god-like being is hidden under his bearskin. For many Native American and Siberian peoples, such as the Khanty, Tungus, Samoyed, and Finns, the bear is a go-between for the heavenly god and the earth goddess. The bear, this animal of Earth and caves, is attributed to the earth goddess and the fertile female realm. But at the same time, it is also attributed to heavenly spheres, highest gods, and fertile weather deities. Like a genuine shaman, it is a being of both worlds. A bear is a forest animal and a forest human, a strong guardian of the threshold to the otherworld. The bear is the messenger of the gods and as such, a benevolent guest of the middle world, the human world.

An Old Stone Age engraving from La Marche, Vienne, France

A bear shaman partakes of the bear's being. He wears a bear mask, bearskin or a necklace, or amulet of bear teeth or claws, all showing that the bear spirit is his totem; he also possesses the ferocious power of a bear, which can cause even the worst demons of sickness to flee in fear. It follows that a shaman who has been called by the bear spirit is one of the strongest healers. For the Kirati, a tribe in eastern Nepal, which still follows an old shamanistic nature tradition, the bear (*balu*) is considered the grandfather of the shamans. Their shamans always have bear claws with them that function as a talisman, a guru, and a protection (Mueller-Ebeling, Raetsch, and Shahi 2002, 177). They also prefer bearskin for their drums. Anthropologist Christian Raetsch tells that bear parts are taken neither from living bears nor from hunted bears—in order for them to be truly powerful, the shaman has to find them in a trance (Mueller-Ebeling, Raetsch, and Shahi 2002, 251). Even the bark from a tree where a bear has scratched can give power. Mongolian-speaking Burjatians, who live east of Lake Baikal, dry and crumble such bark and mix it with their smudging plants in order to give them more power.[3]

Tungusic shaman with bear paws (Witsen 1692)

11

THE PLANT HEALERS' TEACHER

According to northern Native Americans and many Paleo-Siberian peoples, bears not only know plants but can also pass this knowledge on to human beings. In addition to observing these animals when they dig up the roots and try out the herbs and barks, the shaman can receive dreams from the bear spirit that inspire healing. Consequently, one who has a direct vision or dream about a bear has been summoned to be a plant healer, or plant shaman. Ojibwa medicine man, Siyaka, explained it to anthropologist Frances Densmore:

> The bear is quick-tempered and is fierce in many ways, and yet he pays attention to herbs which no other animal notices at all. The bear digs these for his own use. The bear is the only animal, which eats roots from the earth and is also especially fond of acorns, juneberries, and cherries. These three are frequently compounded with other herbs in making medicine, and if a person is fond of cherries we say he is like a bear. We consider the bear as chief of all animals in regard to herb medicine, and therefore it is understood that if a man dreams of a bear he will become an expert in the use of herbs for curing illness. The bear is regarded as an animal well acquainted with herbs because no other animal has such good claws for digging roots. (Densmore 1928, 324)

The famous Sioux medicine man Lame Deer tells that the Wícása Wakan, the shamans, get their power ("medicine") through a dream or vision sent by an animal teacher.

> Much power comes from the animals, and most medicine men have their special animal which they saw in their first vision. One never kills or harms this animal. Medicine people can be buffalo, eagle, elk, or bear dreamers. Of all the four-legged and winged creatures a medicine man could receive a vision from the bear is the foremost. The bear is the wisest of animals as far as medicines are concerned. If a man dreams of this animal, he could become a great healer. The bear is the only animal that one can see in a dream acting like a medicine man, giving herbs to people. It digs up certain healing roots with its claws. Often in a vision it will show a man which medicines to use. (Lame Deer and Erdoes 1972, 152)

Old medicine men of the Sioux used to have bear claws in their medicine pouches. They pressed the claw into the flesh of the sick person so that healing bear power could flow into the patient's body. The songs of the Sioux bear dreamers ended with *mato hemakiye*—"A bear told me this." Then, everyone knew that this medicine man had received his healing power from a bear. The bear dreamers were especially gifted in straightening out and healing broken bones. "These bear medicine people could heal! We had people who were ninety and one hundred years old and still had all of their teeth!" (Lame Deer and Erdoes 1972, 153).

A bear shaman (Catlin 1844–1845)

Sioux medicine man, Two Shields, tells, "The bear is the only animal which is dreamt of as offering to give herbs for the healing of man. The bear is not afraid of either animals or men and it is considered ill-tempered, and yet it is the only animal which has shown us this kindness; therefore, the medicines received from the bear are supposed to be especially effective" (Densmore 1928, 324). A depth psychologist would say someone who can connect with the "bear" in his or her soul, with his or her deeply buried instinct, and also has clear and sharp senses like a bear, will have easy access to comprehending healing plants.

To what degree bears are honored as healers and knowers of wild plants can be seen in the following tale from Algonquians of the eastern forests.

TALE OF THE MEDICINE BEAR

One day an old man appeared in the village. He came empty-handed and was hungry and sick. His skin was full of abscesses, and he gave off a terrible smell. At the first wigwam, he called out, "Help me! I need a place to stay and some food."

He was sent away because the family was afraid he had something contagious and the children could get it. He fared no better at the second wigwam and was sent away again. This was repeated again and again throughout the whole village. Finally, at the very last wigwam, he was taken in. A very poor woman who had only a few relatives and lived alone in a tiny wigwam at the edge of the village took pity on him. She invited him in and gave him something to eat and a place to sleep. Because he was even sicker the next morning than the day before, she tried to cure him with her familiar house remedies; however, it was no use and he got even sicker. After a few days, he told the woman that the Great Spirit had visited him in a dream and shown him which plant would heal him. The old man described the plant in exact detail, and the woman went out in search of it in the forest and found it. After the woman used this plant as the patient had been told to use it in his dream, he got well again, and, after a few days, as he was preparing to say goodbye, he suddenly got an attack of fever and fell sick again. Again, the house remedies of the poor woman could not cure him. He was already on the brink of death when he dreamed of another healing plant. Again, the woman found the plant and he became well afterward. As he was preparing to say goodbye once more, he began to shake and suddenly had to vomit. Again, he was sick and again he dreamed of the right healing plant. This went on for one year. Then, finally, he really was healed. He got up from his sleeping place and turned around one more time before going to the door and said, "The Great Spirit had told me that there was someone in this village who should learn how to heal the sick with plants. I was sent to you to teach you and this I have done."

He stepped out into the sunlight and the dumbfounded woman stared as he left. Just as the old man was disappearing into the forest, he turned into a big bear. It had been the bear spirit who had summoned the woman to become a plant healer.

A bear shaman or bear dreamer is not only a master of healing herbs but also someone—as seen among the Germanics, Romans, and Celts—who can inspire warriors and bestow them with courage, strength, and discretion in battle. The following is a story about a Pawnee who was a bear shaman and a war chief (Spence 1994, 308).

There was once a boy of the Pawnee tribe who imitated the ways of a bear; and, indeed, he much resembled that animal. When he played with the other boys of his village he would pretend to be a bear, and even when he grew up

Black Foot bear shaman during a healing ceremony (Catlin 1844-1845)

he would often tell his companions laughingly that he could turn himself into a bear whenever he liked.

His resemblance to the animal came about in the following manner. Before the boy was born his father had gone on the warpath, and at some distance from his home had come upon a tiny bear-cub. The little creature looked at him so wistfully and was so small and helpless that he could not pass by without taking notice of it. So he stooped and picked it up in his arms, tied some Indian tobacco around its neck, and said: "I know that the Great Spirit, Tiráwa, will care for you, but I cannot go on my way without putting these things around your neck to show that I feel kindly toward you. I hope that the animals will take care of my son when he is born, and help him to grow up to be a great and wise man." With that he went on his way.

On his return he told his wife of his encounter with the little bear. He told her how he had taken it in his arms and looked at it and talked to it. Now there is an Indian superstition that a woman, before a child is born, must not look fixedly at or think much about any animal, or the infant will resemble it. So when the warrior's boy was born he was found to have the ways of a bear, and to become more and more like that animal the older he grew. The boy, quite aware of the resemblance, often went away by himself into the forest, where he used to pray to the Bear Spirit.

On one occasion, when he was quite grown up, he accompanied a war party of the Pawnees as their chief. They traveled a considerable distance, but ere they arrived at any village they fell into a trap prepared for them by their enemies, the Sioux. Taken completely off their guard, the Pawnees, to the number of about forty, were slain to a man. The part of the country in which this incident took place was rocky and cedar-clad and harbored many bears, and the bodies of the dead Pawnees lay in a ravine in the path of these animals. When they came to the body of the bear-man a she-bear instantly recognized it as that of their benefactor, who had sacrificed smokes to them, made songs about them, and done them many a good turn during his lifetime. She called to her companion and begged him to do something to bring the bear-man back to life again. The other protested that he could do nothing.

"Nevertheless," he added, "I will try." If the sun were shining I might succeed, but when it is dark and cloudy I am powerless."

The sun was shining but fitfully that day, however. Long intervals of gloom succeeded each gleam of sunlight. But the two bears set about collecting the remains of the bear-man, who was indeed sadly mutilated, and, lying down on his body, they worked over him with their magic medicine till he showed signs of returning life. At length he fully regained consciousness, and, finding himself in the presence of two bears, was at a loss to know what had happened to him. But the animals related how they had brought him to life, and the sight of his dead comrades lying around him recalled what had gone before. Gratefully acknowledging the service the bears had done him, he accompanied them to their den. He was still very weak, and frequently fainted, but ere long he recovered his strength and was as well as ever, only he had no hair on his head, for the Sioux had scalped him. During his sojourn with the bears he was taught all the things that they knew—which was a great deal, for all Indians know that the bear is one of the wisest of animals. However, his host begged him not to regard the wonderful things he did as the outcome of his own strength, but to give thanks to Tiráwa, who had made the bears and had given them their wisdom and greatness. Finally, he told the bear-man to return to his people, where he would become a very great man, great in war and in wealth. But at the same time he must not forget the bears, nor cease to imitate them, for on that would depend much of his success.

"I shall look after you," he concluded. "If I die, you shall die; if I grow old, you shall grow old along with me. This tree"—pointing to a cedar—"shall be a protector to you. It never becomes old; it is always fresh and beautiful, the gift of Tiráwa. And if a thunderstorm should come while you are at home throw some cedar-wood on the fire and you will be safe."

Giving him a bearskin cap to hide his hairless scalp, the bear then bade him depart.

Having arrived at his home, the young man was greeted with amazement, for it was thought that he had perished with the rest of the war party. But when he convinced his parents that it was indeed their son who visited them, they received him joyfully. When he had embraced his friends and had been

*congratulated by them on his return, he told them of the bears, who were wait-
ing outside the village. Taking presents of Indian tobacco, sweet-smelling clay,
buffalo-meat, and beads, he returned to them, and again talked with the he-
bear. The latter hugged him, saying:*

*"As my fur has touched you, you will be great; as my hands have touched your
hands, you will be fearless; and as my mouth touches your mouth, you will be
wise." With that the bears departed.*

*True to his words, the animal made the bear-man the greatest warrior of his
tribe. He was the originator of the Bear Dance, which the Pawnees still practice. He lived to an advanced age, greatly honored by his people.*

The story tells of the initiation of a bear medicine man. The young man died
and was revived by the animals, and through this his real mission in life was
revealed to him. When Native Americans who live in bear country kill a
bear, they conduct a similar revival ceremony so that the spirit of the bear
can reincarnate.

THE BEAR SPIRIT POSTURE

A bear draws its immense power out of its middle region, out of the solar
plexus, the power chakra that is located between the navel and the heart
area. One can witness such power when observing bears. Bear shamans also
draw their energy from this center, which Hindus call the *manipurna chakra.*
"The yogi who concentrates on this chakra achieves continuous *siddhi* and is
able to find hidden treasures.[4] He is freed of all sickness and knows no fear of
fire," says Sivananda (Friedrichs 1996, 53). Carlos Castaneda (1925–1998)
also describes the solar plexus as the source of the shaman's magical power.

The first bodily reaction to sudden shock or panic is experienced in the
ganglia of the sympathetic nervous system behind the solar plexus. The feeling
can be described as a "punch in the gut." On the other hand, it can be experienced as a sudden surge of energy, which enables the shocked person to react
instinctively and overwhelm the enemy in an instant or save someone's life
by courageous action. Shamans or mediums often feel that their solar plexus

"opens" during their popularly termed OBEs, or out-of-body experiences. The "spirit body" or "subtle body"—according to the testimony of spiritual mediums—floats on a gossamer-thin "silver string" coming out of this energy center and can experience nonsensory dimensions (Storl 1974, 206).

Elaborate research carried out by cultural anthropologist Felicitas Goodman shows the connection of this chakra with the bear spirit and its healing power. She investigated states of trance and different body positions taken by shamans when they connect with a god or an animal spirit. Each spirit being requires that the human take a different body position when seeking contact. The "bear position"—also called the "healer position"—makes it possible to open the soul for the bear spirit and let its healing energy flow in; it is usually a standing position. The fingers are rolled in and held over the navel so that the knuckles of the index finger touch slightly. The knees are slightly bent, and the feet are parallel to each other and planted solidly on the floor (Goodman 2003, 165). This typical bear position can be verified in statues and carvings in many historical and modern cultures.

Left: *Bear spirit posture (drawing by Nana Nauwald, 2002)* Middle: *"Shaman in contact with the bear spirit" (Nivkh wood carving, Siberia).* Right: *Menhir, Saint-Germain-sur-Rance, France, approximately 2000 BCE.*

CHAPTER 2
Bear Caves and Neanderthals

Europa.   "The West."
the bears are gone
                         except Brunnhilde?
or elder wilder goddesses reborn—will race
  the streets of France and Spain
                with automatic guns—
                in Spain,
Bears and Bison,
Red Hands with missing fingers,
Red mushroom labyrinths;
Lightning-bolt mazes,
Painted in caves,
Underground.

GARY SNYDER, "THE WAY WEST,
UNDERGROUND," IN *TURTLE ISLAND*

Husky Carlo lives near the edge of the forest in a small cabin. He has a workshop there where he creates art with metals and other materials. In his folksy manner, he tries out unusual metal alloys, carves horns, bones, and antlers, and polishes various rocks working them all into unique works of art. Some call him a "junkyard bear" because he is often seen looking through "worthless" things in junkyards. He calls himself a free artist, a label that lets him live an unusual life with dignity.

One day, Carlo chugged past our place with a big load of wood for the winter. He stopped to pass the time of day, and our invitation to have some coffee sounded fine to him.

"But don't make a new batch just because of me. Cold coffee is fine, too, as long as there's sugar in it."

When we had settled down at a table outside, he said with a twinkle in his eye, "So, writing books, are you? Just can't leave those trees standing, can you?" And then with sincere interest he asked, "So what are you writing about?"

I told him that, at the moment, I was writing about the city of Berne, Switzerland, where countless old "bear restaurants" and "bear fountains" are named after the city (*Berne* = bear) and a bear park in the city is inhabited by real bears—and that the city was founded eight hundred years ago by the Duke of Zaehringen after he had slain a bear in a beech forest where the Aare River loops.

"When I came home from Berne, something strange happened to me," I continued. "As I walked through the forest and up the mountain . . . I was probably exhausted as I hadn't slept much . . . Anyway, how should I put it? It was suddenly as if I was walking through an enchanted forest. And suddenly, the forest spoke to me—the firs and beeches, the ferns and rocks—and said that it is so sad that there are no more bears here!"

I noticed a look that was hard to place in Carlo's eyes, but he didn't say anything and continued drinking his coffee.

"And then that night I even dreamt of a huge bear," I continued, "I dreamt he was standing over our bed and licking our small son's face; right at that moment, the little guy [our son] woke up and started crying."

"Hmm," Carlo grumbled in a way that sounded uncannily bear-like and stroked his beard as if stroking some deep thoughts out of it.

"Anyway, not long afterwards, my wife also dreamt of a huge bear in the sky that was flailing with its paws and leaving streaks of lightning-like tracks from its claws in the sky," I went on, telling him what had been stirring our souls since we had started this research about bears.

"So, you want to tell people something about bears," Carlo said in a calm voice, which, nevertheless, did betray a little bit of excitement.

"Yes, I do," I said. "Do you know anything about bears?" I asked without expecting much of an answer—Carlo had mainly seen school walls from the outside and did not seem to be much of a reader either. But he looked at me like he was about to tell me an important secret.

"You know bears are like people. They have souls like people. But like people from way back who still lived free and wild in nature before they were constricted into settlements and became fearful and isolated themselves from other living beings. You know what I mean? Look over there. Do you see the Saentis?" Carlo paused so I could keep up with his unusual thoughts. I looked over Lake Constance, over into the area around the city of St. Gallen, which can be seen well from our mountain home. The sacred Saentis Mountain raged up into the sky shining like an opal.

Carlo continued, "There are caves up there. They're named Dragon's Den, Wild Man's Cave, Wild Chapel, and so on. The Neanderthals, early Stone Age people, lived there peacefully with bears. At that time, people could still understand the language of animals. The Neanderthals are called stupid and lacking in culture nowadays, but, really, we are the primitive people, degenerate by comparison. Primitive actually means connected to the pristine, to nature." He paused as if reminiscing. "These Neanderthals didn't really distinguish much between human and animal, and between human and bear anyways. Of course, the bears that lived in the caves with them were seen as especially mighty and sacred. They could protect them from hungry wolves or saber-toothed tigers. The cave people kept the bones and skulls of the bears and buried them ceremoniously so that the bear spirit would stay with them—and whenever they did hunt bears for their warm furs or fat for wounds and sickness, they did it only with permission of the bear spirit and only at certain sacred times. They drank the blood of the sacrificed animal, too, in order to get power from it. They hung bear claws around the necks of their kids so that the mighty bear spirit would also protect them. Yes, these people lived with bears! Even nowadays some primitive hunting peoples in East Asia keep a bear as an honored guest in their village."

Carlo talked like someone who had been there, either as a Neanderthal or as a bear in a cave. He spoke like a visionary. Bears as friends and living companions of Stone Age humans—so to speak, as pets! Theosophists and other esotericists make similar claims: During the "Age of Atlantis," human beings were clairvoyant. They strutted along with gods and divine heroes and communicated with the group soul of animals fearlessly and without superstition; they communicated with them through rites and ceremonies and also, of course, with the mighty bear spirit. But what researcher would take such assertions seriously?

My university professors who taught me prehistory saw things fundamentally differently. It was always a question of the relentless fight for survival, of rivalry with the shaggy beasts for protected caves over which these animal-like hominoids disputed with the beasts using smoke, noise, and pit traps and by rolling stones down cliffs. According to this theory, "survival of the fittest" was the motto of the Stone Age. Not only did they fight over living quarters, they were also greedy for bear meat and fat to stave off hunger. They desired the bear's bones to make scrapers and daggers, its sinews to tie things, its fur as blankets and cloaks, its lower jaw as a bludgeoning weapon, and its teeth for magical ornamentation. The human being has always been an exploiter who knows no scruples, the eternal *Homo economicus!*

According to this same theory, irrational superstition or fear had driven these early hominoids to ceremoniously bury bear skulls and draw bears on the walls of the caves. Cultural anthropologists speak of defensive magic, and psychologists hold it up as proof of the primeval angst inherited by humans into modern times.

Was it as Carlo, who looked ever more like a bear in human form to me, claimed? Or were the learned professors right? Had they perhaps projected their own acquisitiveness and fear onto bears and wild people? Did the scanty finds from excavations and cave expeditions encourage the projection for a worldview that is not unambiguous?

Illustration of Neanderthals hunting a cave bear

AN ENIGMATIC WOMAN

Carlo finished his coffee and headed back to his place. For a long time, I looked over toward the Swiss mountains and thought about bear caves and Neanderthals.

Neanderthals were an old human race, square-built with strong bones and jaws, thick bulges as eyebrows over the eyes, and a brain size that even somewhat exceeded that of modern humans. During the Middle Paleolithic, that is, during the last interglacial and the last ice age, Neanderthals settled in the Near East, parts of North Africa, and the tip of Asia that is now called Europe.

Experts initially believed that the first Neanderthal skeleton, which was discovered by chance in 1856, was a "pathological idiot" or maybe a Cossack who had been left behind and died when Napoleon's army retreated. When more skulls and bones were discovered, Darwinists believed that their theory of evolution had been proven and that the missing link had been found between modern humans and their ape-like ancestors. They proposed that Neanderthals were an inferior human primal species that was completely eradicated by the more highly developed *Homo sapiens*. As ever more facts came to the surface, though, the theory fell apart like a house of cards—not only did Neanderthals use fire, but they also carved blades, hammers, scrapers, and arrowheads out of firestone with distinctive style and sewed with sinews and leather straps to make tents and clothing. It became clear that they had a sophisticated culture that enabled them to endure cold winter snowstorms and extreme drops in temperature.

They also obviously had a spiritual culture (i.e., experience and knowledge about things that are "invisible" to us), which is evidenced by the burial of grave goods with their dead. One grave was found decorated with wild goat horns (in today's Uzbekistan), while the bones of the dead in another grave were colored with red ochre. In Iraqi Kurdistan, pollen analyses suggested several dead had been lain out on a bed of flowers. The plants were mainly healing ones that are even still used today in herbal healing.

For a very long time, it was believed that Neanderthals had no language but communicated like gorillas and chimpanzees. But in 1989, a sixty-thousand-year-old Neanderthal lingual bone (also hyoid, or tongue, bone) (*os hyoideum*) was found in Kebara, Israel. And, in 1995, a fifty-thousand-year-old thigh bone of a young bear with four finger holes in it was found in a cave in Slovenia. Professor Jelle Atema from Boston University was able to play soft, harmonious sounds on this bear flute. Since these discoveries were made, there is not a shadow of a doubt that these people had language and music.

The spiritual life of these early people was especially connected to bears; prehistorians speak of a veritable Neanderthal bear cult. In several places in Europe, in fact (in the Karavanks in Slovenia, in Yugoslavia, and in the Jura

Mountains) researchers have found evidence of the seemingly quite strange custom of ritual bear burial. In Regourdou (Dordogne, southern France), researchers found a rectangular pit with twenty bear skulls in it and covered with a heavy stone plate. In one Neanderthal grave, a bear's humerus was found. Evidence also suggests that some Neanderthals were wrapped in bear-skins when buried (Sanders 2002, 153).

Neanderthals making a bear altar (drawing by Martin Tiefenthaler)

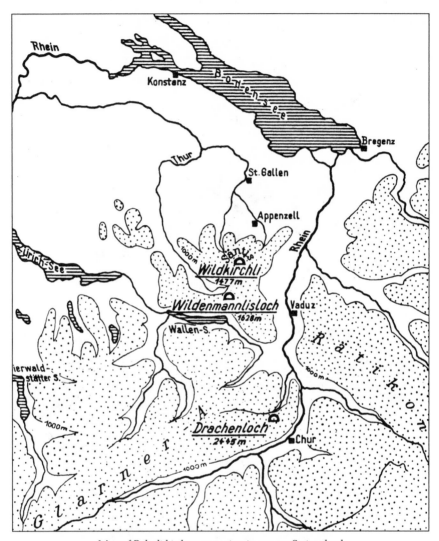

Map of Paleolithic bear cave sites in eastern Switzerland

The most well-known Neanderthal bear ritual centers are certainly the three caves in eastern Switzerland: Wild Chapel (*Wildkirchli*), Wild Man's Cave (*Wildmannlisloch*), and Dragon's Den (*Drachenloch*), where the remains of over one thousand bears were found.[1] The Wild Chapel cave, with an altitude of 4,921 feet (1,500 meters) and located under the sheer cliffs of the Saentis Peak (8,208 feet, 2,502 meters), was long a place of refuge for the hermits of the Abbey of Saint Gall (in St. Gallen, Switzerland). In the tenth century, famous monk Ekkehart is supposed to have written his heroic epos, *The Waltharilied*, there. In 1657, a pastor built a chapel in front of the cave's arch. Because big bones and teeth were found again and again, medieval minds were sure that the cave must have been a dragon's den. For that reason, the chapel was dedicated to Archangel Michael, the dragon slayer. Soon after the last hermit who lived there fell to his death in 1851 while gathering herbs, a guesthouse was built in front of the second entrance to the cave. In 1904, the curator of the natural historical museum of St. Gallen, Emil Baechler, climbed up to this guesthouse, which was built like a swallow's nest onto the cliff. He started digging. The huge bones that he dug up were naturally not from dragons but from long extinct, huge cave bears. When he discovered a piece of flint stone, he realized that early humans had also been active there (Honoré 1997, 208).

Bone altar in the Dragon's Den, Glarner Alps

A few years later, Baechler happened upon an even more significant find above the Alpine village Vaettis in the Glarner Alps: at the altitude of 8,021 feet (2,445 meters) in a steep cliff wall, he found what is now called the "Dragon's Den," one of the oldest human cult sites and the most significant proof of a bear cult. Next to the fire pit filled with ashes, wood and bone remains, and chips from lithic tools, Baechler discovered a "bone altar" at which was placed a bear skull with a bear's thigh bone attached through the zygomatic arch (see illustration 13). In other dark corners of the cave, stone cases stored long leg bones of bears. One of the cases contained seven bleached bear skulls with their snouts carefully placed toward the direction of the cave opening. The analysis of the wood and bone remnants showed that the cases were around seventy thousand years old, which makes them the oldest known objects made by human hands (Lissner 1979, 200).

Seventy thousand years! It is staggering to imagine what that means! Just 2,000 years ago, we began to record our modern history; 2,700 years ago, "eternal" Rome was founded; 4,500 years ago, the first Egyptian pyramid was built; 8,000 years ago, the first village-like settlements were built; and 12,000 years ago, the last ice age ended in Europe and North America. But the bear cult is at least seventy thousand years old and possibly even many thousands of years older than that.

Another very interesting find in one of the caves—this one in the Wild Man's Cave—was a carved and polished figure of a woman about four to five inches (twelve centimeters) tall and located in a niche in the wall.[2] This figure, also seventy thousand years old, is the oldest known human representation in which a cave, a bear, and a woman are connected—a theme that will be seen over and over again with later Stone Age peoples, in myths and legends of many peoples, and which may even also appear in our dreams and in the depths of our own souls. Who is this mysterious woman? We will have the opportunity to get to know her better.

Most modern prehistorians no longer see square-built, stocky Neanderthals as either physically or mentally "primitive." They were completely human and nowadays are classified unquestionably as Homo sapiens. It is also no longer claimed that they were exterminated by a superior race. Indeed, in a 2010 breakthrough, the Max Planck Institute for Evolutionary Anthropology was able to prove the genetic link of Neanderthals with Europeans, northern Asians, and Native Americans.[3] In other words: Neanderthals are also partially our ancestors, and these ancestors of ours honored bears, communicated with them, and shared a biotope with them.

STONE AGE HUNTERS AND BEAR SHAMANS

After the last ice age, human beings of the type Cro-Magnon appeared in northern climates. They were also hunters and lived in the same natural rhythms of the animals they hunted and the plants that they gathered. They roamed the steppes and tundra, following reindeer, horses, wooly rhinoceroses, aurochs, buffalo, and mammoths. Occasionally, and in the summer, they set up their camps (as a few hunting tribes even still do today) in forested areas near snowy mountains with frequent rain where there are lots of berries, fleshy roots, nuts, and fat insect larvae and where there are whole shoals of trout and periodic salmon runs in clear waterfalls. In such biotopes, which biologists describe as "bear biotopes," nomadic bipeds met up with their cousin, the bear, at every turn. They were, so to speak, in the middle of the bear's richly filled pantry.

The senses of these Paleolithic hunters were likely much sharper than those of their civilized descendants—in any case, neither nerve-wracking big city noise nor the constant background sound of the entertainment industry distracted their attention. They were able to intently observe and get to know very well the grumbly, shaggy bears whose guests they were. They understood the bear's wordless language. They would also take encounters with bears into their dreams and express them in dance and ritual. Surely, they admired the strength, cleverness, and natural dignity of the bear no less than modern hunting people do. But a bear is also dangerous, and early humans may have been shy to speak its name. Various nicknames, such as "grandfather" or "grandmother," "the sacred animal" (as some of the forest Native Americans still call it), "honey eater," "honey paw," "gold foot," "the old man with paws," "furry old man" (a name given by Slavs and Siberians), and the like have been passed down the generations. Maybe they also just simply called it Bruin (Dutch for "brown," from Indo-Germanic *bher* = brown) like the northern European tribes did. But no matter what the bear was called, it was known everywhere as a magical, sacred being.

Bears are at home in the wide range of the tundra and forests from Scandinavia to North America and between the Tropic of Cancer and the North Pole. The polar bear lives in the center of this interhemispheric area, in the Arctic Circle. Arctic, from the Greek word *arktos,* actually means "bear."[4] These words go back to the Indo-Germanic root *rktos* = destroyer, demon. (It is questionable whether polar bears are an independent species because polar bears and brown bears can easily mate and have offspring.)

Black bears and sloth bears roam the southern border of this habitat, and Andean bears live in South America. All peoples from this huge expanse, the European, Asian, and North American tribes, have traditionally honored bears with elaborate ceremonies as the undisputed king of the animals and of the forest. In this regard, folklorists speak of a "circumpolar bear cult." Not until one reaches southern latitudes does the predatory cat cult appear. In this southern area, the lion, jaguar, panther, or tiger takes the place of the king of the animals and companion of the goddess.

KINDS OF BEARS

The following kinds of big bears (*Ursidae*) live in the northern hemisphere.

Cave bear (*Ursus spelaeus*): Unfortunately, this mighty bear that lived in Europe during the ice age and the interglacial became extinct about ten thousand years ago. Though this bear lived exclusively as a vegetarian, it exceeded all other bears in height and weight. In the "Dragon's Cave" near Mixnitz in Austria, the bones of over thirty thousand cave bears were found—in the Middle Ages, they were believed to be dragon bones. The clay in that area, which was full of bear manure and bones, was dug up to be used as phosphate fertilizer in the nineteenth century. Sixty freight trains with fifty wagons each were filled with it. A cave near Velburg, Germany, had so many bear bones in it that it was also considered useful as fertilizer. These caves were the homes and also the graveyards of bears for thousands of years (Dehm 1976, 21). Though occasional stone shavings and wood charcoal indicate that Neanderthals also visited these caves, it does not necessarily mean that they killed bears there but that they found bones there that could be useful. If they did hunt bears, then probably only when the bears were in winter hibernation. But then the snow was so deep up in the high mountains and it was so hard to get there that it is unlikely that they made such an effort.[5]

Cave bear (reconstructed according to finds in Mixnitz, Austria, 1931)

Short-faced bear (Arctodus): The American short-faced bear, which also died out ten thousand years ago, was even bigger than the cave bear. It was not a plant eater but a meat-eating predator that could, like wolves and big cats of prey, run very fast and hunt horses, bison, and deer. It presumably died out after the ice age, along with the fauna that fed big game, and was simultaneously squeezed out by the smaller brown bear that had come from Eurasia over the Bering Strait land bridge. The considerably smaller **Andean bear,** or **spectacled bear** (*Tremarctos ornatus*), that lives in South America is a distant relative of the short-faced bear.

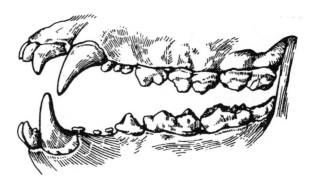

Set of teeth from a brown bear

Brown bear (*Ursus arctos arctos*): As its teeth indicate, the brown bear, which lives in the forests of Eurasia and North America, is an omnivore. Most of the brown bear population, about 100,000 bears, lives in Russia and Siberia; some 32,000 live in the United States, approximately 21,000 in Canada, and roughly 5,000–7,000 in small, isolated areas in Europe. In Ireland, brown bears disappeared during the Bronze Age, and in Central Europe they were almost completely decimated in the nineteenth century. The Alaskan Kodiak bear (*Ursus arctos middendorfii*), the biggest living brown bear; the extinct California grizzly bear (*Ursus arctos californicus*); the blonde Syrian brown bear (*Ursus arctos syriacus*); and the much-feared North American brown bear (or grizzly bear) (*Ursus arctos horribilis*) are each a subspecies of the brown bear, whose habitat once stretched from the North Pole to the mountains of Mexico but today is only still found in Canada and the northwestern United States. The name *grizzly* comes from "grizzled" meaning "with gray-speckled hair."

The American **black bear** (*Ursus americanus*), also called "baribal" in a Native American language (which one is not clear), is smaller than the brown bear. Black bears are excellent climbers and are very adaptable, which has made them into the biggest bear population today with an estimated population of some 500,000.

The **polar bear** *(Ursus maritimus)* can swim a wide sea arm with considerable speed. Compared to other modern brown bears that mainly eat plants and cadavers, it is a predator and hunts. Like the Alaska Natives who share its habitat, it hunts fish, seabirds, seals, and even occasional reindeer or caribou.

Polar bear

The **Asiatic black bear** *(Ursus tibetanus)* is found in China, Japan, and northern India.

The **sun bear** *(Ursus malayanus)* is a small, obstinate bear. Found in forests from Malaysia to Burma, it is unfortunately becoming a rare sight.

The **sloth bear** *(Melurus ursinnus)*, a small fruit- and termite-eating bear, is at home in India and from Bengal to Sri Lanka.

The **panda** represents its own family *(Ailuropoda melanleuca)* and is known worldwide

WWF®
World Wide Fund for Nature

World Wide Fund for Nature

as the mascot of the World Wildlife Fund (WWF). It is an East Asian bear that feeds off bamboo.

The **raccoon** (*Procyon*) is also related to bears, and is from the family *Procyonidae*.

Raccoon washing a corncob

Dogs, wolves, martens, badgers, skunks, and otters are distantly related to bears. They are all descendants of a common Miocene ancestor.

According to the worldview of old hunting peoples, any cave was seen as a womb, the womb of the all-bearing earth goddess who watches over the unborn animal and human spirits in the depths of the Earth. No one may enter her deeply hidden realm of light without a penalty, unless that person has her blessings or is under her protection. To these peoples, it was akin to a miracle that bears could disappear into the belly of the earth and then, as soon as the days grow longer, reappear as if reborn and rejuvenated—with adorable cubs. For this reason, bears were seen in many places as messengers of the earth goddess. They were messengers of the animal/soul guardian who rules over wildlife and whose favor determines all of life, including human life. It was even believed that the Mother Earth—in German fairy tales often called Mother Goose or Mother Hulda—could even take on the form of a bear. Her spouse, the lord of the sky, could also appear as a bear. It is, thus, easy to see how the bear could be the incarnation of the highest mysteries for the circumpolar hunting peoples.

Fearless people, such as shamans, who are summoned by spirit beings, searched for caves to establish contact with the mother or father of the animals. This was not an easy task, but it was necessary because these spirit beings had the power to send the game into the outer world to let it multiply or keep it inside thus causing the people to starve. Similar to approaching a bear itself, one had to approach the goddess with extreme care and know her likes and dislikes. By going into a cave, singing sacred songs there, fasting, drumming, or being completely still, the shaman became like a bear himself. He identified with the mighty animal. Then the goddess, her horned companion, the "lord of the forest," or the bear spirit could appear to the shaman, teach him, and initiate him into the great secrets of nature.

An animal that can go in and out of the womb of the great goddess without incident, like a man's member in a woman's vulva, is surely also a guardian of fertility and birth—an opener of life's door. Consequently, the woman bear shaman was always a midwife. Even as recently as in ancient Greece, the bear goddess Artemis was the patron of women in labor. In some Slavic languages, a new mother is even called "bear." And for the Cheyenne, *nako,* meaning "bear," is the formal name for mother. Such expressions as "to bear a child" come from the Indo-Germanic root word *bher* ("to carry, to bring," and also "brown"); in German, related words are *ge*-baer-*en* = to bear and *Ge*-baer-*mutter* = uterus, with the German word for bear (*Baer*) within each word.

Bear caves in the Pyrenees or in the Alps, which were difficult to reach and to which shamans retreated to find inner visions or youths were brought for initiation into tribal secrets, were cult places and not for living in (not meaning to offend Carlo's ideas). They were cult centers of reindeer and mammoth hunters of the early Paleolithic. These nomads left humanity's very first genuine works of art deep inside of caves; they lived in wigwams similar to those of the Native Americans of the prairie, hunted with spears, fished with fishing hooks, and wore carefully sewn leather clothes. All animals that could be hunted, all species that the earth mother bore from her womb, were drawn on the cave walls—including the bear. In Trois-Frères Cave, for example, a wounded bear can be seen with blood streaming from the mouth. In the same room, there is a dancing shaman with a long beard, buck's antlers, wolf ears, and a horse's tail. His hands are bear paws. He is probably the lord of the animals, the companion of the goddess.

The Lady of the Caves, the bearer of the animals and the companion of the bear, is also found again and again in early Paleolithic art. One finds small statues of a woman carved from ivory, bones, or soapstone that are jestingly called "Venus figures" by prehistorians. They are not like modern fashion models, but are fat with big breasts, fleshy backsides, and big bellies. Their exaggerated genitals make us think of motherhood, pregnancy, and fertility.

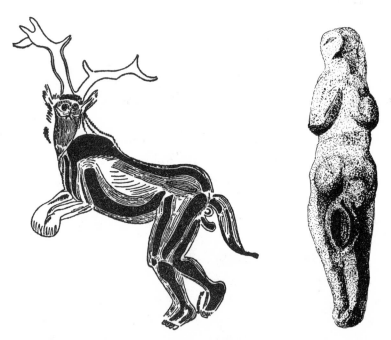

Left: The magician of Trois-Frères (Ariège, France, early Paleolithic) Right: One of the many "Venus figures," the goddess of the cave, birth, and bears (small statue from Montpazier, Dordogne, France)

CHAPTER 3
Bear Ancestors

Women, protect your womb from the bear!

SIBERIAN PROVERB

I t is not uncommon for woodland peoples to refer to clans, as well as entire tribes, as descendants of mystic bears. They claim to be bears in human shape. In Homer's *Odyssey,* too, it is suggested that the superhero Odysseus comes from bear genes. His father, Laertes, is described as "bear-like" and his forebears go back to Cephalous, who is claimed to have sired a bear son, an *Arkeisios,* with a female bear (Sanders 2002, 164).

Anthropologists call this widely spread belief of having wild animals as forebears "totemism."[1] Consequently, members of the same clan or small tribe who originate from the same totemic animal are not allowed to marry each other as that would be incest. The members of a kin group are said to have the qualities of their totem animals. For instance, eagle people have large noses and especially piercing eyes; wolf people are courageous and wild and have a lot of stamina; ant people are always busy; buffalo people are stubborn. Bear people are called thick skulled but clever; they appear to be slow and cuddly, but woe to whomever crosses them. They are often of strong, sturdy stature and, like their animal relatives, have a weakness for sweets. Clan members often have names that allude to their totem animal.

It was believed that the elders, priests, or shamans of the clan could communicate with the totem animal or even occasionally turn into this animal and roam through the wilderness. Of course, a totem animal is not hunted like other animals, which would be like killing a relative. Its flesh was also

taboo except on very special days when it was hunted ritually and eaten ceremoniously. At such sacred totemic feasts—which anthropologists compare to
the Christian Last Supper—the clan members take in the strength, wisdom,
and other virtues of the sacred animal and reconnect with the ancestral spirit
that blesses and protects them.

OSBORN (ASBJØRN), THE DIVINE BEAR

Many European peoples, such as the Goths and the pagan Danes, also
believed that they were descendants of a bear ancestor. This bear was not
a common bear, however, not the kind one can meet up with in the woods.
He was *Osborn* (Scand. *Asbjørn* or Old High German *Anspero*), the *Asen-* or
god-bear himself who was none other than mighty Thor (Donar, Thunar).
Thor is the full-bearded, red-haired storm god. His firestone hammer causes
lightening to sear across the sky, and, while thundering loudly, it pulverizes
the skulls of monsters, lindworms, and ice and frost giants that make life hard
for farmers. He is the hero and friend of the spring goddess, Freya, who drives
winter numbness and infertility from the countryside. His hammer spews
fiery, starry sparks out into the cosmos and, at the same time, causes fertile
rain to fall, refreshing the dry earth.

It is surely no coincidence that for peoples in East Asia and Siberia, such
as the Ainu and natives of Kamchatka, the weather god is a cosmic bear.
They hear it roaring during storms and howling wind and see its shape in
mighty, dark thunderclouds. For the Navajo, a whirlwind is a huge grizzly
bear in the sky (Arens and Braun 1994, 48):

> *With zigzag lightning projecting from the ends of my feet I step.*
> *With zigzag lightning streaming out of my knees, I step . . .*
> *With zigzag lightning streaming out from the tip of my tongue I speak.*
> *Now a disc of pollen rests on the crown of my head.*
> *Gray arrowsnakes and rattlesnakes eat it.*
> *Black obsidian and zigzag lightning streams out from me in four ways.*
> *Where they strike the earth, bad things, bad talk does not like it.*
> *It causes the missiles to spread out.*
> *Long life, something frightful I am.*

Now I am.
There is danger where I move my feet.
I am whirlwind.
There is danger where I move my feet.
I am a gray bear.
When I walk, where I step, lightning flies from me.
Where I walk, one to be feared.
Where I walk, Long Life.
One to be feared I am.
There is danger where I walk.

Nearly everywhere bears stand for fertility. God-bear Thor is no exception. He increases fertility in the gardens and fields and also helps people have children. His sparkling hammer symbolizes a man's member, and Germanic tribes used to put a hammer, Thor's hammer, in the lap of the bride at the wedding to ensure that the blessings of fertility would accompany the marriage.

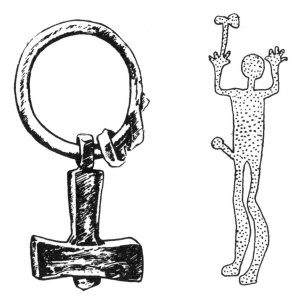

Left: Thor's hammer as an amulet, tenth century. Right: Cave painting in Sweden
from the Bronze Age, probably representing the hammer god, Thor.

Thor, son of the heavenly king, was also worshiped as *Jardar Bur,* the son of the earth. He is earthy and bawdy, like a bear, and the biggest and strongest of the gods *(Asen).* His ravenous hunger and sheer unquenchable thirst are infamous. Only a chieftain or a coarse farmer who works the earth can drink and eat as much. Like the forest bear, he also loves the sweet honey of the bees—but preferably in the form of mead, or honey wine. Over the course of time, the characteristics of Thor were transferred to the first and mightiest of men, to Charles the Great (Charlemagne). Just as the bear is the king of the animals, Charles the Great is the king of men, chosen by the goddess. We will learn more about Charles the Great, bear among men, later.

BEAR CHILDREN

Throughout Siberia, one finds peoples who proudly claim they are descended from bears. The Ainu claim to be descendants of a bear goddess and a human to whom she gave her love. Some tribes tell that they are descendants of children who had been set out in the woods and adopted, nursed, and raised by female bears. Someone raised on bear's milk would inevitably become strong and courageous—the perfect tribal founder for tribes that have a healthy portion of self-esteem. The Oroqen, a tribe of hunters and fishermen living on the banks of the Amur River in Siberia, believe that a mystical female bear that lives in a cave on the dark side of the moon was their first ancestor. She nurses the unborn human souls before they descend to earth into a womb. When an Oroqen dies, the soul returns to this ancestral bear. The Evenks, to whom we are indebted for the word "shaman," are also a Siberian tribe that subsists from fishing, hunting, and reindeer husbandry. The following legend tells of their first ancestor, a girl named Kheladan:

> *Kheladan lived many, many years ago, at a time when hunters still stalked game with stone-tipped spears. One day, the young woman rambled deep into the forest where she encountered many animals. When she met a bear, it said: "Kill me and butcher me! And then when you lie down to sleep, put my heart very near to you. Put my kidneys on the hearth where it is nice and warm and the spirits go in and out. Put my head near the fire too. Put the duodenum and the anus opposite yourself on the wall. Spread my fur coat across the ditch*

outside in front of the door so that it can dry well, and, finally, hang the intestines in the trees near the door to dry!"

The fearless young maiden did as she was told. When the merry chirping of the forest birds woke her up the next morning, she discovered, instead of the bloody bear's heart, a beautiful, strong young man lying next to her. Next to the hearth where she had put the kidneys, there were two rosy-cheeked children sleeping peacefully. The bear's head had turned into an old man who was watching over the children. On the opposite wall where she had put the duodenum and anus, an old grandfather and grandmother were sleeping and snoring.

When she opened the door of the yurt and squinted into the sun, she saw that the fur coat had turned into a herd of fat reindeer. There were so many that they filled the entire valley. The intestines in the trees had turned into reindeer halters. That is how the bear sacrifice of the ancient ancestor brought forth not only the Evenk race but also their entire livelihood.

Other Evenks tell the tale of their primeval ancestor somewhat differently. They trace the origin of their tribe back to the marriage of the young woman to a bear rather than the bear's sacrifice. Some tales from Siberia and North America tell that it was not at all a case of humans descending from bears, but that bears originated from humans. According to an Altai-Turk legend, only two humans remained on earth after a deluge: an old man and his wife. They fled into the forested mountains, ate bark and roots, and gradually turned into bears. This is why bears have an almost human intelligence.

The Cherokee also believe that humans are not descended from bears, but, to the contrary, bears come from a human ancestor. The following story about the origin of bears emphasizes the similarity between bears and humans (Mooney 2011, 148):

In the long ago time, there was a Cherokee Clan call the Ani-Tsaguhi (Ahnee-Jah-goo-hee), and in one family of this clan was a boy who used to leave home and be gone all day in the mountains. After a while he went oftener and stayed longer, until at last he would not eat in the house at all but left at daybreak and did not come back until night. His parents scolded him but it did no good. The boy still went every day until they noticed that long brown hair was beginning to grow all over his body. Then they wondered and asked him why it was that he wanted to spend so much time in the woods and why he would not even eat at home. Said the boy, "I find plenty to eat there, and it is better than the corn and beans we have in the settlements, and pretty soon I am going into the woods to stay all the time." His parents were worried and begged him not leave them, but he said, "It is better there than here, and you see I am beginning to be different already, so that I cannot live here any longer. If you will come with me, there is plenty for all of us and you will never have to work for it. But if you want to come, you must first fast seven days."

The father and mother talked it over and then told the headmen of the clan. They held a council about the matter and after everything had been said and thought over they decided: "Here we must work hard and do not always have enough. He says there is always plenty without work. We will go with him." So they fasted seven days, and on the seventh morning all the Ani-Tsaguhi left the settlement and headed for the mountains as the boy led the way.

When the people of the other towns heard of it they were very sorry and sent their headmen to persuade the Ani-Tsaguhi to stay at home and not go into the woods to live. The messengers found them already on the way and were surprised to notice that their bodies were beginning to be covered with hair like that of animals because for seven days they had not taken human food and their nature was changing. The Ani-Tsaguhi would not come back, but said, "We are going where there is always plenty to eat. Hereafter we shall be called Yonv(a) (bears). But you will always be our relatives and when you yourselves are hungry come into the woods and call us, we shall come to give you our own flesh. You need not be afraid to kill us, for we shall live always." Then they taught the messengers the songs with which to call them and bear hunters still have these songs. When they had finished the songs, the Ani-Tsaguhi started on their way again and the messengers turned back to the settlements, but after going a little way they looked back and saw a drove of bears going into the woods.

GOLDEN BEARS

Sir Francis Drake, who sailed the world's oceans by order of Her Majesty Queen Elizabeth I of England and lightened numerous Spanish galleons of their freights of gold, also reached, among other places, the coast of what is now Northern California. There, he discovered a beautiful park-like country-side where simple, friendly people lived. They appeared to him to be so happy and healthy that he called them "Arcadian people." He could not compare the beautiful country to any other than classical Arcadia, the Greek province in which simple shepherds lived in peace and natural grace. The old pirate—for the Spanish, Sir Francis Drake was nothing but a pirate—certainly hit the mark with his choice of words. Arcadian means "bear country," and there was an exceptional number of bears in the Northern California wilderness at that time; they were also especially beautiful with their golden, shiny fur. The white settlers, who came to the area later, called them "golden bears." This American Arcadia was a blessed land with a mild climate and never lacked rain. The oak, manzanita, and madrone forests, which were interspersed with flowering meadows, transitioned into pine forests at higher altitudes and offered humans and bears—whose tastes are not very different at all—a rich and nourishing food supply.

The main nourishment for both humans and bears were acorns from different kinds of oak trees. The Native Americans gathered them, ground them to meal, and filled finely woven baskets with it. They then placed the baskets in flowing water in order to filter out the indigestible bitters and tannic acid. The treated acorn meal was then stored for winter and used to make soups and bake a kind of unleavened flat bread. The bears definitely had an easier time of it—they ate acorns until they were fattened up and could spend the entire winter lazily hibernating in their cozy dens.

The food supply was not restricted to acorns, however. All kinds of fish, river crabs, small animals, seeds from wild grasses, roots, wild onions, oil-bearing pine nuts, mushrooms, berries, the strawberry-flavored fruits of madrone trees, chestnuts, and sweet-sour manzanita berries enriched the menu. With such abundance, the native peoples were not only able to survive without hard work and technology but were also able to live a truly good life—and the golden bears had it just as good. The indigenous tribes of the area respected bears and did not hunt them for they felt closely related to them. The bears were able to prosper and have a large population without any rivalry with humans. It was a true paradise, an Arcadia.

For the Pomo, a tribe of Californian natives, the bear spirit initiated young people into the hidden secrets of life and revealed the duties of adulthood to them. A young Pomo adult would spend four days in the forest, completely naked and without water. During this time, a big bear appeared to him, tested his courage, "killed" him with blows from his paws, taught him, and then gave his life back to him in the end. The scars that were left from the bear claws were to remind the victims of this meeting with the bear for their entire life, and the sacred teachings the bear had imparted to them.

The Shasta, from farther north, are said to be nearly indistinguishable from bears. That is, for them, human beings are simply a cross between the forest bear and the Great Spirit. The bear was something along the lines of the father of humanity. How it came to be human is told in the following legend:

The Great Spirit once roamed the earth but was not pleased because the earth was dry and there were no animals. He picked up dry leaves and tossed them up into the air while singing magical songs; hence, the dry leaves turned into colorful birds and flew off into the distance. Then he took the stick that he had been using to walk with and broke it into many pieces. He strew the tiny splinters from the bottom of the stick into the water where they became fish and swam off. The rest of the short and long pieces were turned into different animals that now populate the mountains, forests, prairies, and deserts.

He put a lot of effort into the top end of the stick that was very hard and thick and had been the knob. Out if it, he formed the crown of his creation—the bear. The bears became so big and strong that the Great Spirit almost became worried about his own creation. These golden-furred beings went on two legs and were gifted with their hands like human beings later were. They grouped into big clans and lived from hunting. They used clubs to stalk other animals.

The Great Spirit left the earth to them and retreated into the inside of Mount Shasta. In the middle of this mountain, there is a sunny land where all gods and spirits are at home. The souls of dead animals come to this land to gather up strength until they are reborn in the outer world. The Great Spirit felt very good with all of these beings.

One day a horrible hurricane rampaged in the outer world so that even the huge mountain quaked. The Great Spirit told his young daughter she should go out to see what was going on and tell the wind to calm down. As soon as the little red-haired girl peeped out from behind the cliff, the wild wind snatched her and flung her to the foot of the mountain. What wonderful things she saw in the outer world! She marveled and admired everything until, completely exhausted, she fell asleep under a tree. A bear found her there asleep when he came back from hunting. He grabbed the helpless girl's arm and dragged her along to his hut. The bear wife took pity on the cute little being and gave her milk from her breast so that she could regain her strength. She raised the child with her own son as if she were her own child.

The years passed and the girl grew up to be a beautiful young maiden. The bear's son fell in love with her and they married. The children that were born of this union were especially beautiful. They all had smooth reddish skin and an especially fine spirit—after all, their mother was a child of the Great Spirit. At the same time, they had the courage and strength of the bear lineage. The entire bear population was very happy about the finely developed children. With great pride, they sent a messenger to the Great Spirit to tell him that his daughter was now a married woman and a mother.

When the Great Spirit heard this, he was not at all pleased. This had all happened without his knowledge and agreement. He charged down the mountain to the bears, raging in anger. The old bear mother died straight away of fear when he appeared, and the other bears were completely at a loss. They wailed and begged for forgiveness, but that only made the Great Spirit even angrier.

"Be quiet! Be quiet forever!" he cursed them, and since then bears cannot express their thoughts in words.

"You will have to walk on all fours like ordinary animals," he continued, "and instead of with clubs, you will have to use your teeth and claws to fight."

Then he drove the new race, which was half bear, half Great Spirit, away from the bears. From then on, they were to live separately. He took his daughter and disappeared with her into Mount Shasta.

These new beings—half animal, half god—were the first human beings, and, because they were descendants of bears, real human beings respect bears and would never hurt them.

47

Sacred Mount Shasta, a dormant volcano, crowned with eternal snow, and 14,179 feet high (4,322 meters) reigns majestically over the forest and lava landscape of Northern California. The children of the mountain, the Arcadians and the golden bears, have long since disappeared. For the gold diggers, who swarmed to California like locusts in 1848, the "redskins" were nothing but bothersome, unpredictable savages, who stood in the way of civilization and progress.

During the time of the gold rush, the repeating rifle came onto the market, an advance in technology that made the brutal land conquest considerably easier for the newcomers. The government paid ten dollars apiece for slain bears. In those times, ten dollars was good extra income for hunters, and some of them even killed up to two hundred bears a year. In 1870, bait laced with strychnine sped up the extermination. In 1922, the mission had been accomplished and the last golden bear of California was shot. Ironically enough, that same year the golden bear was chosen as California's heraldic animal that still graces the state flag.

Meanwhile, the plight of native peoples in California also carried on. In 1911, the local sheriff captured and jailed the last free native who had been found hiding in a slaughterhouse when he previously still had been in the wilderness. The starved and exhausted man was the last of a small clan of Yahi, who had hidden from trigger-happy white men under an overhanging cliff out in the wilderness. They had called their last refuge Grizzly Bear Hideout, as if hoping to conjure up the mighty spirit of the most powerful inhabitant of the country. Anthropologist Alfred Kroeber of the University

The California state flag

of California, Berkeley, read about the capture of the wild native in the newspaper and, in the name of science, took him under his wing. Ishi, as he became known, lived in a university building where he then died in the spring of 1916, the last Stone Age human being of California.

Hippies who built communes in the late 1960s in Northern California and cultivated marijuana revered Mount Shasta as a sacred mountain. A full-bearded forest dweller once told me that the bears and the Native Americans live inside Mount Shasta, but one day they will come out again when the world becomes a less evil place.

CHAPTER 4
Forest Maidens and Feral Mountain People

*What seems so odd to us about bears is how humanlike their move-
ments are, the way they tread on their soles, stand up, and the way
they use their front paws like hands.*

R. GERLACH, *DIE VIERFUESSLER*

For modern city people of today, a bear is just another animal like any
other. It is known in zoos as a clumsy, ravenous, over-sized "teddy bear"
or from books and television films as a funny and dumb cartoon character. Except in some more serious media, such as *National Geographic* articles,
bears are often portrayed as cute, cuddly creatures. The bear itself seems less
interesting than the fantasies about it.

The idea of a godly bear sounds as strange to modern city people as
it does to cowboys and ranchers who see a bear as an incarnated devil
and a dangerous beast of prey that ravages cattle and sheep. Ranchers
are not willing to admit that bears, by nature scavengers, usually do not
kill animals but are just the first to find the perished creatures, chase all
other scavengers off, and make a meal of them. But bears have no chance
against ranchers' firearms, which they use freely even though the state
reimburses such loss of livestock.

Bears as objects of fantasy (illustration from a sheet of music, England, 1910)

Native peoples, who learn about the secrets of nature starting from childhood, see the bear as a hunter, fisher, and gatherer just like they are themselves. The kind of thinking that puts humans, animals, plants, and spirits into neatly separated categories, the way that so-called civilized people do, is foreign to them. They see bears not only in the forest but also in their visions and dreams. The bear spirit appears to them in the rituals of the shamans, and they know that bears speak in a language that can be understood if one listens deeply to one's own heart. They know bears and it is no problem for them to see them as god-like, or at least as beings similar to humans. Consequently, for them it is conceivable that their ancestors were bears, that a mother bear may adopt lost human children, or that a bear might even occasionally steal a human woman.

Indeed, who can deny certain similarities between bears and humans? Bruin does not walk on his toes, like most four-legged mammals; he walks on the soles of his feet like humans do, stepping down on the whole foot, from the toes to the heels. He often stands up like a two-legged being, and, when he comes out of hibernation, his soles are soft and tender like human feet are when they kick off their shoes for the first time in the spring. He has thick fur, but Siberian hunters find it uncanny how skinned bears resemble humans. When a female bear is skinned, they say for example, it looks astonishingly like a human woman particularly in the breast area, the hips, and the thighs.

Bears use natural caves for their dens or dig holes in bushy embankments and cover them with branches, earth, and sod. They make themselves comfortable beds of moss, leaves, or hay and strew bracken and aromatic herbs on them to keep fleas, ticks, and other parasites at bay. Nomadic Stone Age humans, prehistoric Native Americans, and Siberian forest people hardly did things much differently; they, too, built cave homes for the harsh time of winter then left them in the summer (for leather, teepee-like tents).

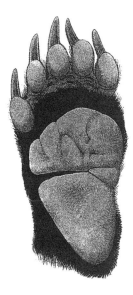

25a: Sole of a bear's foot.

25b: Skeleton of back legs and back paws of a bear.

GLUTTON AND GOURMET

A bear's favorite bill of fare is hardly different from that which human foragers eat. Its dentition shows that, just as the human being, it is an omnivore. Bears use their front paws when they eat, bringing them up to the snout, just as human beings use their hands. They are regular gourmets with a liking for sweet and sour. They are renowned for their love of wild honey, and they also cherish the sweet spring sap of maple trees, which they lick after slicing the bark with a claw. They are also fond of sweet and sour berries. They have even been seen slurping sweet clover blossoms and other blossoms that are especially rich with nectar. As a special sour delight for the taste buds, they like ant larvae and ant eggs. Bears like sour tastes so much that they will even lick batteries that have been tossed in garbage dumps. They can resist the sour smell of the silage in farm silos as little as they can resist honeycombs.

When Bruin awakes from winter hibernation, he first quenches his tremendous thirst with fresh water. Then he searches for fresh, juicy grass, wild onions, young ferns that are just beginning to unroll, fresh stinging nettles, sour dock, taro roots, young yarrow shoots, skunk cabbage, and various other fresh greens. Whenever he comes across a squirrel's nest, he will plunder that, too. Not a few half-starved trappers and mountain men have eaten that which a bear will eat to survive themselves when their supplies had run out during the severe Rocky Mountain winter. Many believe that primeval humans also learned quite a bit by observing bears.

In the summer, bears continue eating herbs and roots, skillfully swat fish straight out of the water, and unearth mice, snails, grasshoppers, caterpillars, frog spawn, mussels, and other small animals. They scratch small crevices open and turn over big rocks to find worms and bugs hidden there. The lenses of their eyes function like magnifying glasses from which none of these small creatures can hide. Behavioral scientists have been surprised at how many moths—up to thirty thousand a day—a black bear eats in the summer months.

All in all, bears have a well-balanced, protein-rich diet on which they thrive very well. We modern people, who are used to cellophane-packed foods, find the thought of eating such foods horrible, but for native peoples who shared and still, to a degree, share the same habitat as the bears—such as the native peoples in Siberia—most of these things are also welcome human nourishment. Bears are mostly vegetarian; about 75 percent of their nourishing calories come from plants and the rest from animals. Anthropologists have recorded the same ratio in most hunters and gatherers.

Bears also like to eat slain animals as much as humans do. But whereas humans cook, cure, or dry the meat, bears bury it for a few days to make it tastier. Bears also like small portions of raw meat, like human gourmets relish a medium rare steak or the Inuit like rancid, raw meat with maggots as a very special delicacy. But they are not enthusiastic hunters. Instead of hunting, they tend to rely on the "might is right" principle and steal freshly slain prey from wolves, pumas, and even Siberian tigers! In 1996, a bear was observed driving nine wolves off a fresh stag cadaver. Studies in Yellowstone and Glacier National Parks have shown that grizzlies are able to take away up to one fourth of a cougar's prey (Busch 2000, 85).

In the fall, bears fatten themselves up with beechnuts and other nuts, acorns, rowanberries, wild fruits, mushrooms, and other delicacies. Research in behavioral science shows that bears strip bushes of up to 200,000 berries a day. In ancient Roman times, bears were veritable pests in the vineyards, which, for them, were nothing but abundant feeding grounds.

Bears seem to have a weight regulator that works similarly to a thermostat and is of interest to nutritionists. In the summer, they keep a steady normal weight and do not carry any extra weight around at all; in the fall, their metabolism adjusts to fattening up for the winter. Through these studies, nutritionists hope to find out how humans might also learn to control weight gain and loss (Bates 2013).

Each bear has its own cherished territory that it has been familiar with since it was a cub. However, contrary to other animals that mark and defend their territories, bears do not have a fixed range. The so-called scratched trees at the edge of the territory belong as much to the realm of fairy tales as the old belief that bears are born as a formless clump and the mother licks them into bear shape.[1] But there are trees at strategic places (for instance, at bear crossings), and bears rub themselves on them to leave messages for each other—these are the billboards of the bear world.

A symbol of maternal care: according to fables and myths, the bear mother licks her newborn to give the cub its form.

Bears, just as human foragers and nomadic hunters and gatherers, move around following the seasons. They follow the staggered ripening of berries and wild fruits into the mountains and up into high altitudes, and, when the salmon run, they come back into the river valleys. If there is an especially big supply of nourishment, very many bears can be in one place at the same time. But they do not act like a pack or herd; instead, they are individualistic, knowing each other personally and greeting one other. Fairly rowdy tussles, which may look like fights to one who doesn't know them well, are completely nonaggressive. The young bears tussle like this, too, and two bears in love may also seem to be fighting. The pecking order, based on size and strength, makes for peaceful cohabitation. The smaller bear is naturally respectful of the bigger one.

Bears even tolerate human beings in their berry paradise or on the salmon runs. Cheyenne elders told me that they remember picking berries where bears were eating the same berries, sometimes even on the other side of the same bush. They could hear them smacking their lips. There were no problems as long as the humans always showed them respect and yielded them the absolute right of way. If a bear licked its snout during a meeting like this, it was not because the thought of human meat made his mouth water but because, with a moist nose, he could smell them better. Bears do not like to smell cold sweat, a sign of fear, and become unpredictable in such situations.

Bear researcher Helmut Heft, who observed these animals for many years in their natural environment, claims that bears usually meet people in an observant and patronizing manner and basically prefer to leave them alone. Bears are chivalrous and do not attack for no reason. It is more the case that dull, civilized humans are the ones who are aggressive. When attacked, a bear will defend itself fearlessly and is never cowardly. A bear will become mean and deceitful only in captivity. *Cruel* and *bloodthirsty*, as bears are often called, are terms that fit human beings almost exclusively. A German expression goes, "What I think and do, I trust others to think and do" (*Was ich denk' und tu', das traue ich dem anderen zu*). In this case, the expression could be changed a bit to "That which humans think and do, they trust bears to do."

Meeting a bear in the forest (Erik Werenskiold, nineteenth century)

BEAR LOVE AND MATRIARCHY

Many years ago, I lived in the mostly pristine forests near the Oregon coast before the environmental degradation in California drove many of its residents there. There were still free-roaming bears in that area. Inexperienced young bears would often be attracted to human settlements by the smell of garbage where they would most likely be greeted with a hail of bullets. I knew a strapping young man who, like so many hippies of the times, had turned his back on civilization. He hunted with a bow and arrow and shot a black bear that was following him up a tree. He proudly wore the claws as a necklace. The neighbor woman shot a bear each fall and turned the meat into sausage. I knew bears from various meetings in the woods, and I never liked the thought of killing them.

Long before my time in Oregon, I worked for a couple of summers, in my youth, at Yellowstone National Park. One summer, I had the opportunity to observe a black bear mother with her two cubs. It was like a window into a paradise we humans have long lost, a picture of happiness and unadulterated love. The two furry cubs scrambled all day long, played tag, teeter-tottered on pine tree branches, chased butterflies, and curiously sniffed crawling bugs. They played with stones and pieces of wood with the same abandonment as human children do when playing with conventional toys. When the first snow came, it was especially fun to watch them. They were very surprised and curious, sniffed the snowflakes, and tried to catch them. The next day, they slid down the hills in the snow, obviously having great fun. Occasionally, the mother bear hugged them tenderly, licked them clean, and stroked them with her claws as if combing their fur. If a lone hiker showed up, the mother called the cubs with a "woof" and chased them up a tree. When they got out of hand, she grumbled and boxed their ears. She actually even seemed to talk to them. Behavioral scientists have reportedly distinguished a bear "vocabulary" of some thirty sounds.

Like human beings, bears do not have a mating season. They nurse their offspring for about a year and a half, also the average nursing time for humans. Bears have six teats but only the two top ones swell and give milk. When the cubs are some three years old and leave their mother to strike out and try their luck on their own, the mother starts looking around for a new mate.

A bear mother with her cubs

While mating, which is done in the mild springtime, the bears seem to be in love. They dance and scramble around exuberantly. The female bear teases the male and acts uninterested, seeming to possess all the human female allures. The male tries to impress her by boxing around on bushes and carrying out various other demonstrations of strength. After a few days of such games, they pair up, and they are not puny in this act either. They copulate two to three times a day and each time for more than a half hour. One should be careful not to disturb this love play. Especially the female will be very upset, and the male will be eager to show her that he is no wimp.

If no insemination happens after this first meeting, the menstrual cycle sets in again. Just as with *Homo sapiens*, the cycle is twenty-eight days. If the female is pregnant, then the male bear can leave without further ado.[2] He is not included in the education of the youngsters; she alone is responsible for that. If prehistorians are hard put to find a nonadulterated matriarchy, here is one.

Like humans, bears sleep at night. Only where they are mercilessly hunted or constantly disturbed do they develop into reclusive night animals. They suffer the same frailties as human beings do: colds, pneumonia, rheumatism, and arthritis. Only the garbage bears suffer toothache due to eating sugar-sweetened foods, leftovers from humans.

Compared to many other animals, bears are biologically capable of living a fairly long life. They have a thirty-year life span on average—Stone Age humans are said to have not lived much longer than that either. In that amount of time, they become fairly wise and experienced. The bear's life expectancy today, however, is only about six years, and the reason is not a natural one: some 80 percent of bears killed in the wild are victims of trigger-happy, greedy, or fearful human beings (Busch 2000, 46). Nearly all native peoples claim that bears have a human-like intelligence. Mongolians and tribes of the Altai Mountains say they have a natural, intuitive intelligence like that they say women tend to have.

Bears also have an excellent memory. It is claimed that a bear will always remember a person that it has met only once. Bears can reason—and have humor! They will often throw hunters off by disguising their tracks, by jumping from stone to stone, from sedge tuft to sedge tuft, walking backward, or sidestepping. Some bear hunters have sworn off bear hunting after they have heard the human-like death screams of a mortally wounded bear, or been brought to their senses by hearing the pitiful whimpering and crying of a baby bear. It is no wonder that bears were sacred animals to whom native peoples attached taboos. For the Gilyak in Manchuria, bears are "mountain people" and messengers of the god of the forest. Transylvanians believe the bear is a "forest human," and theosophists and anthroposophists believe bears are descendants of "Atlantean humans" who have sunk to the level of an animal. Anthroposophist Karl Koenig expresses it like this: "Bears avoid humans; I doubt, though, that they are afraid of them. They avoid them out of a feeling of shame, which is at the same time also a feeling of dignity. Bears sense a deep kinship with humans. They sense that they were also once upright, like humans still are today" (Koenig 2013, 98).

CHAPTER 5
Meeting up with Maheonhovan

The bear possesses power—spiritual power. He can heal himself and other bears. He is a great medicine animal.

STATEMENT BY A CHEYENNE
(GRINNELL 1923,105)

The bear was a special creature for the native peoples of North America. In the legends about the animal world, the bear is the animal of leadership because of his fairness, strictness and courage. For most tribes, the bear clan is a clan of medicine, leadership and defense.

SUN BEAR, *MEDIZINRAD*

Commissioned by the National Parks Administration, we hacked our way through endless virgin rain forest immersed in green, translucent light. We were making the first trails into the forest. Paying no attention to startled deer that fled from us, or silent white-headed eagles swooping high above us, we made our way over slippery moss-covered cliffs and through endless groves of dripping giant ferns. The giant ferns made up the first story in the forest. Above the ferns towered hemlock spruce, fir, Douglas fir, and cedars. Our small troop of youths in their prime had been sent in to open up the Olympic Wilderness for tourists. Where until now hardly a white person had set foot, trails, stairs, and lodgings were to be built. It was during this time that I personally experienced the proverbial strength of bears for the first time.

At one of the planned rest areas, a garbage pit—large and bear-proof—was to be dug out. We shoveled and shoveled for nearly a week. Stout Fjørd horses pulled thick cedar logs, one by one, to the pit, and it took several of us to lay each one over the pit snugly next to the one before it. Then we secured the massive lid with cross beams. We figured it could now be put to use—the first garbage that plopped down into the deep bottom of the pit was our own. Bears have noses that can only be compared to bloodhounds. Researchers have determined that they can smell as far away as some twenty miles (approximately thirty kilometers). Since they have the same tastes as humans, it was not surprising that we heard loud crashing the very first night. The painstakingly built garbage pit was ruined. When we looked out of our hut to see what was going on, we saw a bear pulling the heavy logs aside like so many toothpicks. Then it slid into the pit and happily licked the tin cans clean, munched on steak bones, and ate whatever other leftovers were there.

A BEAR IS NOT A TAIL-TUCKING DOG

An old cowboy I met in Montana was personally convinced of the extraordinary strength of a bear's paw. While emptying a bottle of whiskey, he told me how he had met up with the king of the forest in the wilderness. The grizzly bear that he had taken by surprise hit his horse so hard on the neck that it fell down dead right under him. The cowboy was just able to pull his Colt out and shoot the bear. "Take a big-caliber gun along when you go into the mountains," he advised me. The good advice was superfluous, as the rancher's sons I rode out with always had a rifle within quick and easy reach on their saddles. Luckily, though, we did not surprise any bears. In the daytime when we fished in the crystal-clear mountain streams for trout or in the evening when we stretched our legs by a campfire, Bruin never let himself be seen. When the campfire was almost out, with only a soft ruby-red glow, we heard the bears sniffing around, attracted by the smell of our provisions that were hung up a good distance from us and well out of reach of their insatiable hunger.

Everyone knows the stories about careless campers using as pillows their backpacks full of cookies, apples, chocolate, and sandwiches. Bears have a notoriously voracious appetite and do not know their own strength nor just how frail humans are—they can push someone's head aside to get at the food and break their neck.

It is easy to become careless when one sees bears day in and day out in the wilderness. One thinks one has gotten to know them plenty well enough. That is what I thought when I was grilling hamburgers at one of the restaurants in Yellowstone during my second summer in the park. Cartons of fresh ground beef that had been delivered in the morning were still in the parking lot in the afternoon when I took a break from tourists ordering colas and hamburgers. When I went out to gather them up, a black bear was licking with relish the bits of hamburger that still clung to the cartons. Because I was so used to seeing bears all over the place by then, I thought I could shoo it away like a stray dog. I went toward it waving my hands and yelling, "Get out of here! Get! Get!" But bears are not like dogs! The bear looked up, sized me up, laid his ears back, snorted angrily, and whisked one of the cartons with its paw as far as a World Cup kicker would have sent a soccer ball. And then it headed for me.

I was a good runner and even won a couple of medals in high school in running sports—but no human can run as fast as a bear. These otherwise unhurried and ambling animals are almost as fast as a horse and can

Black bear, or baribal

effortlessly run forty miles per hour even at a short distance. I just reached the back door of the restaurant with the bear on my heels when the cook's wife, who had witnessed the incident, opened the door and doused the bear's nose with ammonia from a squirt gun, thus saving my life. It wasn't the first time a bear had been at the door. The bear turned heel immediately and went off to a distance where it sat down and rubbed its nose with both paws. Even though it hadn't been able to teach me my well-deserved lesson, it certainly taught me to have more respect for the king of the forest.

SHINING LIGHT IN THE BEAR'S SOUL

Later, in the Montana highland wilderness, I was given a chance to see far deeper into the unfathomable bear's soul. I had been hiking on a summer's day without seeing a single person. The characteristic, delightful aroma of prairie sage filled the air, elk grazed in the swamps below, prairie dogs whistled their short communications to each other, and eagles circled up high in a cloudless, azure-blue sky. As the sky began to turn into a glowing red-pink-yellow with the approaching sunset and the coyotes began their evening songs, I climbed up a steep slope toward a solitary and knotted old ponderosa pine where I planned to roll out my sleeping bag for the night. Just as I reached the crest of the hill, I saw three grizzly bears standing directly in front of me—so close that I could have touched them. They were standing upright with their paws raised.

I was overwhelmed. All thoughts and feelings were gone in an instant. I can only remember that I looked into the eyes of the bear nearest to me, and it was like looking directly into the sun. Bright light came out of its eyes toward me and I experienced what can only be described as a moment in eternity. Then the bear suddenly made a sound, "woof," as if it meant "hmm," went back down on all fours, and trotted leisurely past me. The other two followed. Most likely, it was a mother bear with two almost completely grown cubs.

The Cheyenne, whom I had befriended, told me later that I had seen maheonhovan, "the heavenly bear," in his earthly appearance, the bear that is seen at night in the sky near the North Star. He is the guardian of the wild animals, knows the strongest medicine, and can speak. He appears to humans as a white, shining bear.

Primeval spirits and the white bear (painting by Dick West, Cheyenne)

At that time, I was young and still believed in the exclusive validity of objective science too much to put much stock in such tales. But I did remember this meeting often. It awakened memories of stories about shining bears that my grandmother used to tell me. *Snow White and Rose Red* tells about a bear that spends the cold winter in the isolated hut of a mother with her two daughters. In the spring, when they let him back out into the forest, some fur gets caught on a nail in the door and golden light shines out from under it. In the fairy tale *Bearskin*, a golden soul is hidden under Bearskin's rough,

65

wild appearance. I also remembered some Siberian tales, which tell about the starlight that a bear carries inside. We will go into this subject more later on.

Just as I was writing this book, a friend sent me a book about the meaning of meetings with animals (*Tierisch gut* by Regula Mayer). One of the first meetings discussed is one with bears. "The bear's message for modern people is to remind them of their roots, which they are beginning to long to understand but have nearly lost. The bear connects us to our primeval roots. Bears remind us of our earthly origin and show us the pathway through our human life; they connect us to our human purpose" (Mayer 2004, 20). Bears connect us to our ancestors, primeval human beings, who honored bears, and from whom we have inherited the same genetic pattern. "Just as we have driven bears from the forests, we try to distance and free ourselves from our ancestors and their experience. Human beings must learn to live within nature's laws and grant space for the internal and external animals of prey" (Mayer 2004, 21).

The bear warns us to come back to a natural consciousness. "Let instinct, intuition, curiosity, and the force of life itself become the tools that guide your zest for life and bestow you with ever new experiences and joy. And when the time is appropriate, have the awareness to sink into the inner depth, the deep inner darkness, where you can draw strength from these experiences in peace" (Mayer 2004, 20).

CHAPTER 6
Grandmothers' Stories

The bear is wiser than the human being because he knows how to survive the winter without eating.

AN OLD SAYING OF THE ABENAKI PEOPLE

Old medicine man Bill Tallbull was worried about his people on the Cheyenne reservation. They were drinking too much alcohol, fighting too much, and getting sick too often in the winter months. Despite traditional sweat lodges, they caught colds and fell sick with pneumonia and the flu. He himself was also not feeling completely well. His heart was constricted and feeling too tight in his chest. He did not go to the doctors in the towns who wore white jackets and recommended pills, vaccinations, hospitals, and operations, which he did not trust. He had long ago chosen the path of his forefathers, the "old ways," which meant seeking healing through visions by fasting, waking, and praying—done at remote, traditional places of power in the countryside. But so much sacred knowledge had been forgotten. The reservation that had been allotted to the Cheyenne was far away from the places where old medicine men used to find healing plants. And the old medicine people who knew the plants were long dead. In addition, many of the diseases were of a new kind. They had come along with the invaders, just like "firewater," horses, and the book of religion.[1] Many new wild plants, European weeds that now grew on the prairie and in the mountains, had also come along with the white settlers.

Bill Tallbull had heard about my classes in healing plant lore at the college in Sheridan, Wyoming. "Maybe this 'pale face' can tell us something about the new plants and their uses," he thought, and discussed the prospect with the other elders who decided it could be a good idea to make contact—and that is how we became friends. We took many excursions into the prairie and the pine forests of the Big Horn Mountains. I showed him how to make a heart-strengthening tea out of hawthorn (*Crataegus* spp.) leaves and blossoms. He tried it and was happy to notice that it actually did help. I suggested hemp agrimony (*Eupatorium* spp.) and other plants to counter the flu, as they strengthen the immune system. I was expecting an exchange for plant information and that Tallbull would tell me some of the secrets he knew about the plant world, but I was very disappointed how little he was willing to tell me. I knew that Native Americans are generally not talkative, especially regarding what they know, but I had never experienced it personally. Bill Tallbull, in his defense, felt it was disrespectful toward the plant world to reveal their secrets. Idle talk could take away the healing power.

When it comes to sharing personally accumulated medicine power (*mayun*), most Native Americans are downright miserly. If I had taken a rifle from the wall or taken off with his car without asking or saying thanks, it would bother him less than taking his personal medicine knowledge without going through the right channels.

The "spirit-animals-of-down-below," mainly the bear but also the badger and the buffalo, can reveal knowledge about healing plants. The bear, which radiates like the sun in visions and can talk to human beings, is especially close to the grandmother *estsheheman*, who lives deep down in the earth and is the mother of the plants. The "spirit-animals-of-up-above," such as wolves, eagles, or cranes, reveal to us the secrets of the clouds and the sky. The human being who has been blessed with a vision given by a spirit animal is the owner of the vision and the power that comes along with it. That person will provoke the anger of the spirit animal if he or she is not respectful and careful regarding the vision.

So I had to rein in my desire for knowledge and be patient. But one day finally, after Tallbull had been on a vision quest for four days in a cave at Bear Butte, he told me a story he had inherited from his grandmother—just like healing knowledge, tales have magical power and are basically the personal property of the teller, who is the only person who may tell them unless he or she decides to give them as a present. He gave me the following story, which tells of the hero Little Bear and a Cheyenne woman who lived in magical primeval time. Since he gave it to me, I feel sure he would not mind that I share it here, so to say, in typical Western fashion:

It was late summer. The men were hunting buffalo herds in the prairie and the women went into the mountains looking for wild fruits and berries to gather. As the women were happily singing and chatting while filling their leather pouches with ripe berries, a huge grizzly bear appeared out of nowhere, grabbed one of the women, and took her off into the forest. The others ran back to the camp to get the men, but the men were not back from the buffalo hunt yet. They began to cry and lament the loss of their sister, believing that she was surely dead now.

In the meantime, the bear had brought the woman to his cave where she heard a baby bear crying pitifully. Something had happened to its mother and it was starving. The grizzly shoved her over to the baby, letting her know in its way that she should take care of the little creature. She began to nurse it and immediately loved it as mothers do.

The bear rolled a huge rock in front of the cave every morning when he left the cave so that the woman could not escape. In the evening when he came back, he brought her fresh meat and edible roots, grunted in a friendly manner, and left her in peace otherwise.

Many moons came and went, and the little bear grew bigger and bigger. One day, he suddenly began to speak. "Dear mother, why are you always crying?" he asked her.

"Oh, little bear, it is because I want to go back to my people," she answered.

Then she sighed because she didn't believe that the little bear was strong enough to roll the rock away. But the next morning, as soon as the old grizzly disappeared into the prairie and could be seen through the small opening as only a small dot on the distant horizon, the little bear shoved the rock effortlessly aside. They both then ran as fast as they could. When they came to a river, they swam a long stretch so that the old grizzly, who had soon enough discovered their escape, could not smell their trail.

They walked for many days until they finally reached the Cheyenne camp. The long-lost woman was greeted joyfully, and everyone admired her bear son. Only the dogs didn't like him and tried to nip his heels. He was given an appropriate name: Little Bear.

Soon Little Bear played with the other children, and three of them became his best friends. The first one was Fast Foot, who could run faster than anyone, as his name suggests. He often ran the antelope down just for the fun of it, grabbed them by the horns, and stuck their heads under his belt. It was great entertainment for the others and they very much enjoyed watching him.

American antelope

Another boy with whom Little Bear became friends was especially strong. He liked to catch buffalo and toss them up so high in the air that it took days for them to fall back down—as bleached skeletons—from the clouds. Even today one can still find such bones sometimes in the prairie. The third friend carried a hammer wherever he went and enjoyed smashing rocks with it. It seemed that the bigger the rock, the easier it was for him to smash it.

Once, as the four friends walked over the dry prairie in the direction of the setting sun, they came upon a huge cliff that went from horizon to horizon and was so high that only an eagle could fly over it. Little Bear, who was the leader, said, "The cliff is blocking our path, so let's rest here. Tomorrow Fast Foot can run to the south and see if we can get past it there."

Fast Foot did not return until very late in the evening the next day and could not report any success. "The cliff just doesn't end," he groaned. "Tomorrow I will try to get around it in the north." But in the north, it was the same story. Here, too, he did not return until late in the evening, saying it was impossible to get around it in the north, too.

Rock Smasher spoke up, "I will smash the rock," he said and swung his hammer with all of his might against the cliff. There was a thunderous echo in all directions, and the huge formation split into thousands of pieces—and that is how the Rocky Mountains were formed out of a huge cliff. Now humans and buffalo could cross. Rock Smasher's hammer stayed stuck in the rocks where it (as Obsidian Cliff) can still be admired today near Yellowstone.

Native American of the prairie

The Assiniboine ("the people who cook with hot rocks"), nomadic buffalo hunters from north of the Cheyenne, also tell a story of a woman a bear captured. This story also proves to be a key in our search for the secret of the bear's being:

It was late summer again, the time of ripe berries, when a bear took a group of women pickers by surprise. The beast grabbed one of the women—she was pregnant—and dragged her into his den. Instead of eating her, he made a prisoner of her in his den by rolling a huge rock in front of the entrance.

In the spring, she had a child with thick fur. She named the child "Thick Fur."

The little fellow was very strong, and as soon as he was big enough, he pushed the rock from the entrance so that he and his mother could flee. When the old bear came home in the evening and found the cave empty, he began to track them down.

After they had been walking for days on end, the woman fell to the ground completely exhausted. But the little thick-furred fellow packed her onto his shoulders and carried her to the village of the Assiniboine. As the custom required, they had to spend four days in the guest teepee, but then they celebrated their reunion. The woman's husband was happy to have such a strong son.

When Thick Fur played with the other children, he killed several of them unintentionally. He had no idea how strong he was. He was then banned from the village and had to go out into the world alone. After a few years, he met two men who were also very strong. One was named Tree Dragger because he could drag huge trees. The other one, whose name was Wood Spinner, could spin pine trees into strong, long ropes. Thick Fur made his home in the woods with these two friends. They agreed that Tree Dragger should stay home and cook while Wood Spinner and Thick Fur went out hunting.

When the two hunters came back home the first evening, they found Tree Dragger lying dead on the ground. A bear-like forest ogre had killed him for no other reason than pure lust to kill. Thick Fur, who had gotten medicine power from the old bear, sang a medicine song and brought the dead man back to life. Thick Fur said, "Tomorrow I will take Tree Dragger hunting with me, and, you, Wood Spinner, can stay here and cook!"

The next morning, just as he had gathered up wood for the fire, the wild forest ogre broke into the hut and hit unfortunate Wood Spinner so hard that he dropped dead on the spot. That evening, Thick Fur had to bring him back to life as well. At this point, Thick Fur decided it was time to put an end to this nonsense and said, "Tomorrow, you two can go hunting and I will stay here and cook."

The next day, Thick Fur filled leather pouches with water in which—according to Assiniboine custom—he intended to cook the meat. He was just getting the hot rocks out of the fire to put them in the pouches when the ogre stuck its ugly head through the door of the hut. Thick Fur knocked it down as fast as lightning. The beast did not move again. "What a weak ogre," he thought. "I don't understand why the other two didn't just strike it dead."

Soon the three companions moved on. One day they came upon a big camping place. The chief welcomed them in a friendly manner and told them that ungodly beings from the netherworld had kidnapped his three daughters. No one, not even his strongest medicine men, had been able to free them. If the three could free them, the chief promised to give his daughters to them as wives.

Thick Fur thought it would be good to have a wife as then he wouldn't have to cook and sew anymore, and, besides, he would have a pleasant time with her. Tree Dragger and Wood Spinner thought the same. They made their way to the entrance that led to the netherworld. Tree Dragger dragged trees over and Wood Spinner spun them into strong ropes. Thick Fur, who knew no fear, let himself down with the rope. Deep down under the earth, at the end of the den, he saw a light and then he saw the three maidens sitting there crying. A mountain lion was watching over the first one, an eagle was watching over the second one, and a cannibalistic giant was near the third one.

When the maidens saw the stately young man, they entreated him to leave. They were sure that the netherworld beings would kill him. But he flung the mountain lion against the rock wall so that it fell into a swoon. Then he grabbed the eagle and twisted its neck. The maidens called out to him again, "Leave! Flee!" and at that moment twelve horrible giants jumped at him. But Thick Fur took a slingshot into each hand and killed six of the screeching attackers with each slingshot. As a sign of her thankfulness, each maiden gave him a token of appreciation: the eldest gave him her necklace, the middle one gave him a colorful scarf, and the youngest gave him her ring.

"Come quickly," Thick Fur said, "my friends will pull us up." And he led them to the end of the rope. Tree Dragger and Wood Spinner pulled the eldest maiden up first. Her beauty stunned them. The second maiden was just as beautiful.

"What do you say? We will take these two for ourselves and leave Thick Fur and the third one down below," said Wood Spinner. Tree Dragger did not dare contradict him and cut the rope.

Thick Fur and the youngest maiden, who had already been halfway to the entrance, plunged into the depths. Fortunately, an eagle caught them. The eagle was even willing to bring them back up to the world above, but Thick Fur first had to bring him something to eat so that he could build up enough strength for the extremely strenuous flight. Thick Fur slayed three elk and gave them to the bird to eat. After eating them, the eagle had enough strength to lift off and rise ever higher. But shortly before reaching the upper world, it started to lose height. Thick Fur cut some pieces of his own flesh and fed them to the giant bird.

When they were finally back in the upper world, they quickly made their way to the village. The village was abuzz as the two traitors were preparing to marry the chief's two daughters. The maidens were already adorned in wedding colors and wore gowns decorated with colorful porcupine quills. The buffalo that had been slain just for the wedding festivities was already sizzling over the fire pit, and horses, blankets, and other gifts were being given. Thick Fur and the chief's youngest daughter had come just in time. Wood Spinner and Tree Dragger turned as pale as if they had seen a ghost and fled immediately.

When the chief asked who had saved his daughters, Thick Fur showed the necklace, colorful scarf, and ring that the maidens had given him. The chief ordered that the festivities continue and Thick Fur married all three maidens.

CHAPTER 7

The Cave, the Bear, and the Woman

The others had all gone down
From the blackberry brambles, but one girl
Spilled her basket, and was picking up her
Berries in the dark.
A tall man stood in the shadow, took her arm,
Led her to his home. He was a bear.
In a house under the mountain
She gave birth to slick, dark children
With sharp yellow teeth, and lived in the hollow
Mountain many years.

GARY SNYDER, *MYTHS & TEXTS*

In both of the previous two Cheyenne und Assiniboine stories, we have the recurring theme of the cave, the bear, and the woman. Again and again, the woman turns out to be the mother of an extraordinary hero who accomplishes fantastic deeds. No one who has an intense interest in myths and tales of different peoples can learn these stories without noticing these themes. To the contrary, one must realize immediately that this theme is old, that it is, in fact, ancient. It goes back as far as the Old Stone Age and back to the very beginnings of human culture.

Is it possible that these stories that were told for thousands and thousands of years while sitting around the fire have lived on until the present day? There is quite a lot of evidence that indicates this must be the case.

For instance, the Chippewa tell of huge "buffalo" with thick reddish fur that their ancestors hunted with spears "at a time before bows and arrows existed." These buffalo were strange looking: a long, enormous nose that moved like a snake grew out of the middle of the face. This snake nose had a hand on the end with which it grabbed grass and leaves and stuffed them into its mouth. Unlike the buffalo we know, its horns did not grow on its head; instead, two pointed horns grew out of its mouth on each side of its nose.

One could shrug this Chippewa story off as the result of a childish, primitive fantasy. But on closer inspection, one realizes that a mammoth is being described, an animal that died out in America some ten thousand years ago. The story has to be a primeval memory that has been passed down until today—and that must also be the case with the stories of the cave women and their bear sons. The theme must have already had considerable importance at a time when the ancestors of the Native Americans still lived in the glacial Old World, a time before they had crossed the Bering Strait (which at that time was still a land bridge) over to North America. Asians and Europeans tell the very same stories. They tell about bears and women from whom strong sons and daughters emerge. They also tell stories about stolen or abandoned children who are raised by bear mothers in caves.

In a Russian tale, we hear of a woman who was surprised by a bear while picking mushrooms and conceived a son with him. The child that is then born is human above the navel and bear below it. She names her son Ivan Medviedko (or John Honeyeater), who turns out to be exceptionally clever and who even outsmarts the devil, wangling a cart full of gold out of him.

In the French Alps, the Pyrenees, and in Valais, Switzerland, the story of a woman who is captured by a bear, held captive in a cave, and gives birth to a hairy son is very common. The child, Jean de l'Ours (or John Bear) is exceptionally courageous, strong, and clever. Even at one year old, he tries to push the stone from the cave opening where he and his mother are held captive. He succeeds when he is only three years old. The woman goes back to her kin, but her son prefers to stay in the forest. In the course of his roaming, he overcomes wicked witches, kills horrible giants, and ultimately frees a young maiden from sure death.

In Berne, Switzerland, the story of a poor girl who is so plagued by her stepmother that she flees into the forest is still told today. The girl preferred the risk of being torn up by wild animals to the relentless torture of her stepmother. Freezing, starving, and without any hope, she strayed through the wilderness when suddenly a bear appeared in front of her. Instead of eating her, it tugged on her dress and grumbled in a friendly way. The bear led her to a cave and brought her dry moss as a cushion for her to sit down. He gave her strawberries, honey, and other delicacies to satisfy her hunger. She understood that the bear wished she would stay with him, so she made herself at home, cleaned and cooked, and slept close to him when the nights were very cold. Over the course of time, she bore a big family of sturdy sons, who resembled her but were as strong and courageous as the bear. When they became adults and went out into the world, they were very popular in the entire region because they were so good-natured. The emperor awarded them generously for their brave deeds as warriors. They always won at the "Schwingfeste"—a festival featuring a special kind of wrestling still practiced in Switzerland today by men nearly the size of sumo wrestlers. They were the primeval ancestors of the Bernese lineage. Folklorist Sergius Golowin, himself half Bernese, claims with a knowing smile that there might be something to this story (Golowin 1986). If scientists claim that humans evolved from animals, then certainly not from ridiculous monkeys—in any case, not the citizens of Berne! (As mentioned earlier, Berne even means "bear.")

THE STRENGTH OF THOSE RAISED ON BEAR'S MILK

All of the stories have one thing in common: anyone who is sired by a bear or raised on bear's milk will grow up to have a bear's strength.[1] Ancient Greek legend claims that even Zeus, the Olympian ruler of the gods, has such immense strength because he was nursed by two bears who reared him in a cave in the mountains near Cyzicus.

The Arcadian king's daughter, *Atalante*, is another one claimed to have been raised on bear's milk. After her birth, her father set her out in the woods where a mother bear found and adopted her. She grew up to be a stately and courageous young woman. With her bare hands, she slayed the lustful centaurs that were stalking her, and, with her spear, the courageous young bear maiden wounded the wild Caledonian boar, a monster that had been sent out by the hunting goddess Artemis.

The tale of John Bear, which we do not want to leave out in this context, tells of a typical child raised on bear's milk.

A poor charcoal burner and his wife lived in a hut deep in the forest and had a son whom they named John. Already as a baby, he was so strong that he strangled three dogs by mistake while playing with them. Of course, his parents scolded him, but they were also secretly proud to have such a strong child.

One day, as little John was playing in front of the hut, a grimly growling female bear lumbered by. Heartless hunters had killed her two cubs, and she wanted to eat a human child in revenge. The child defended himself so bravely that the bear mother was touched. She involuntarily thought about her two lost little rascals. So, she picked up the little fellow and carried him into her cave, just like she would have carried a little bear cub. She gave him as much bear milk as he could drink and played with him until he squeaked for joy. But every time she left the cave, she took the precaution of rolling a huge rock in front of the entrance. As time went by, she grew to love the child ever more, and she even hoped he would stay near her and take care of her when she grew old one day.

John thrived and prospered. One day, he tried his strength on the huge rock in front of the entrance. He pushed and pressed until it rolled away. Now he roamed the forest with eyes wide open. By chance, he happened upon the hut of his parents who recognized him immediately and thanked God that he was still alive. They took him back in and tried to teach him good manners and the necessary skills to survive in the world.

When he was old enough, he set out to find someone he could work for, and soon he was taken in as a farmhand on a big farm. It just happened to be fruit-harvesting time, and many helpful hands were necessary to bring in the harvest. But, unfortunately, every branch that John touched broke under his mighty grip. His angry boss sent him to fetch wood in the forest, thinking there he could let off steam. Sawing and chopping went too slowly for him, though, so he pondered for a moment how it could be done faster. Then he put his conclusion into action and just pulled the trees out of the ground and started to stack them up carefully. The other forest workers got scared when they saw this and started to plot how they could kill him as this was the only way they figured they would be safe from him.

"John," they called out to him with false friendliness, "go down into the well. There is a treasure down there that only someone as strong as you are can bring back up." John, who was as good-natured as he was naïve, went right down into the well shaft without a second thought. When he was at the bottom and was looking for the treasure, the others started throwing heavy rocks down on his head. He thought it was just a hailstorm. The others lugged a millstone over and let it fall into the well, which fell right around his neck. Without having found anything below, he climbed back up. When he saw the shocked faces of the others as he came back out, he laughed out loud and said, "With this stiff collar I must look like a preacher!"

When his boss heard about this incident, he was very shocked. "This stupid farmhand is driving the others crazy and it is also possible that he is dangerous to boot," he thought to himself. He gave him his earnings in gold and sent him on his way to be rid of him.

John went back to roaming the countryside looking for work. He heard all kinds of rumors and stories and one of them made him especially pensive: There was a horrible giant in the land that was intent on marrying the king's daughter. The poor maiden was beside herself, and her father didn't know where to turn. Three of the bravest warriors had already been slain by the giant.

John Bear had no doubt that he could deal with the giant. With his earnings in gold, he bought the best sword available and set out to find the giant. When the fiend saw John, he made fun of him and laughed until he shook. But his laughter was quickly stifled. With one felicitous swing, John beheaded the bruiser, and its black blood spouted out as if from a fountain.

In thanks, the king gave John Bear his beautiful daughter to wed. John was very happy, and the princess was also happy because, not only was he incredibly strong, but he was also good looking.

When the old king died shortly afterward, John became his successor. The first thing he did was move his parents from the old charcoal maker's hut into the palace. Then, with his wife, he went to the cave of the old she-bear. He came just in time as his bear mother was dying. She was already too weak to even get herself berries to eat. When she recognized John, she grumbled contentedly. Then she put her head into the lap of the young queen and died in peace. It had been her last wish to see her foster child once more.

A BEAR-LIKE MOTHER HULDA, OR MOTHER GOOSE

European lore also knows of the old grandmother of the Cheyenne (*estshe-heman*) who lives deep down in the earth. In old European lore, she is known as Mother Hulda, Mother Goose, or Mother Holle (the woman of the cave), who is also linked to the medieval goddess, Diana (*Dea Ana* = the divine ancestor woman, the primeval goddess), or Artemisia, the goddess of the wilderness, or "the devil's grandmother." Her realm is the otherworld, where animal and human souls wait to be born again. She is the Paleolithic "lady of the animals," and the bear is her favorite companion. She herself is somewhat bear-like: she could appear as a beautiful young woman or as an ugly old witch, but she was usually described as having tangled, disheveled hair and very large teeth. In caves, springs, wells, and also in very deep forests are found the portals to her green realm that is full of light, blossoming meadows, and forests.

The fairy tale *Mother Holle*, which was written down by the Grimm brothers, is ancient. The message about death and rebirth and the reason for individual fate as the old pagan, European forest peoples knew it, is related in this fairy tale. It tells of an industrious young lady who sits near a well, spinning with a spindle. She spins so much that her fingers start to bleed and the spindle slips out of her hands, which is symbolic of losing the thread of life. While looking for the spindle in the deep well, she falls in herself and lands on a sunny, flowering meadow. She begins a journey through the netherworld—the world of the dead. She comes upon a tree full of ripe apples. The tree asks her to pick the apples, and she is glad to do so. Then she comes to an oven full of bread that is finished baking, and the bread asks her to take it out of the oven because otherwise it will burn.[2] She also gladly helps out here. Next, she meets up with Mother Holle herself, who asks her to help in the house, telling her how especially important it is to shake the featherbeds out each day, as this action causes it to snow on earth. She selflessly does everything Mother Holle asks her to do, and, when the time is up, she is led to the portal back into life. When she crosses the threshold, a shower of gold rains down upon her.

Back on Earth, her lazy stepsister is jealous of her golden fate. The stepsister finds out how it happened and throws a spindle into the deep well and jumps in. But she is lazy and greedy for the shower of gold, so she takes no time to pick the apples or take the bread out of the oven. She works hard for Mother Holle for one day but already on the second day refuses to get up early in the morning. When her time is up, and she is led to the portal, a shower of tar rains down on her as she crosses the threshold. She will have bad luck her entire life.

A similar tale is told by Paleo-Siberians. In this story, the otherworld is a cave deep in the forest and Mother Holle is a bear. Nana Nauwald recorded the story (Nauwald 2002, 87):

A brother would not allow his sister to watch when he whittled the tips of his spears because then they would lose their magic and break. When his curious sister did watch him, after all, he tossed her down from the house that was built on stilts. She ran into the forest, got lost and finally came to a bear cave. A bear girl came out and jumped up and down for joy because now she had a playmate. She bit into the seam of the girl's dress and tugged at it. The bear mother came out of the cave, too.

"Don't be so rough with her," said the bear mother. "See here, you have torn her dress. Let her come into the house." The girl came in and sat down to sew her dress. The bear mother watched her sewing and thought, "She sews very well; she is very industrious" and then said out loud, "Soon my sons will come back home. You should hide from them because they are rambunctious and they could hurt you." The girl wasted no time in finding a good place to hide.

Shortly after, five young bears came into the cave. "I say, it smells like human flesh in here," they grumbled.

"Oh, come on! You stroll around all day sniffing this and that and when you come home you talk about all kinds of smells. Now eat supper and go to bed!" retorted the mother.

After the meal they went to sleep and the bear mother spoke to her guest, "Now go away, otherwise they will find you in the morning." The girl slipped quietly out of the cave and went on her way.

At midnight the old mother bear woke up her youngest son and said to him, "You really shouldn't sleep so soundly. While you were sleeping, a pretty girl came into the house and now she is gone again. She would be a good bride for you. Go out and see if you can't find her and bring her back!"

The young bear went out to search for her but she was already near her village. The people came out to welcome her back, but when they saw a bear behind her, they hurled a spear at it and killed it. The girl skinned the bear but as soon as his hide was off, he turned into a handsome young man, who wooed and then married her.

The girl had a cousin who was worthless and also jealous of her for having found such a handsome young man. She also had a brother, who forbade her to watch him whittle his spears. She watched anyway, but since nothing happened, she grabbed them and broke them herself. Then because her brother did not toss her out of the house, she jumped down from the stilt house herself.

After walking for a long time in the woods, she found the bear cave. Just as before, the bear girl came out and tugged at her dress until it tore. The old mother bear came out, just like with the other girl, and asked her into the cave. When she sat down to sew her dress, the old bear noticed that she was unskilled with the needle. When her sons were to come home, the mother bear told the girl to hide. At first she did not want to, but the bear convinced her. When her sons fell asleep, the mother bear told the girl, "Go now!" To herself, she thought, "This girl is really a bad one." She did not wake any of her sons when she was gone. A big shaggy dog was lying at the entrance to the cave and the bear told him to follow the girl. When she came back into the village, she called out, "A groom is following me!" The villagers came to look and killed the dog with spears as they had done with the bear. But when the dog was skinned nothing was under the surface—it was and remained a dog.

A bear with a fish in its mouth (carving from the Paleo-Siberian Koryaks; Schlesier 2013)

CHAPTER 8
The Vital Spirit of the Vegetation

Tell us of the birth of Otso!
Was he born within a manger,
Was he nurtured in the bathroom
Was his origin ignoble?"

This is Wainamoinen's answer:
Otso was not born a beggar,
Was not born among the rushes,
Was not cradled in a manger;

Honey-paw was born in ether,
In the regions of the Moon-land,
On the shoulders of Otava,
With the daughters of creation.

KALEVALA, RUNE 46

The archetypal imagination that linked the cave, the bear, and the woman in a large mythological web lived on beyond the hunters of the Old Stone Age. This god-like woman, primeval mother of all game, healing plants, and shamans, lived on with the first sedentary farmers and became Mother Earth, whose cornucopia showers onto the fields filling them with grains and all of the other fruits of the field.

Mother Earth was, to express it in modern language, the personification of nature itself. Primeval peoples, especially the matriarchal first planting peoples, would hardly have understood our word "nature," which was a word created much later by Latin Church scholars. They did not think abstractly, but in pictures. They saw their world as absolutely alive and animated. That which we noncommittally call nature was for them the Great Mother, the one who bears and nourishes all of life, but also the mother of death who takes her creatures back, mourns, and weeps for them, only to bear them once more anew in the great cycle of all that is.

The first planters, including the megalithic farmers in Europe, scratched open the virginal skin of this great mother and planted bulbs or sowed grains into her—a process that they saw as a sort of sexual procreation.

BLOODY SACRIFICES

Because Mother Earth was a woman who was to become pregnant and bear many children, she needed a lover and sire who was worthy of her. And who would be more suitable than the wild bear, who goes in and out of her subterranean realm with impunity? As has been mentioned earlier, already the old hunters regarded bears as potent, libidinal, and fertile. It was only fitting that the bear was integrated into the Neolithic fertility cult as the son and lover of the goddess. Of course, his relationship with her is, in fact, downright incestuous, but, after all, we are dealing with gods who are often allowed to do things forbidden to mortals.

Contrary to the self-domesticating human beings with all of their artificial behavior, bears live in harmonious unison with nature and its seasonal rhythms. They appear with the balmy breeze and first green in the spring and disappear when the leaves fall and the vegetation retreats into the root realm below the ground. Bears follow their drives just like wild human beings did, who were still untouched by civilization. For this reason, the bear was suited to be honored by many tribes as their primeval forbear. Bears are still bonded with pristine, unbridled fecundity, with the pure beginnings of life. Because primitive and primal are regarded everywhere as potent and fertile, the bear is the natural fitting paramour of the goddess.

"Fertility cult" is a favorite but fairly nebulous concept often used by anthropologists. It refers to the rituals regarding the welfare of humans (and animals) and their "daily bread" (in reality, in earlier times, it was the daily mush as bread was not yet baked). In order to ensure prosperity, magical help from the old, experienced clan members who knew about the secret of the goddess and her lover was necessary. So it followed that, amid the first sedentary farmers, a caste of priests developed to carefully guard their knowledge. Their purpose was to influence the goddess with strict rituals, ceremonies, rites, and sacrifices during which often plenty of blood flowed. These priests even often sacrificed a son or lover for the goddess so that his blood—this precious red juice of life—would give her womb new strength. They had observed that blood and fertility are obviously connected: blood flows when women lose their virginity as well as during birth, and the beginning of menstruation is the beginning of fertility for women just as menopause presages the end of fertility. These observations supported their conviction about blood and fertility in a wider dimension.

It is possible that late Neolithic planters, lake dwellers, and megalithic farmers sacrificed bears in elaborate rites believed to ensure fertility for humans and fields. There is also reason to believe that young bears were raised in villages as honored guests and then sacrificed, as eastern Siberian tribes still did until recently. In northern Europe, bear figures carved into amber were found from this time period; in the Balkans, terracotta figures of bear-headed women nursing bear children[1]; and in many places, especially in the late Neolithic lake dwellings surrounding Swiss lakes, well-polished bear teeth with many holes drilled in each one.

Soon, though, other animals superseded the bear as lovers of the great goddess, such as bulls, billy goats, boars, and rams. Especially powerful, drooling bulls, as the very incarnation of male virility, were favored as a sacrifice. (Spanish bullfights with their culminating sacrifice are remnants of such archaic sacrificial rites.) Despite its wild nature, a bull is a domesticated animal and therefore more accessible to farming peoples. With

Sandstone figure from a Neolithic field of graves near Tomsk, Siberia

remarkable virility, a bull sires an entire herd. In some of the old agricultural cultures that were known to be matriarchies, even young men in their prime were sacrificed within the framework of orgiastic festivals.

"STRAW-BEAR" AND "PEA-BEAR"

Even though fertility cults took on new forms as times changed, they could not completely displace the ancient bear cult. Even in modern traditional farm culture, the bear plays a role as a bringer of fertility. In this context, anthropologists describe the bear as a "vital spirit of fertility." Northern Germanic peoples also called Thor, the god of farmers, by the nickname "Bjørn," which means "bear." Thor roars over the fields in a wagon pulled by two goat bucks when there is a thunderstorm, thus bringing fertility to the fields. In the countryside in Sweden, it is still said, when the wind blows over a field of grain, "there goes the grain bear." In Saxony, the grain bear is believed to be the son of the grain mother. In many places, the "bear" is believed to be in the last sheaf that is cut and bound during the harvest. In lower Austria, the "bear"—usually a young man dressed as a bear—comes to the farm that finished harvesting last. Such harvest customs are even still widely practiced in Europe despite modern machinery.

At the time of the winter solstice when, during the twelve days of Christmas, the cosmos revitalizes the earth and the new light is born, festivals of fertility were also traditionally celebrated. All of the festive foods, the nuts and apples and cakes, represent—in the language of symbolism—the renewal of life, the seeds for new harvests. Cakes and cookies were already baked in pre-Christian times in the Old Nordic-Celtic midwinter festivities. Motifs of men and women as well as boars, roosters, the Christ child, stags (also an ancient symbol of the sun), oxen, white horses, or bears in favorite festive breads and cakes developed into baked Santa breads, as one still finds in northern Europe at Christmastime. These festive breads were usually baked from the grain of the last sheaf. They represented the concentrated power of life sprouting out of the earth and were given, just as apples and nuts, as nourishment for the dead. They were offered to the ancestors, who were waiting in the depths of the earth under the protection of the great goddess until they returned to life on earth.

The grain mother, a typical symbolic Christmas cookie

On these holy nights in Europe at Christmastime (also the winter solstice), here and there a "bear" appears, or some other wild animal, usually
accompanied by a holy man, such as Saint Nicolas, or by a servant, such
as "Servant Ruprecht" (German *Knecht Ruprecht*) in Austria. Here again,
the bear is associated with fertile prowess, just as the hazelnut rods that the
old man carries are. Originally, this rod of life was used in a playful way on
women and cows so that they would be fertile; there are still festivals today
in which the young men of the village run around and playfully "beat" the
young women with hazelnut rods on the holy nights of midwinter.[2] On these
nights in which the spirits promise fertility, treats used to be offered to the

bears. In Norway, the leftovers from the Christmas feast were brought into the forest for the bears; in northern Bohemia, the leftovers were tossed under the fruit trees for them.

But especially during the wild post-Christmastime, the time of fasting, but more traditionally the time of carnivals and bawdy fooling around, the old bear spirit appears. The Church and the Enlightenment, which both agitated against this ancient survival of heathen fertility festivals, had their hands full trying to curb this wild, often obscene behavior.[3] But it did not work. Even today in many areas in Europe, young men with blackened faces, wild animal masks, and furs run around at night and ritually tease the young women, who are more than happy to play along.[4] During this time of year, the powerful, uninhibited bear comes very much into its own. It represents the wild energy beyond civilized manners and mores without which sexuality and proliferation are hardly possible.

Long ago, in most of Europe, it was custom to thrash all of the grains before fasting time. The young fellow who thrashed the last grain sheaf, or pea sheaf, was masked and wrapped in straw and chosen to be the pea-bear (or straw-bear, oat-bear, or rye-bear).[5] A "gypsy" or bear trainer led him through the entire village with loud music and tra-la-la where he danced on all fours and scared the women. He was brought into the stables to drive out wicked (invisible) witches and scratch at cracks in the walls with his claws to drive out bad spells that may have been put into them. One of the customs was to have the pea-bear refuse to enter a jinxed stable until the farmer gave his trainer a coin or until he recited the right phrase. The pea-bear also showed a lively interest in the supposed flirts of the village because he also symbolized manly drives that are hard to rein in. In some villages in mainland northern Europe and England, the pea-bear simply trotted from house to house asking for alms.

In many places, the pea-bear was brought to court after his rounds. He was accused, inevitably found guilty, and "beheaded," at which time pig bladders hidden under the pea-bear's disguise and full of blood were emptied. In other places, a bear made of straw was burned as a symbol of the old winter leaving to make way for spring. In even other places, there were "bear hunts" during this fasting time. A man dressed as a bear was hunted by a pack of "dogs" and a bunch of other carnival fools and "slain." In the Rhineland, a bear, as the embodiment of the wild, crazy time, roars and romps for the last time on Ash Wednesday. Women pluck some of the straw out of his fur coat to place in the hens' nests for fertility. Then, the bear's fur coat is also burned to ashes. (In medieval Rome, a real bear is supposed to have been shown around like this and then ritually killed.)

The bear of the fasting time (Lent), doing the rounds in a Bohemian village

In some of the regions in French-speaking Switzerland, the bear appears once more as a May Bear or Pentecost Bear. For example, in Ragaz, Switzerland, a six-foot (two-meter) figure decorated with flowers and colorful ribbons is paraded through the streets by loud youths. This "bear" also has an inglorious end and is tossed into the river. Once again, civilization and law and order triumph over wildness and chaos, but only after the beast has bestowed its power and blessings for fertility. And finally, the old Scandinavian and Russian wedding custom should be mentioned, in which a hooded guest represents the honey-loving bear and crawls around on all fours during the festivities!

These customs, which live on as superstition and are barely understood, are surely remnants of the first sedentary peoples' religions. The decorated young bride symbolizes the great goddess, and her companion, the wild bear, is the bringer of fertility. As is shown in so many of the folk tales, its death is not its end but a necessity for its transformation. By being sacrificed, it is freed of its animal existence, and, as a stately groom, it celebrates its resurrection as a human being.

In the year's cycle, the bear, the companion of Mother Earth, symbolizes death and rebirth in harmony with the sun cycle. It is sacrificed into the earth, fertilizes the earth, and is then transformed into new life. The mystery dramas of antiquity (ritually celebrated plays) of the great goddess—Ceres, Cybele, Isis, Nana, and so on—and her mistreated lover and son—Adonis, Attis, Tammuz, Osiris, Baldur, and so on—are a distant echo from Neolithic farming cultures. They even live on, changed beyond recognition, in modern decadence, detached from the moist, fertile earth and cosmic rhythms: Who has ever thought about the deeper meaning of the Elvis Presley cult, for instance? His house, Graceland, where he apparently still appears, continues to be besieged by hysterical fans.

Baby, let me be your teddy bear.
Put your chain around my neck,
and lead me anywhere.
Oh, let me be your teddy bear.

Elvis sang this refrain while gyrating his hips slowly to the rhythm, as if he had a girl in his hands and not his guitar. But, as he said himself, it was always his "mom" who he worshiped.

Even Christianity shows some heritage of this Neolithic imagination. God's mother's son is sacrificed in a bloody ritual—his flesh and blood are our bread and wine. His mother weeps over him, and his body is put into a grave with a heavy rock closing the entry. The stone is later rolled away, and he is resurrected and glorified. The first witness to this was the eternal woman.

CHAPTER 9
The Bear King of the Celts

Al primo die febbraio l'è fuori l'orso della tana;
se l'è nuvolo dall'inverno siamo fuori
e se sereno per quaranta giorni si ritorna dentro.

(On the first day of February, the bear comes out of his cave,
If the sky is overcast, winter is over.
But if it is sunny, there will be forty more days of winter.)

ALMANACCO DEL GRIGIONI ITALIANO, 1937

The warring cattle nomads came to Europe from the West Asian steppes. Their shiny bronze swords and battle-axes, but especially their battle-wagons drawn by horses, terrified the late megalithic hoe farmers in Europe. The haughty invaders brought along herds of cattle, of which ownership was considered the very epitome of wealth. They also brought warring gods, and they worshiped light. Not even willing to give their bodies back to the earth, they burned their dead to ashes.

These Indo-European tribes, whose descendants included the Celts, soon subjugated all of Central Europe. They began to extract iron ore from the earth and forge iron swords; their rule ranged all the way to the Atlantic coast, to Britain and to Spain. Their warriors, who honored the strong, unflinching, and fearless bear as their totem, took over the earthen fortresses of their predecessors and used them for banquets. Their priests, who honored the sensitive, nervous stag as their totem, retreated into the forest and became known to us as "wise hermits," or Druids. These Druids, adopting the stone circles and menhirs that had been built in honor of the earth goddess, recognized the cosmic rhythm and order, including the summer and winter solstices, by observing the shadows thrown by the stones.

For farming peoples, it is a matter of survival to know the right time to sow the fields, when to bring the animals to pasture, when to harvest. The Celts mixed with the peoples and came under the influence of the time-measuring stones and the great goddess. They recognized the daughter of the heavenly goddess, Dagda, the white goddess, in the earth mother. The shadows thrown by the megalithic stones measured her steps as she tread upon the earth, the phases in her life: her appearance in the spring, her marriage in the joyful month of May, her birthing in the early fall with the fruits of the earth, and her disappearance into the gray fog in the fall.

Celtic bear amulet from Lancashire (Northern England, made of anthracite/jet)

Warrior fighting a bear-like monstrosity

The white goddess chose the first of the warriors, whose totem was the bear, as her hero and lover. She chose the chieftain of the tribe as only a chieftain, the bravest and best among the people, was worthy of her. The bear was the king of the animals, so it only followed that the king of the people, her spouse, would also be called "bear." *Artur, Arto, Mato, Matus,* and similar Celtic names represent the terrifying king of the forest. Thus, they named their tribal rulers as such, from King Math of the Irish with his magic powers to the king of kings, King Arthur of the Round Table.

King Arthur with Merlin (Arnulfus de Kay, Plusieurs Romans de la Table Ronde, 1286)

The Celts saw the royal loins, male potency, as a prerequisite for ensuring the thriving and fruiting of the earth. The bear was the plow and the goddess was the virginal furrow. If he became old and weak, the fields and herds would also decline; then, it was time to dethrone or ritually sacrifice him so that the merciless fair lady could choose herself a new king.

Just like the bear that disappears into a cave when the green of the summer has passed, the king also disappeared into the "otherworld," the realm of the dead, only to come back later, completely rejuvenated. Even if he appears to die, the king is immortal. *Rex quondam, rexque futurus*, the once and future king, refers to King Arthur, the bear king, who comes back again and again to love the goddess anew. This pre-Christian culture seems strange to us today, but a lot of these ideas are still alive. Let us have a look at how diverse country customs and festivities have their roots in the cult of the white goddess and her bear lover.

THE WHEEL WITH EIGHT SPOKES

The Celts divided the rural year into eight phases and celebrated the transition from one to the other with fire festivals and sacrifices. The four solar cardinal points, the so-called quarter days—the fall equinox, the spring equinox, and the longest and shortest days—divided up the year. The four segments were then halved, resulting in the cross-quarter days: the full moons of February, May, August, and November.[1] In this way, the wheel then had eight spokes. The goddess danced over the earth in eight steps.

These so-called witches' days had special meaning for the Celts. They were in-between times, times of transition, times in which the old was passing but the new had not yet completely taken hold. During these short pauses, when everything was hanging in the balance, ghosts, gods, elves, and other ethereal beings from the otherworld could slip into human beings, take on their shape, and tell the future. The bear, who needs no calendar stones to recognize cosmic rhythms, celebrated the festivals of the goddess in his own way.

THE FESTIVAL OF LIGHT

The beginning of these sacred festivals took place during the February full moon. Irish Celts called this festival *Imbolc*. Although northern climates are still in a frozen winter state at such a time of year, the days slowly are getting longer and the sap unnoticeably begins to flow in the trees. In this new light, the goddess appears as a beautiful maiden of light. In pre-Christian times, it was called the Festival of Lights, and, in Christian times, it became known as Candlemas Day (in the United States, Groundhog Day). Spirits of fertility and nature spirits were believed to come out of the earth with the goddess of light, who in other northern European countries was known as Birgit (from Indo-Germanic *bhereg* = radiant, shining). The bear, the goddess's furry, divine companion, also ventures out from the earth at this time.[2] According to legend, Bruin, still quite stiff and drowsy, sticks his nose out for the first time on this day to see how far spring has come along.

Celtic peoples greeted Birgit with festive fires and consulted oracles. The goddess of light was so adored as a muse, poet, healer, and magician that not even the Christians wanted to discontinue the festivities honoring her. After renaming the festival Candlemas, household candles that would be used for religious purposes for the rest of the year were blessed on that day.

Some country folk still shake the trees on Candlemas to wake them up and tell the bees, "Bees, be happy, for today is Candlemas!" "If the sun shines on Candlemas, it will be a good year for the bees" is a saying in the countryside in England. On this day, it is time to take down the holly and pine branches that were winter decoration. Traditionally, by the time Candlemas comes around, the threshing and spinning should all be done because the new grain bear, or pea-bear, comes around (as has been described earlier) and brings new fertility. The day is also traditionally seen as an oracle day— who will marry, who will die, and how the harvest will be. To find out how much longer the winter will last, the animals that have been hibernating in the ground are observed. Foxes and badgers are observed as substitutes for bears. In many northern European countries, this saying is known: "If it is warm and sunny on Candlemas Day, the bear has to stay in his cave for six more weeks." According to this saying from Baselland, Switzerland, "As many hours as the bear can sun himself up above, so many more weeks of winter" (*So maengi Stund der Boer z Liechtmess dr Doope cha sunne, so maengi Wuche wird's no Winter*) (Hauser 1973, 114). In France and England, the saying goes, "If the bear sees its shadow on Candlemas, it will have to go back into its cave for forty more days." In the United States, the groundhog has taken over the role of the bear. After forty days, it will be spring equinox and then Bruin can really shake off his winter drowsiness and the bane of winter is broken.

Bears, which bring fertility, and bees that produce beeswax out of which golden, shining candles can be made, are radiant Birgit's favorite animals. In the colorful ways of country thinking, the two extremes belong together: massive, virile, lazy Master Bruin and tiny, chastely, industrious bees.[3] Bees were especially admired because they draw the nectar out of the blossoms without destroying them. For the early Europeans, honey, which was not replaced by cane sugar until the seventeenth century, was the only sweetener. It was so sacred that it was given to the gods and ancestors as an offering, and only in the holy nights of midwinter were cakes sweetened with honey eaten as sacred food. The Indo-Europeans saw honey as a remnant of a long ago, golden age, when honey was the dew on the primeval world tree. It is truly a divine food for the chosen one of the white goddess, the honey-eating king of the animals in the forest, as well as for the king of the people. The king and his noble companions drank wine made of honey (mead), and the peasants, servants, and workers drank beer made of barley.

MAY JOY AND AUGUST FIRES

When nature begins to turn green again in the spring and flowers begin to blossom, when the sun shines ever warmer and the queen bee swarms out for her nuptial flight with her entourage, the goddess of nature also celebrates her wedding. When the hawthorn blossoms and the full moon in May light up the landscape, the goddess becomes the radiant bride of the sun god. In honor of the divine couple, young men and women dance around the maypole, which has been decorated with colorful ribbons, and fall in love with each other. The bears in the forest also fall in love in the joyous month of May if the female bears no longer have small bears with them. They romp around joyfully in flowering meadows. Their wedding lasts until the summer solstice, which the Christians named Saint John's Day. Then the female bear is pregnant.

Forty days after the summer solstice, another magical point in time arrives: the fire festival *Lugnasad* (Anglo-Saxon *Half-mass, Lammas* = festival of the bread loaf) in the full moon days of August. Again, the bear appears,

The spring goddess riding a bear

this time in the form of the last sheaf, as the grain bear. The goddess now appears as the mother of the grains. She is no longer a shy young maiden or freshly married bride. She is a matron whose cornucopia is over-abundantly filled with fruits and grains. We recognize her in the *Dea Artio*, the Celtic-Roman bear goddess, whose statue was found in 1832 in Muri, near Berne, Switzerland. She is sitting majestically on a throne, in front of her is her companion, a big bear, and she holds a full basket of fruit.

Dea Artio (bronze, from Muri near Berne, second century BCE)

For the Celts, the August fire was at the height of the summer. At this time, the goddess pours out her blessings—but she also already begins to retreat from the outer world and head back toward the otherworld again. Under the custody of the Church, this festival became known as Mary's Assumption. At this time, when God's mother leaves the earthly world, the herbs are at their peak as far as their healing virtues are concerned. In Alpine regions, country women and herbal healers bring a bouquet of healing herbs to be blessed during mass.

This is also the time of the so-called dog days, these hot, humid summer days when the grasses dry up, the water in the ponds evaporates or dries up completely, and nasty gadflies pester the animals in the pastures. They begin in late July when Sirius, the Dog Star, ascends above the horizon, and end in late August when Arcturus, the bright guardian of the bear, ascends. The bear guardian walks along near the oxen driver, Booetes, protecting the heavily laden wagon from the hungry Big Bear (*Arctus Major*), which is filled with grains and wine, gifts from the goddess. In any case, this is how the old Greeks saw it when they looked up into the August sky. Harvest time continues beyond the fall equinox. The bears in the forest also harvest as much as possible and celebrate regular eating orgies. They become sluggish and fat like aging lovers. Soon the time will come when the goddess lets them be hunted or calls them into her cave.

MODRANIHT (MOTHER'S NIGHT)

The Celts called the November days *Samain* (Irish *samhain*; Gallic *Samon*; English *Halloween*). It is the time of year when the light begins to leave the northern climate, the birds flock and fly south, and the pasture animals return to the barns for the cold time of year. It is the time of the dead, the time of gray fog, of quiet, the time for hunting and butchering. The bears, these virile symbols of fertility, and the nature spirits descend down into the sphere of the roots.

The goddess, now seen as a wrinkled old woman, also descends into the netherworld; or, according to other Celtic versions, she turns on her husband, the sun-bear, sun-god, or sun-stag, and marries the god of the underworld, to reign in his realm of the dead and ghosts. (In the Celtic-Welsh tale of King Arthur, this motif also surfaces: Sinister Mordred wounds the bear king fatally and takes his wife, the white fairy, Genevieve, as his mistress.)

In November, when the days grow ever shorter and darker and snow begins to fall, the bears in the forest become very drowsy. Soon, they will be sleeping cozily on soft beds of moss, dry grass, and leaves in their dens. They are not in torpor when they hibernate, such as, for example, rodents are. Their state during hibernation is more like a trance, similar to that of yogis in India when they go into *samadhi* (these yogis are also able to survive the entire winter in Himalayan caves, snowed in and without any nourishment). The bear's heartbeat and breathing slow down during hibernation. Its pulse decreases to twelve beats per minute, and its body temperature sinks from 38°C (100°F) to 32°C (89°F). Bears do not excrete during this time and live from their fat reserves, so to say, on automatic pilot.[4] In the spring, they weigh one third less than when they went into hibernation.

At the time of the winter solstice, or Christmastime, the bear cubs are born—one to three naked, blind, and helpless cubs, no bigger than puppies, weighing about 500 grams (one pound) each. The ancient Celts and Germanic peoples of the north called this sacred time of year Modraniht, "Mother's Night"—a time when the new light, the child of the sun, is born deep in the earth. In earlier tales of Christ's birth, he was also born in an underground stone cave and not in a manger.

For the early Europeans, it was evident time and time again that a bear's life unfolded in synchronicity with the sacred yearly cycle. Just like the vegetation, bears appear in perfect harmony with the sun in the spring and disappear again in the fall. Bears are natural sons and daughters of the earth and have not removed themselves as far from their origin as the species *Homo sapiens* has. According to Rudolf Steiner, founder of anthroposophy, early humans in northern European latitudes were much more bound into the natural sun rhythms. They also wooed only in the early summer, and their children were born nine months later during the winter solstice. This pattern slowly changed as they became more independent of natural rhythms, and cultural acclimation (clothes, tools, institutions) replaced biological acclimation (pure instinct).

So far, we have mostly pursued ancient Celtic customs and their bear mythology because they are closer to native English-speaking, European cultural roots; however, other peoples also saw the bear as closely related to nature's yearly cycle. For the Abenaki in Maine, for example, the seasons are mirrored in the life cycle of the cosmic bear: In the spring, the bear appears in the sky, and all summer long it is hunted by hunters with dogs. That is, the constellation of the Northern Crown (Corona Borealis) is a cave to the Abenaki; the shaft of the great wagon (the Big Dipper), Arcturus, and some of the stars in Booetes are the dogs. When the hunters shoot the bear down in the fall, the leaves in nature turn bloody red, orange, and yellow. The first snow is the fat of the bear dripping down to the earth when the hunters melt it down. After the heavenly hunters have eaten the flesh and put his bones back together in the right order, the bear comes back to life and goes into hibernation. In the spring, the eternal drama of the bear hunt starts over once again.

Animals, including the bear (Celtic Cross from Drosten,
St. Vigeans, Forfarshire)

CHAPTER 10
The Guardian of the Treasures

Two fellows pressed for cash, averse to labour,
Sold a bear's skin to Furrier, their neighbour—
Skin of a bear uncaught and living still,
But one, they said, they were about to kill.

"The very king of bears," they cried,

"You'll make a fortune by his hide;

Of sharpest winter it will stand the test,
And furnish lining for two coats at least."
Dindenaut did not rate his fleecy kind
So high as they this bear they had to find.
They bound themselves, without the bear's consent,
To give it up at farthest in two days.
The price was fixed, and off our hunters went.
Towards them trots the beast to their amaze.
The bargain's broke: and thunderstruck they stare,
Without a word, or claim upon the bear.
One gained a tree—the other, cold as lead,
Fell on his face, pretending to be dead
Held in his breath, for he had heard it said
That bears but very seldom vent their spite
On bodies motionless and breathless quite.
Sir Bear was cheated, as the story goes,

He thought him lifeless, and stretched out in death;

Yet to have no remaining doubt,

Close to his nose

Applied his snout,

And smelt the issues of his breath,

Turning him round and round about.

"A corpse," he cried, "away, it stinks too strong,"
He said, and through the forest moved along.
Our marchant left the tree, surprised to hear
His neighbour had no other hurt than fear.
"Where's now the skin," he cried, "we praised so much?
But tell me what he whispered in your ear,

As you together were so near,

And he was turning you with snout and clutch?"
"He told me to look after other wares,
Nor deal in skins of uncaught living bears."

JEAN DE LA FONTAINE, "THE BEAR
AND THE TWO COMPANIONS"

D o you remember, dear reader, the fairy tale of Snow White and Rose Red who lived in the deep forest alone with their mother? No need to look for the dusty volumes of Grimms' Fairy Tales; we will retell the story here because it reveals another secret about the bear.

Once upon a time, a poor widow lived alone in a cottage and in front two rose bushes grew—one of them had white blossoms and the other one had red blossoms. The widow had two daughters who were like the rose bushes—one was called Snow White and the other was called Rose Red.

One evening when the cold autumn wind was already blowing over the pines and a merry fire was burning in the hearth, they heard a knocking at the door. The mother said, "Rose Red, open the door. It is probably a wayfarer looking for a place to stay the night." Rose Red went and unbolted the door thinking it was probably a poor wayfarer who had knocked. But it was no wayfarer—it was a bear that poked its big black head into the door as soon as it was opened enough! Rose Red screamed and jumped back. The lamb bleated, the dove fluttered, and Snow White hid behind her mother's bed.

But the bear began to speak, saying, "Do not be afraid. I will not hurt you. I am half frozen and only wish to warm up a bit."

"You poor bear," said the mother, "lie down near the fire and be careful not to burn your fur!" Then she called out to her daughters, "Snow White, Rose Red, come out of hiding. The bear will not hurt you. He means it honestly." Both girls came back out and the lamb and dove also came closer and lost their fear.

The bear spoke, "Children, come closer and brush the snow out of my fur." They got a broom and brushed his fur and the bear stretched out near the fire and grumbled in a happy and satisfied manner. It did not take them long to become good friends and play happily with each other. The girls would tousle his fur with their hands, put their feet on his back and push him back and forth mischievously, or they grabbed a hazel switch and playfully hit him, laughing when their clumsy guest grumbled. The bear put up with it all but when they got too rambunctious, he would say, "Let me keep on living, children. Snow White, Rose Red, do not slay your suitor!"

Evenings, when the others went to bed, the mother said to the bear, "You can stay here near the hearth. Here you are protected from the cold and the bad weather." As soon as the morning began to break the children let him out and he wandered off to spend the whole day in the forest. The bear came back the same time each evening to spend the night near the hearth and let the children play with him as much as they wished. The children became so used to having him there that the door was not bolted in the evening until their furry guest was back.

When spring came and everything began to turn green outside, the bear said to the two girls, "Now I must leave and cannot come back for the whole summer."

"Where will you go, dear bear?" Snow White asked.

"I have to go into the forest and protect my treasures from the wicked dwarves. In the winter when the earth was frozen, they had to stay below the ground and could not reach the surface. But now that the sun warms the surface of the earth, they climb up to search for and steal treasures. Whatever they get their hands on and hide in their caves is not easy to find again." Snow White was very sad to see him go. When she unbolted the door and he pushed through, he got stuck. A piece of skin was scratched open on the door hinge and Snow White thought she saw gold shimmer through the torn skin, but she was not completely sure about it. The bear hurried on out and was soon out of sight.

Sometime later, the mother sent the girls out to gather some brushwood for fire. They found a big tree on the forest floor that had been felled. Something was jumping up and down between the tree trunk and the grass, but they couldn't tell what it was. When they got closer, they saw it was a dwarf with an old wrinkled face and a long white beard. The end of his beard was stuck under the tree trunk and the dwarf jumped this way and that like a puppy on a leash, not knowing how to get out of the predicament. The children tugged and tugged, but they could not get his beard out from under the tree.

"I will go get some other people to help!" Rose Red said.

"Crazy blockheads!" the dwarf snarled. "Why would you go get more people? You two are already two too many! Can't you think of anything better?"

"Don't be impatient," said Snow White, "I will think of something." With that, she took a pair of scissors out of her apron pocket and cut off the end of his beard.

As soon as the dwarf noticed he was free, he grabbed a bag of gold that was between the roots of the tree and grumbled, "Uncouth girls, cutting my fine beard! Go to blazes!" With that he swung the bag over his shoulder and went off without once looking back.

On another occasion, Snow White and Rose Red went to the stream to catch some fish for supper. As they approached, they saw something that looked like a big grasshopper hopping toward the water as if it wanted to jump in. They came closer and realized that it was the dwarf. "Where do you want to go?" asked Rose Red. "You surely do not want to go into the water!"

"Do I look like such a fool," the dwarf yelled, "don't you see that accursed fish wants to pull me in?" He had been sitting there fishing and the wind had tangled up his beard with the fishing line. A big fish had taken the bait and was stronger than the dwarf, so it was pulling the dwarf toward the water. The dwarf grabbed onto the rushes and stalks, but the fish was getting the upper hand just as the girls arrived. They held on to him and tried to loosen his beard from the fishing line, but it was too entwined. There was again no other choice than to cut the beard free from the line, resulting in a very scraggy-looking beard.

When the dwarf saw his reflection in the water, he yelled at the girls, "You dumbbells, what kind of manners do you have—how do I look now? As if it wasn't enough you cut the bottom off. Now I can't show myself in front of my people! I wish the two of you have to walk and have no soles on your shoes!" Then he grabbed a bag of pearls he had in the rushes, and without another word he disappeared behind a rock.

It was not much longer after this last incident that the girls had been sent to town by their mother to buy thread and needles and colorful ribbons. The pathway to town went through a big patch of heather that had huge rocks strewn here and there. They saw a big bird circling slowly in the sky and then it dived near one of the rocks. Right afterward, they heard a piercing, pitiful scream. They ran up to the rock and saw that the eagle had grabbed their old acquaintance the dwarf and was preparing to fly off with him. The girls had pity on the dwarf and pulled at him so long until the eagle finally let him go.

As soon as the dwarf got over his shock he yelled with his screechy voice, "Couldn't you have been more gentle with me? My elegant gown is torn and full of holes. Clumsy and awkward riffraff, you are!" Then he grabbed a sack full of jewels and slipped off into his cave. The girls had become used to his thanklessness and continued on their way. After taking care of their business in town as they were on their way home they happened upon the dwarf again, who had emptied his bag of jewels in a clearing and was admiring them. He did not think someone would come by so late in the day. The setting sun shone on the jewels, and they shone so brightly that the girls had to stop and admire them.

"What are you two gaping at?" the dwarf yelled at them, his otherwise ashen face turning bright red and looking furious. He wanted to continue ranting at them when a loud grumbling was heard and a big black bear appeared out of the forest. The dwarf jumped up in shock, but he couldn't reach his bolt hole as the bear was already on top of him. Terrified, he called out, "Dear bear, spare me. I will give you all of my treasures. Look, the beautiful jewels there. Spare my life. What could you want with a small fry like myself? You would not even feel me between your teeth. Take those two godless girls there, such delicate tidbits, eat them, in God's name!" The bear did not listen to the dwarf but gave him an ear cuff with his paw and the dwarf did not budge again.

The girls had run off, but the bear caught up with them. "Snow White, Rose Red, do not be afraid. Wait, I want to walk with you." They recognized his voice and stood still. As soon as the bear was near them, the bearskin fell off and a handsome young man dressed in gold stood in front of them. "I am a king's son," he spoke, "and that godless dwarf that had stolen all of my treasures cursed me to be a wild bear in the forest until I would be redeemed by his death. Now he has gotten his well-deserved punishment!"

Snow White married him and Rose Red married his brother. They shared the huge treasure that they found in the dwarf's cave. The old mother lived happily for many years with her children. She took the two rose bushes with her and planted them near her window where they flowered every year, one white and the other red.

Snow White and Rose Red riding the bear

The bear kills the wicked dwarf

THE CROESUS OF THE ANIMAL REALM

In the tale of Snow White and Rose Red, it becomes evident that the bear, despite its wild appearance, is not only noble, but also rich—tremendously rich. How else could it be? Do we not know him as the companion of the earth goddess who pours her cornucopia over the fields and meadows, causing crates, barrels, and warehouses to overflow? We meet the king of the animals here as a guardian of immeasurable treasures, as the owner of precious jewels, pearls, and piles of gold. Because the inner earth is not closed off from him, he has access to secret chambers where jewels grow, buried gold lies, and veins of silver crisscross the rock substrata. This story seems to relate to another legend in which a bear shows Saint Mang the gold and silver veins in the mountains, which made affluent the monastery in southern Germany, Saint Mang's Abbey, Fuessen. It is also surely not by chance that, according to legend, the cellar underneath the city hall in Berne, Switzerland, was once a bear's cave. The oldest silver coin (from the thirteenth century, called a *Batzen;* see illustration) of the city shows a striding bear and, on top of it, the crowned head of the king.

Bernese coin, "Der Batzen," thirteenth century

The word *Batzen* spread far and wide in German-speaking areas, and etymologists believe it goes back to the words *Betz* or *Petz,* which is the German equivalent to the affectionate *Bruin* (bear) (Roehrich 2001, 1:158).

Even in the nerve centers of the modern financial world, on Wall Street, in Frankfurt, or Zurich, one can hear the bear grumbling in bear markets, bear operations, and bear sales. This term used by stock exchange speculators goes back to a pan-European adage that one should not sell a bear's fur before having skinned one.[1]

Bruin is fabulously rich without having to work hard and without having to be stingy and miserly. Wealth simply falls to him. It is part of his being. Even when he is lazy, lying around, and taking it easy, his wealth never becomes less. After all, he is a king. Astrologers attribute a

Jupiter nature to the bear. Jupiter, the gold-crowned king of the planets, ruler over thunder and lightning, is the giver of fullness, wealth, and joy that can also turn into their opposites: gluttony, sloth, and obesity. Hardly any other animal is so Jupiter-like. A tale from Lapland tries to tell how Bruin became so blessed:

> Once, when the Lord was still with us here on earth, he came to a raging river that he could not cross. He asked a horse that was grazing on the riverbank if it would take him on its back and bring him across. The horse whinnied proudly and turned away. Not long afterward the Lord met a bear that was catching fish in the stream. He also asked him if he would carry him across. The bear did not hesitate and, as if he were Saint Christopher himself, he carried the Lord over to the other side.
>
> The Lord said to the horse: "Because you refused to render me even only this small service, you will have to spend your life with hard work, pulling coaches and plows and carrying heavy loads on your back—and that with only meager fare!"
>
> Turning toward the bear he announced: "And you, dear bear, you will be granted a pleasant life without work. You may sleep the whole winter and in the summer the best tidbits, berries, honey, and other treasures will be yours!"

KRISHNA HUMBLES THE BEAR KING

The wealth of bears is also well-known in India. They know that *Jambavat*[2] (the king of the bears) has a never-ending treasure of gold and precious jewels, but he also has wisdom. Because he is wise, he has always honored Vishnu, the Preserver of the Universe. Whenever meanness and injustice get the upper hand, Vishnu appears as an earthly being to save the world with Jambavat right there at his side.

When Vishnu appeared incarnated as a dwarf, took three strides across the world, and so saved it from the despotic rule of the demon king, Bali, it was the bear who blew into the big horn announcing the victory to the entire world at once. When Vishnu incarnated another time as Rama to slay the demon king of Sri Lanka, Ravanna, the bear king marched along-side the monkey army with an entire army of bears, helping the mission to succeed.

Only once has Jambavat been blinded by possessiveness and crossed the great god. A fabulous jewel, *Syamantaka,* shone as bright as the sun and generated a wagon full of gold every day; those near it lost all fear of bad omens, wild animals, dangerous fires, robbers, and famine. This miracle jewel belonged to the sun god who once gave it to his most loyal worshiper in recognition of his devotion. His devotee accepted the gift with gratitude; however, soon doubt crept into his mind. He felt unsure that he could measure up to such a jewel. In addition, the sun devotee was afraid that Vishnu, who was at that time incarnated as the cowherd Krishna on earth, might take the jewel away from him because he loved jewels as much as he loved women. So, he decided to give the jewel to his brother, Prasena, who was stronger than he was.

> But the jewel had another characteristic: It brought luck to the good, but the bad could only expect misfortune. Prasena had a bad core, and no sooner had he received the jewel than great misfortune befell him. A lion attacked and ate him, and then took off carrying the brilliant sun jewel in its mouth.
>
> Jambavat happened along, and he wanted to show the lion who was really the king of the animals. He swiped the lion with his paw and the lion staggered. Then the bear grabbed the lion in a bear hug and squeezed so hard that the lion quit breathing for good. Grumbling in a satisfied manner, the bear took the jewel in his mouth and trotted off to his palace down under the ground. No one except God himself would be able to take his prize away from him.
>
> In the meantime, the sun worshiper began to worry about his brother who had disappeared without a trace, just as the jewel had. He wondered if cowherd Krishna had snatched the jewel and maybe even killed his brother to get it. Krishna assured him he was innocent and even promised to help find the magical jewel. He immediately took off following the tracks of unlucky Prasena. After some time, he saw Prasena's tracks seemed to disappear into a heap of dust and turn into lion tracks. Soon enough these tracks turned into bear tracks and Krishna followed them to the mouth of a cave. He entered and demanded the jewel. Jambavat had given it to his son and he was playing with it. A terrible battle ensued. After seven days

Krishna's friends and devotees thought the divine human would never return alive from the bear's cave. Crying and lamenting, they cut off their hair in mourning and put on white mourning clothes.

It was not until the twenty-first day that the bear surrendered to the divine supremacy and handed over the loot. As an extra gesture of conciliation, the bear also gave Krishna his daughter in marriage. After all, not only all treasures but also each woman's heart (each soul) belong to the blue god—who symbolizes the higher being in each of us.

Krishna's fight with the bear king

ZALMOXIS AND IMMORTALITY

The Getae and Datians, who once ruled over southeastern Europe (the Balkans), worshiped a bear god they called Zalmoxis—the name allegedly means "bearskin." This god, who occasionally disquieted the people with roaring thunder and lightning, was seen as the giver of all goods. Every five years, a messenger presented the humans' concerns to the bear god. To send the messenger on his way, the priests grabbed him by his hands and feet, swung him for momentum, and then threw him up as high as possible. Three upright spears caught him when he came back down, and his immediate death was considered a good omen and guarantee that Zalmoxis would continue to be benevolent (Eliade 1981, 4:57).

Herodot, the Hellenistic historian, has this bear god as a human being. In ethnocentric self-aggrandizement, he claims that Zalmoxis was a slave belonging to the great Greek philosopher Pythagoras from whom Zalmoxis learned about immortality. How else could such a primitive barbarian have ever come upon such a lofty idea? Zalmoxis, though a slave, is supposed to have been outrageously rich. When he returned to the barbarian Datians, he is said to have built a giant festival hall where he hosted his fellow tribesmen with fine wines and opulent meals. During the feasts, he instructed them, telling them that their souls were immortal and would go to a place where they would live forever and have precious possessions. One day, Zalmoxis is said to have disappeared into a subterranean chamber. Since he did not come back, the barbarians believed he must have died and they mourned him with great lamentation. But after three whole years, he came back up—like a bear out of hibernation—looking healthy and lively. Since then, reports Herodot, these people believed in eternal life.

The Greeks were the first to practice anthropocentrism and were the founders of humanism. They humanized their gods and put the human being in the midst of all that took place. In this respect, we have taken over their inheritance. However, it is probable that this Zalmoxis, the god of the ancient Getae and Datians, is the very bear that goes in and out of the realm of the goddess of death and that is so immeasurably rich because all the riches of the depths are available to him. The feasts described by Herodot and Zalmoxis's three-year residence beneath the earth were probably part of an ancient initiation ritual. It was also said that Zalmoxis gained great wisdom under the earth as well as the ability to predict the weather.

The eastern Siberians also know about the wealth of the bear, and they, too, send a messenger to the sacred bear spirit every two years or so to ask for luck and material wealth for the tribe. But they do not send a human being—like the Getae and Datians did—instead, they send a forest bear that is sacrificed in an elaborate ritual.

MASTER OF FIRE

The Kaska Dena, who live in the cold subarctic coniferous forest belt in the northern Rocky Mountains, hunt caribou, trap fur-bearing animals, and fish in icy-cold glacial waters. In this cold, inhospitable country, there is hardly anything more precious than a warming fire. One of the favorite stories of these people is about a bear from long, long ago that was a master of fire. He possessed a rock that was more valuable than all the sparkling jewels in the world. It was a firestone out of which he could make sparks anytime and start a fire (Campbell 1991, 277).

Long ago, in the beginning of time, people did not have fire. Only the bear could warm himself in the winter thanks to firestone. The bear was very much on guard to protect this possession that he carried tied tightly to his belt. Once, when he was warming himself near his cozy fire, a small bird flew into the cave. "What do you want here?" he asked in a not very friendly tone.

"I am nearly frozen," the bird peeped, "please let me warm myself here near your fire."

"Well, ok," the bear answered, "but while you thaw, you can pick the lice out of my fur."

The little guest hopped here, there and everywhere and picked lice here and there, and once in a while, it also picked at the rope that held the firestone. When it had finally picked enough that the firestone came free, it grabbed it in its beak and flew off with it. At the mouth of the cave other animals were waiting at various intervals because they had planned to steal the firestone for a very long time.

The angry bear chased the little feathered thief, which could only barely carry its heavy booty. Just as the bear almost grabbed him, the next animal took the stone and ran off with it as fast as he could. When the bear caught up with it, it tossed the stone to the next animal, and so it went all day long. The firestone was passed from one to the other like in a relay race until it came to a fox. The fox ran up a mountain so that the bear would get completely out of breath by the time he reached the top. The fox then lost the stone and it fell down the mountain breaking into many pieces and that is how the humans got the firestone—as they happened to be camping at the foot of that mountain.

Native American bear illustrations from the northwest. Left: Tsimshian; right: Haida.

CHAPTER 11
Berserkers and Guardians
of the Threshold

The berserkers are ready,
Wolves will escort them,
Whether Middle Ages
Or modern times, is all the same.

They came once more from up above
But this time not to run riot,
Instead to give their power
For the earth and Life on earth.

The berserkers are back again,
So that the earth can come back into its own,
They are bringing all the gods along
And dedicating themselves to Mother Earth."

NORBERT J. MAYER, FROM *DIE BERSERKER SIND*
ANGESAGT! (AUTHOR'S TRANSLATION)

Positivist scientists would hardly join company with primitive peoples and their storytellers in their belief in a realm of light under the surface of the earth, inside the mountains where gold and precious jewels are strewn all over, where white stags with golden antlers graze peacefully near bears, and where the dead and unborn dance lovely round dances together.

However, those who research the vast depths of the soul presume we are not dealing with a material, geographical place that can be found by following a map, but a realm in our unconscious that is usually blocked off from our daily consciousness. And there, under the surface, is the very real primeval fountain of all vitality, beauty, and wisdom—precisely such riches of the soul that are waiting to be discovered—there in the realm where the bear is at home.

Only great shamans, noble spirits, and gods, such as Krishna or Zalmoxis, are allowed to enter the cave and find treasures on the sunny meadows of the otherworld and then return to this world. Terrible "guardians of the threshold" keep those who have no business in these realms at bay. Fire, poison, and gall-spewing dragons and sphinxes, hell hounds with huge red-glowing eyes, or giant bears with their paws raised and jaws wide open guard these treasures from wanton seizure. (For the people of ancient times, these monsters were real beings—psychoanalysts see them as psychic repressions or fears that have taken form in the imagination.)

The devil is also never far away from such mysterious places. In Goethe's most well-known work, learned Dr. Faust conjures the son of Mother Night, the spirit of hell, Mephistopheles. He turns out to be the ancient "earth daemon" that has command over all earthly treasures and possesses all the wisdom of the earth. Justifiably, the poet has him appear as a black poodle—in many old religions, a black dog is the guardian of the threshold to the netherworld. However, in the old medieval tales that tell about the excessive life of corrupt Dr. Faust, Mephistopheles usually appears as a black, or fiery, bear, or a bear with a human head—who comes out from behind the fireplace.

Anyone who wants to reach the hidden hoard of treasures has to deal with this bear. The hero must be willing to put aside the false pretenses and phoniness of the civilized world and must bathe in dragon's blood or slip under a bearskin. He must be pure-minded, be uncorrupted, and have clear instincts, like a bear or a "noble savage." This is the only way to find the precious gem of life. This is the only way to save, or even be able to save, the "maiden in distress" who is "captured" in the depths of the soul.

This is the heroic path that the young warrior embarked upon in the following story, "Bearskin."

Once upon a time, there was a young fellow who signed up for the military, was very brave, and was always the first one forward when the bullets flew. Things went very well as long as there was a war somewhere. But when peace came, he was dismissed and his commander told him he could go wherever he wished. His parents were dead, and he no longer had a home to go to, so he looked up his brothers and asked if he could stay with them until another war started. But his brothers were hard hearted and told him to move on. "There is nothing for you here! We can't use you around here. Move on and find a way to make it on your own!" they said.

The soldier had no other possessions than his gun. So he shouldered it and took off out into the world. He came upon a big area of heather and moorland where nothing was to be seen but a ring of trees. He sat down under the trees and mused about his fate. "I don't have any money," he thought, "I haven't learned anything but the trade of war, and now that we are living in times of peace, it looks like I will starve."

Suddenly, he heard a boom and just as suddenly an unknown person stood there in front of him. He had a green jacket and was quite smart looking, although one of his feet was a horrible-looking horse's hoof. "I know what you need," said the man, "you shall have money and property, as much as you want, but first I have to know whether you are afraid so that I don't spend my money for nothing."

"A soldier and fear, how does that go together?" asked the soldier, "You can put me to the test."

"Well, then," the man answered, "look behind you."

The soldier looked behind him and saw a big bear that was trotting straight toward him, grumbling loudly. "Look at that," the soldier called out, "I will tickle your nose so much you won't be grumbling anymore!" He grabbed his gun, aimed, and shot the bear so that it dropped dead in an instant.

Bearskin, bear, and the devil

"I see that you certainly do not lack courage," the stranger spoke, "but there is one other condition that you must fulfill."

"If there is no damage to my soul, I will," said the soldier, who very well knew who was standing in front of him, "otherwise, I will make no deal."

"You will see," answered the man with the green jacket, "you may not bathe for the next seven years, may not comb your hair or beard, not cut your nails, nor say the Lord's prayer. I will give you a jacket and overcoat that you have to wear during this time. If you die within the seven years, you are mine. But if you stay alive, after seven years you will be free and will be wealthy for your entire life."

The soldier thought about his needy situation and decided to accept the offer. The devil took off his green coat, gave it to him, and said, "As long as you wear this coat and search the pockets, you will always find a hand full of money." Then he skinned the bear and said, "This will be your overcoat and also your bed because you have to sleep on it and use no other bed. And because of this overcoat you will be called Bearskin." The devil then disappeared.

The soldier put the jacket on, reached right away into a pocket and found that things were as had been promised. Then he put the bearskin on, went out into the world, and left nothing undone that did him some good and didn't do the money quite as much good. During the first year, it went quite well, but already in the second year he looked like a monstrosity. His hair almost covered his whole face, his beard looked like a piece of coarse felt, his fingers had claws, and his face was so packed with dirt that if one had sown cress into it, it would have sprouted. Anybody who saw him ran away. But because everywhere he went he gave the poor money to pray for him that he would not die during the seven years and because he paid up front for everything, he always found room and board. In the fourth year, he came to a lodging where the innkeeper did not want to let him stay. He did not even want to give him a place in the stall because he was afraid his horses would get spooked. But when Bearskin reached into his pocket and pulled out a handful of ducats, the innkeeper softened and gave him a room in the far back, but he had to promise to not show himself lest his inn get a bad reputation.

As Bearskin sat there alone in the evening and was wishing from the bottom of his heart that the seven years were over, he heard loud crying in the room next to his. He had a compassionate heart, so he opened the door and found an old man sobbing and wringing his hands. Bearskin came closer, but the man jumped up and wanted to flee. When he heard a human voice, he sat back down, and, with his friendly manners, Bearskin convinced him to tell him the reason for his grief. Bit by bit, he had lost his wealth and he and his daughters had to live in utmost poverty. He could no longer pay the innkeeper and was soon to be sent to prison. "If that is all," said Bearskin, "I have enough money." He sent for the innkeeper and paid the old man's debts. Then he gave him a bag of gold to put in his pocket.

When the old man saw that he had been saved from his dire state, he thought about how he could thank Bearskin for his help. "Come with me," he said to him, "my daughters are very beautiful. You may choose one as your wife. When she hears what you have done for me she will not refuse. You do look mighty strange, but she will get you nice and cleaned up."

Bearskin liked the sound of that and he went along. When the eldest saw him, she was so shocked that she screamed and ran away. The second daughter stayed put but after looking him up and down quite thoroughly, she asked, "How can I accept a man who no longer has a human form? I liked the shaved bear even better that was once here pretending to be a man—at least it wore hussar's cloak and white gloves. If it were only that he is ugly, I might be able to get used to that."

But the youngest daughter said, "Dear father, if he helped you out of your troubles, he must have a good heart and your promise must be kept." It was a real shame that Bearskin's face was so caked with dirt and covered with hair; otherwise, one would have been able to see how his heart leapt for joy as he heard these words. He took a ring out of his pocket and broke it in two, giving her one half and keeping the other half for himself. He wrote his name in her half and her name in his half and asked her to guard it well. Then he took his leave, saying, "I must continue to roam for three more years. If I do not come back, you are free, because I will be dead. But pray to God to protect me and keep me alive."

The poor young betrothed bride dressed in black, and, when she thought of her groom, tears came to her eyes. Her sisters mocked her. The eldest said, "Be careful, when he comes back and you want to give him your hand, he will hit it with his claws!"

The second sister said, "Be careful, bears love sweet things and if he likes you he might eat you!"

"You will always have to obey him," the other one chimed in again, "otherwise he will growl."

Then the other added, "Well at least the wedding will be fun because bears can dance well."

The youngest sister remained silent and did not let them vex her. In the meantime, Bearskin traveled from place to place doing as much good as he could and giving generously to the poor while asking them to pray for him. Finally, at daybreak of the last day of the seven years, he went to the moor where the ring of trees stood and sat down again near the trees. It did not take long for a wind to come up, and there was the devil standing in front of him again with a peeved look on his face. He tossed Bearskin his old coat and asked him to give the green one back. Bearskin said, "We are not that far down the line yet. First you clean me up!" Whether the devil wanted to or not, he had to go get water and scrub Bearskin clean, comb his hair, and cut his nails. When he was done, Bearskin looked like a gallant warrior and was even more handsome than before.

When the devil disappeared, Bearskin felt very lighthearted. He went into town, bought a splendid velvet jacket, and took a coach drawn by four white horses to go to the house of his bride. No one recognized him and the father thought he must be a very high colonel, so he brought him into the parlor where his daughters were sitting. He had to sit between the two elder sisters; they poured him a glass of wine and offered him special tidbits to eat. They both thought they had never seen a more handsome man before. But the young bride sat in her black dress across from him and did not speak a word or even raise her eyes to look at him. When he finally asked the father if he could have one of his daughters as a wife, both of the elder sisters jumped up to put on their best dresses because each of them was smug and believed she would be the chosen one. As soon as the stranger was alone with his young bride, he put his half of the ring in a glass of wine and reached it across the table toward her. She accepted it, but, when she saw the ring in the bottom of the glass, her heart began to pound. She took her half of the ring that she wore on a necklace, fitted the two halves together, and saw that they fit perfectly. Then he spoke, "I am your promised groom that you saw as Bearskin. Through God's grace, I was able to get my human form back." He went over to her, hugged her, and gave her a kiss. Right then, her two sisters came back into the room. When they saw that the handsome man had chosen the youngest and heard that he was Bearskin, they ran outside in a rage. One of them drowned herself in the well, and the other hung herself on a tree. That evening someone knocked on the door, and, when the groom opened the door, he saw it was the devil with his green jacket on. The devil said, "You see, now I have two souls in place of your one!"[1]

The fairy tale tells of brave souls, who are not afraid of their own untainted, instinctive side, their "bear nature." It also tells of those who are pure and humble, such as the youngest daughter, who dares to trust the bear and follow him through the dark labyrinth of life to achieve wholeness and the marriage of the opposites (the marriage of animus and anima, the male and female aspects of being). Souls like this will not be in need of anything. The devil is also not a problem for them because, after all, he is also only a servant of the pure and divine human being.

In this sense, it may very well be true that it is a sign of good luck to happen upon bear tracks, as believed by gypsies, Transylvanians, and many native peoples (who often hardly distinguish between internal and external reality).

Bear tracks

INTERPRETATIONS

Let us go back now to the story of Snow White and Rose Red. The hero in this story is also a "bearskin." The bear that appears so late at night at the cottage is in reality a young man who, after his trial as a wild animal, will discard his bearskin, return to society, marry, and come into his true inheritance. Depth psychology would see here the process of spiritual individuation, of finding one's true being. In most Western European cultures, the true being of a young man, the innermost noble spirit, was traditionally usually seen as a prince. It is his destiny to free the maiden, who symbolizes the human soul, from prison or some other distress, marry her, and rule the country—symbolic for human life—with wisdom and justice as the king with her as his queen.

But before things get that far, a drama happens. The ugly lower self, the ego that feels shortchanged—this godless dwarf—is envious of the higher self and its treasures: the gold of wisdom, the pearls of tears spent while gaining clarity through catharsis, the gems of a crystal-clear spirit. The cunning gnome hexes the prince into a wild animal and steals his treasures. As a bear clothed in shaggy fur, the hero experiences the forest and wilderness—the dark world of the unconscious. He gets to know primeval, wild nature that is older than civilization. In this wilderness, he meets the female anima. She is his bride, the other half of his soul. But not until he overcomes the venomous dwarf—this appropriate symbol of lower, egotistical intelligence and materialism—can the bear cast aside his disguise. The soul then recognizes that its other half is waiting there beneath the rough exterior of the enchanted prince, and, through the marriage of the two halves, the human being becomes complete.

A cultural anthropologist would interpret the fairy tale, with regard to the cultural history of Europe, as follows: The three women, Snow White, Rose Red, and their mother, who live deep in the forest, represent the female trinity that was once prevalent in the entire Indo-European cultural area. Fairy tales that were recorded by the Grimm brothers and other collectors—and thus saved from being lost forever—contain many treasures of spiritual vision and wisdom common to the pre-Christian forest peoples of Europe, the Celts, the Germanics, the Slavs, and others. The three women are different aspects of the same one goddess. It is the goddess who reveals herself in the yearly changing of the seasons: as a white virgin; as the beautifully blossoming whitethorn goddess in the spring (Celtic *Brigit*); as the red goddess of the blood of life, summer warmth, and plentiful harvest; and as the dark lady of wisdom and death in the fall.[2] We see here the ancient Paleolithic goddess of the cave, Mother Goose, in her changing appearances.

The bear, who finds shelter with the three women and from under whose fur pure gold shines, is the sun—is the sun god himself. Like the bear in the wilderness that holes up in a dark cave, the sun conceals itself mostly under the horizon in the winter (in northern climates), and a gray coat of fog muffles its light. In the spring, the bear tosses off its bearskin. When the whitethorn and blackthorn are in full blossom, the sun radiates like a young hero—bringing them to blossom. As *Belenus* (Celtic for "radiant, shining"), he woos the whitethorn goddess. His "brother," who marries Rose Red, is the hero in the form of Celtic Lugh or *Lugus* (Celtic for "burning brightly"), representing the fiery sun in August that drives everything into ripeness and completion. As an old woman, as a grieving widow, the black goddess (Celtic Morrigan) accompanies the dying sun god in the late fall into the womb of the dark earth. On the darkest day of the year—the winter solstice—she bears the new light, the new sun, like a bear does its young.

Fairy tales are not clear cut; instead, they are usually ambiguous. Each interpretation can be correct. The shiny jewels guarded by a mystical bear not only exist in the womb of the earth or in the depth of the soul but also shine as stars in the high heavens—inaccessible to mortals. In the imagination of the alchemists and also some primitive peoples, crystals and precious gems are magically connected to the stars by invisible threads. According to the alchemical law "as above, so below," precious jewels are reflections of the stars in earthly matter.

Both the depths of the earth and the distant heavens were regarded by archaic people as the otherworld, as the barely reachable "beyond," as the realm of the gods and ancestors that is full of mystery. Bears and other guardians of the threshold watched over the thresholds to these worlds. Consequently, these peoples also saw bears in the heavens at night—shining, godly bears that roam along paths near the stationary North Star. We will now follow the star tracks of these heavenly bears.

The three-fold goddess (Renaissance representation, Vincenzo Cartari, Venice, 1674)

CHAPTER 12
The Heavenly Trail of Ursa Major

Ursa Major, descend, shaggy night
nebula-furred animal with those ancient eyes,
Star eyes,
your clawed paws break shimmering
through the thicket,
Star claws,
We keep vigil over our herds,
yet you hold us in your power, and we mistrust
your tired flanks and sharp,
half-bared teeth,
old Bear.
Your world is a pinecone
and you its scales.
I propel them, roll them
from the firs at the beginning
to the firs at the end.
I blow them, test them in my mouth
and grasp them with my paws.

FROM *INVOCATION TO THE GREAT BEAR*
BY INGEBORG BACHMANN,
TRANSLATED BY ANGELIKA FREMD

In the myths of the peoples of the northern hemisphere, one happens again and again upon the imagination of a big bear that roams around the North Star. We all know the constellation of the seven bright stars called Ursa

Major (or the Big Bear, also known as the Big Dipper and in older times in northern Europe as "the Wagon"). It is easy to identify and often the first constellation that beginning astronomers learn. Close by, one can see the small bear, Ursa Minor, whose long tail points to the North Star.

Ursa Major and Ursa Minor

THE POWER THAT MOVES THE HEAVENS

In India, the seven stars in the constellation Ursa Major are called "the seven luminous ones" or "the seven rishis" who are gathered around God (the North Star) on the top of the world mountain (Mount Meru). According to an even older version, the Hindus speak of seven shining bears. The

North Star is the hub around which the heavenly vault turns, and the bears represent the elemental power that makes the turning possible. They drive the stars that rise and set daily. They push and shove the wheel that turns summer to winter and back to summer, brings rain and harvest, but also wind and drought.[1] These bears are identical to the *Maruts*, the storm gods that whirl around the god Shankar-Shiva with thunder and lightning bolts. The androgynous god of yoga, Shiva, sits in the quiet eye of the storm, and out of the unfathomable depths of his meditation the entire creation emerges. The North Star is the spring out of which the worlds flow, the place of birth, and the bears are the guardians of this cosmic womb.

For the ancient Germanic tribes, the North Star that was surrounded by vital bear power was not only a physical point of orientation but also a spiritual one. It is the tip of the conical firmament, the tip of the mystical mountain of glass; in the Edda, the North Star is called *Leidharstjarna* and in Old High German, *Leitesterre*, which means "leading star." It is the star one looks for to avoid getting lost, to "get one's bearings." For some Siberian tribes, the heavenly bear appears in the constellations *Booetes* and *Arcturus*—the same constellations in which the ancient Greeks saw the oxen driver and the bear guardian. They call Ursa Major a huge elk that the hungry heavenly bear is chasing.

But no matter where the hunting peoples of the north see the divine bear in the starry sky, it is always the center of their religious life. The bear appears on earth, the middle world (of the three-fold heaven, earth, and netherworld), as a benevolent visitor. He is the cosmic shaman who connects the higher cosmic and lower earthly worlds. He is a higher being created by star power but at the same time the son of Mother Earth. Only to deceptive, everyday consciousness does he appear as a wild animal, bulky and clumsy and covered with fur. This ancient view lingers in the fairy tales that we sometimes tell our children. As we have seen, they also tell about the light and starry secrets of the bear. According to ancient Finnish belief, the heavenly bear descends from the northerly regions in the sky to the earth in a golden crib. Finnish reindeer herders describe dying as "mounting the bear's shoulder," what we know as "going to heaven."

THE GUEST FROM THE TWELFTH HEAVEN

The Algonquian tribes lived as hunters and corn farmers in the northern forest areas of North America. They also worshiped the mystical bear and saw it in the four brilliant stars that form the square in Ursa Major (the dipper part of the Big Dipper). The three other stars that are the handle of the dipper, or for the ancient Germanic tribes the shaft of the wagon, were seen as three hunters with their dog, the star Alcor,[2] who are hard on the bear's heels. A star song of the Passamaquoddy, an Algonquian tribe that lives in Maine, goes like this:

We are the stars who sing,
we sing with our light;
We are the birds of fire,
we fly over the sky.
Our light is a voice . . .
We make a road for the spirits,
for the spirits to pass over.
Among us are three hunters
who chase a bear.
There never was a time
when they were not hunting.
We look down on the mountains.
This is the song of the stars.[3]

In the deepest wintertime, shortly after the January new moon, when it seemed that everything was going to petrify in the freezing cold, the Mohicans celebrated a twelve-day festival for the rejuvenation of creation. At that time, the cosmic bear, as a messenger for the Great Spirit, descended from the Twelfth Heaven down to the wintery world on earth. He took on the shape of a simple forest bear and appeared to a woman in a dream, revealing to her where he was hibernating. When it became known that a woman had dreamed the sacred dream, twelve hunters, under the leadership of a flawless bear ceremony master, set out to find the hibernation place. Without speaking a word, the hunters made their way through the deep snow in the forest. When they found the bear's den, they waited—fasting and still not speaking—for one more day and night in the bitter cold. Only then did the ceremony master enter the den, greet the heavenly messenger as the lord of all animals, and ask him to follow him. Presumably, the master successfully contacted the bear telepathically because it is said that the drowsy bear followed the men willingly into the village. There, the divine guest was brought into a longhouse. The bear was tied to the center pillar and sent back to its star-lit, heavenly home when it was killed at the end of the all-night ceremony. The bear was then to tell the Great Spirit that everything on earth is in good order, that people are faithfully carrying out their duties, and that they deserve divine blessing.

The spacious sacrificial longhouse was covered with elm bark, built on an east-west axis, and seen as a reflection of the cosmos. The center pillar, on which the bear was killed, was seen as the world tree. The two fires that burned between the pillar and the two doorways symbolized the all-permeating duality: day and night, male and female, life and death. The bear on the martyr stake was the universal messenger, the being in which all dualities were obliterated. The seats in the longhouse represented the stars in the heavens. The ceremonial dances portrayed the movement of the stars and the life of the cosmic bear.

After the killing, the ceremony master skinned the bear with an obsidian knife, cutting in the opposite direction of that used for normally slain furry animals. Afterward, the bear's body was carried out of the longhouse on the east side through the women's doorway, the doorway of life, and prepared for a sacred communion meal. Neither salt nor vegetables were allowed in the broth. The dogs were shooed away. Under no circumstances were they to gnaw on the bones, which were all gathered and burned to pure ashes in the fire on the east side of the center pillar.

In the last four nights of the bear festival, as the full moon was approaching, the Mohicans danced until dawn. During this time, the festival escalated into an orgiastic, trance-like celebration. The bear that was now shining down from Ursa Major again was to watch over them. Through the festival, the necessary bear's strength was given to the tribe so that all could grow and prosper for another year. Around 1850, the Mohicans were converted to

Christianity. They were a defeated people, demoralized and decimated. No woman ever dreamed of the divine bear again—and, consequently, as the Mohicans came to say, compared to the height of their culture, hardly any bears roam the New England forests in modern times.

The winter bear festival of the Mohicans (painting by Dick West)

THE FORBIDDEN NAME

The children who merrily play among the car junkyards, trailer houses, and army barrack–like prefab houses on the northern Cheyenne reservation play hopscotch and tag like any other children do. But sometimes they also play a bear game: A girl hides in a dark hole and the other children come as hunters. They have sticks and try to pry the girl out of the hole. They act like they don't know what animal is in there and try to guess. A badger? A mountain lion? A prairie dog? A porcupine? They name all the animals they can think of. Only one animal they are not allowed to mention by name—the bear! It is a sacred animal, and its name is taboo. If one of the little hunters mistakenly calls out the bear's name, the "enraged" little "bear" storms out of the cave to punish the excitedly squeaking and fleeing culprits.

This simple child's game has its roots in the mythology of the Cheyenne. In the myth, the godly bear storms down to earth to punish those who have called out his name and insulted him. Medicine man Bill Tallbull told the following story regarding this myth:

> A very long time ago, a tribe had their teepees set up near the Black Hills, in what is today called South Dakota. It was a careless tribe that did not honor traditional taboos. Because they constantly called the bear by name, it got so angry that it stormed down from the heavens, destroyed their settlement, and killed all of the people. Only one girl escaped his claws. She ran out into the prairie as fast as she could. But he chased her with great strides. He wanted to wipe her out, too. The seven brothers, the constellation Pleiades, heard her heartbreaking cries. They tried to obstruct the bear, but they could not.
>
> The earth felt sorry for her, too. Mother Earth quickly let a glass mountain grow up right under her feet. It grew very high, and so the girl came out of the bear's reach. The mighty bear tried to climb it, but it constantly slid down and its claws left deep crevices in the mountain. It did not give up though. Because it was a magical being, it painted its face with red mud and yelled at the Pleiades with its voice of thunder, "Toss the girl down to me or I will squeeze the mountain until you all fall down and I will eat all of you!"
>
> Although the bear yelled this threat four times (four is a magical number, universally, for Native Americans), the seven brothers did not waver. The bear grabbed the mountain with its front paws and squeezed it with all of his might. The mountain became so small that it looked like a gigantic tree stump. The Pleiades were shocked and flew back up into heaven with the little girl. The bear chased them. When we look up into the night sky, we see the bear that is still chasing the Pleiades.

Anyone who doesn't believe this story should travel to eastern Wyoming. There, Devil's Tower, the core of an extinguished volcano, looms as a lonely pillar or huge "tree trunk" above the sagebrush prairie. The Cheyenne call this pillar *Nakoeve*, "the bear's peak," which the angry heavenly bear formed.[4]

Grizzly trying to climb Devil's Tower

ARTEMIS'S CHILDREN

For the peoples of the Mediterranean region, the image of the cosmic bear—which they saw as female—leisurely walking around the North Star was also familiar. The Greeks saw Ursa Major and Ursa Minor either as (1) the hands of the divine mother of the gods, Rhea, that are turning a spindle out of

136

which come the threads of fate or (2) two bears that keep the heavy mill-wheel—its hub is the North Star—in motion for the goddess. The Hellenes also saw the nymph Phoenicia who was having a secret affair with Zeus. When his jealous wife, Hera, found out about it, lightning-bolt-slinging Zeus turned his lover into a bear and placed her in the stars. In the constellations of the big and small bears, the people of Crete saw the two bears that sheltered baby Zeus in their den and suckled him.

Each of these legends is from another epoch and another tribal mythology that over thousands of years grew to be the mythological treasure of antiquity. However, the most popular legend of this region regarding the bears in the northern sky comes from the cult of the wild female hunter, Artemis. Artemis, the "bear goddess," who immigrated to Greece from the cold hyperborean forests of the north along with her brother, the sun god, was seen as the lady of all the wild animals. The beautiful, lithe hunter was untamable like the wild animals themselves. Her arrows brought quick death to forest and wild game desecrators. Only to childbearing women did she reveal herself as a gentle helper—as these conditions find themselves outside of conventional behavior patterns. In temples and groves dedicated to the goddess, often wearing a silver crescent moon as a crown, bears and other wild animals were free to roam.

In Athens and on the eastern coast of Attica, the festival of Artemis-Brauronia was celebrated as part of the midsummer festivities. Girls danced cult dances naked or in saffron-colored robes during the rite called *arkteia*. They were the virgins of Artemis and were called *arktoi* (bears). A ten-year-old and a fifteen-year-old girl played the roles of the big and little bears. They wore fur-like gowns the color of the Syrian bears that were at home in the forests of the Near East. Similar to the Cheyenne children's game, the Brauronia "bears" lunged at the boys who came too near and pretended they would devour them.

Artemis was honored in the entire ancient world, but nowhere as much as in Arcadia in the mountainous, inaccessible Peloponnesus, the home of fauns, nymphs, and lustful Pan. The Greeks saw the "acorn-eating Arcadians" as bear people who were "older than the moon." The temples of the aboriginal people were decorated with bear paws and skulls from bears that had been sacrificed, and the female priests wore bearskins.

They were rumored to be, just as the Arcadian warriors were, very ferocious. The warriors wore bear's heads with wide-open mouths on their
helmets.

In these impassable, forested mountains, there once lived a girl named
Kallisto who joined the wild band of virgins who honored the goddess and
roamed the countryside. Just as her name indicates (*Kallisto* = the most beautiful), she was enchantingly lovely. This fact had not escaped Zeus, the father
of the gods, and, driven by desire, he stalked her.

Artemis (Roman representation)

Kallisto's father, Lycaon, the king of Arcadia, was a werewolf that delighted in feasting on human sacrifices. Zeus was so angry about the heinous crimes of Lycaon's sons that he even sent a deluge because of them. But before it came to that, he was possessed by the desire to seize Lycaon's beautiful daughter. However, the beautiful virgin had devoted her life to Artemisia and had sworn, like the goddess herself, to remain untouched. And so, wrapped in a bearskin, she roamed the mountains and forests with the other wild women and wild animals. She fended off all of lustful Zeus's advances. But the father of the gods was a master of deception and could take on any shape he wished to. He had seized beautiful Europa in the guise of a wild bull, and he had even seduced Phokos's daughter while disguised as a bear. This time he approached the innocent girl disguised as a female bear and was able to kidnap her and impregnate her.

The maiden kept a secret of what had happened and did not tell the goddess. But one day, as Artemis was bathing with the nymphs in a forest pool, Kallisto was hesitant to take off her cloak. When she did at last, her bulging belly revealed that she was expecting a child. The goddess was enraged, "Leave my circle of virgins immediately, you perjurer, and do not desecrate our water." As punishment, she turned the girl into a bear, and the poor girl who still had a human heart and mind had to roam all alone as a shaggy, pregnant bear. Soon, she bore a strong son whom she named Arkas (the bear). Because his father was a god, he was a hero. He became the founder of the Arcadians, and the idyllic country praised by poets was named after him.

Very soon, fate separated small Arkas from his mother so that he could not remember her. The irony of fate also let him turn into a passionate bear hunter. One time, he encountered his mother in the dark forest. She recognized him and came up to him grumbling in a friendly way. But he did not recognize his mother who had given him his life. He only saw a wild animal and began to chase it mercilessly until they came to a sacred region of the Wolf's Mountain where Zeus was worshiped as a wolf. Those whose shadow was seen in this sacred place were doomed to die and damned to go to the underworld into the realm of shadows. However, Zeus took pity on his lover and her son. He put Kallisto and Arkas up into the night sky in the most beautiful spot, as the big bear (Ursa Major) and the star Arcturus (in other versions as the small bear, Ursa Minor). Up there, the son is still stalking his mother, but he will never catch her.

However, Zeus's jealous wife, Hera, did not grant the poor girl who had enjoyed her husband's favor any pity. She arranged it so that Kallisto could never take a refreshing bath in Oceanus, the world stream that flows around the Earth and the seas; for that reason, the constellation of Ursa Major never dips below the horizon.

Bear hunter Arkas (Arcturus) in Booetes

THE ONCE AND FUTURE KING

All of the ancient indigenous peoples, the early hunters and gatherers of the northern hemisphere, saw a mighty bear circling the North Star in the night sky. In Neolithic times, when people became sedentary and started cultivating grains and building wagons, their imagery regarding the constellation changed. The Romans saw the seven main stars in Ursa Major as seven threshing oxen that unceasingly walk around the axis of the North Star. When they looked up into the night sky, the Germanics and Celts saw a huge wagon that slowly drives around the North Star. Three horses, or three oxen (the three stars of the shaft), pull the wagon. The small Tom Thumb, or rider, sits on the middle star of the shaft as a coachman (Fasching 1994, 102).

The pagan Swedes called this heavenly wagon "Thor's Wagon." But have we not just learned that Thor was also called "Bear"? Indirectly, the bear is still connected to this constellation for these peoples. These Swedes of long ago also believed that Thor sometimes came loudly clattering down close to the earth at midnight and that peace and fertility came in the wake of these nightly journeys.

In the early Middle Ages, this heavenly vehicle became hero king Dietrich of Berne's hearse. When this Gothic king died, a wagon appeared and drove him up into the sky where he still sits in it circling the North Star. Christian zealots of the early missionary times tried to change this hearse to Elias's or Paul's coach of triumph, but it did not strike a chord with the only recently converted peoples.

In England and Scandinavia, Thor's Wagon eventually turned into Charles's Wagon (*Charles Wain*). This Charles is none other than mighty Charlemagne, and the wagon is his hearse in which he circles the North Star until his return. Like the Celtic King Arthur, Charlemagne is the great *Rex quondam, rexque futurus*, the once and future king, the archetypal universal king; he is not dead. He is only sleeping in the beyond, far removed. The beyond is in the stars, or, without it being a contradiction, deep in a mountain (such as for German King Friedrich Barbarossa and also Charlemagne) or on a faraway island (such as for King Arthur or Irish King Bran). It could also be a megalithic tomb, such as, for example, where the Bernese giant

Botti rests. Botti sleeps in this grave and will only then awaken when the Bernese are in great need and call for him.

In these images of the faraway sovereign, we recognize the archaic legend of the bear king and his lover, the great goddess. Just like the king of the animals hibernates in the winter and returns in the spring, the human king withdraws until he rides down to earth again in a golden heavenly wagon, bringing a new time of happiness and justice. The Greeks called the Goths *Amaxoluoi*, "Men of the Wagon," which may go back to the covered wagon, the vehicle in which this nomadic warrior people had arrived from the hyperborean north. But *Amaxa* is also occasionally used to describe the Big Dipper and Little Dipper. The Goths described themselves as descendants of a totemic bear. Fabled *Berig* (bear) is their ancestor, and their chieftains also called themselves *Berige*. The bear, the totem and coat of arms of the Goths, became the coat of arms of many cities that they conquered or founded, such as Bjorneborg, Hammerfest, Novgorod, or Madrid (Sède 1986, 63).

CHAPTER 13
The Warrior Bear

Close the door, there's growling in the forest!
When the sun hid itself today
the weather was balled up on the riff,
and now one hears it seething and boiling.
Hush, hush, little one!
Do you hear? Beneath us, in the stall—hmm?
Do you hear? Do you hear? Clink, clink.
The werewolf is rattling his chain!

ANNETTE VON DROSTE-HUELSHOFF,
DER LOUP GAROU (THE WEREWOLF,
AUTHOR'S TRANSLATION)

Nearly every tribal society has brotherhoods of wild warriors possessed of nearly superhuman strength and fierceness and who, fearing neither noose nor fire, lunge eagerly at any enemy. Here we are dealing with an asocial type of warrior, a warrior for whom the civilized manners of society do not count and who identifies with a wild beast of prey. The Cheyenne knew such a warrior as a "contrary warrior," or *hohnohka*, because he said "yes" when he meant "no" and "right" when he meant "left" and only attacked when his comrades drew back. The Crow called them "crazy dogs that want to die," and the Sioux called them "clowns."

Similarly, in India, the naked ascetic *(naga-sadhu)* rubs cremation ashes from funeral pyres on his naked body, does not cut his hair or beard, and, roaming the countryside with a trident (not seldom used as a weapon of self-defense), steps aside for no one. Such a naga-sadhu does not heed any rules or laws of caste or society as he has already passed beyond this life and has already become one with the wild, ecstatic god Shiva. (See more on this topic in my book *Shiva: The Wild God of Power and Ecstasy*).

BERSERKERS AND *ULFHEDINN*

As shown in the beginning of this chapter, we see that "bearskins," the *berserkers* (from Old Nordic *beri* = bear and *sekr* = robe, garb) of the Germanic peoples, are not a singular phenomenon. They lived outside of society. They were ritually declared as already dead and beyond normal laws; therefore, they had no need to fear death as ordinary mortals do. The ecstatic god of death and magic, Odin (Wotan), had taken possession of them. He fanned their wrath, their inner embers, so that they plunged into the heat of battle with no protection, helmet, or shield, even often completely naked or only with a bearskin on. Their hair-raising looks—wild, matted hair, faces painted black like the color of death, crazed expressions, unrestrained behavior, bear-like roars, and wolf-like howls from a drooling mouth—made their opponents hesitate and become weak-kneed even before any physical violence had taken place.[1]

Berserker motif on a helm dress plate (Ölland, Sweden, seventh century)

Bronze plate from Torslunda, Sweden (sixth century)

In times of war, these berserkers and their comrades, the "wolfskins" (*Ulf-hedinn*), were invaluable to their tribes, but in times of peace, they were more a disservice. They had neither homes nor fields, knew no family obligations, and just hung around. They lived off others as uninvited guests, squandering the goods of their involuntary host, and lazing around. Their behavior was always unrestrained, menacing, and erratic. They knew no bounds in eating and drinking, and sometimes they also molested the women. So, it is no wonder that decent citizens drove them off into the forests and often did not even let them enter the villages. There are even reports that they were occasionally chained up like vicious dogs. In German, "bearskin" (*Baerenhaeuter*) is even still an expression today for an ill-mannered bully.

Bearskins were so named because they did not wear tailored, sewed garments. For clothing, they only wore a bearskin, which usually came from a bear they had killed themselves, often with only a knife as a weapon. They also slept on this bearskin. According to archaic belief, those who did not cut their hair and wore the fur of an animal had the power of that animal. Thus, the long-haired berserkers had "become animals." They had become one with the unpredictable, magical god, Odin-Grimnir, who constantly changes his shape and often likes to appear as a wolf, raven, or bear.

In the bearskin fairy tale from earlier, a distinct memory of the Germanic bearskin phenomenon lives on. The young man is a warrior, a soldier who fears neither death nor the devil, nor a wild bear. The pact of loyalty to Odin turns into a pact with the devil in the fairy tale. Seven years of wearing the bearskin—seven years of not washing, cutting or combing his hair, cutting his nails, praying, or working—remind us of the saying, "going berserk" (Berserkergang), the initiation of the wildest warriors that lasted for many years.[2]

Going berserk was originally part of an initiation for male youths (which was essentially no different from similar such rituals of tribal peoples the world over). To make pubescent boys into responsible men, they were separated from the rest of society and sent into the wilderness. Under the guidance of older bearskins or Wotan initiates, they learned to endure pain and deprivation. Often with the help of entheogen drugs—ethnobotanists presume marsh Labrador tea (Ledum palustre), belladonna, henbane, and fly agaric—they experienced, again under the strict guidance of the elders (as some of these plants are poisonous), the spiritual cosmos of the tribe and learned about their animal nature in order to grasp it and ultimately merge in harmony with it. During this time in the wilderness, they were regarded as "dead" and preparing for their rebirth as grown-up tribal members. After going berserk, which could last several years—the number seven in the Bearskin tale is magical rather than real—their hair and nails were cut, and the fresh initiates received new clothes. Now they could marry and lead lives as valiant, free, and weapon-carrying men, as it turned out for Bearskin in the tale.

In later times, during the commotion of the Migration Period in Europe and into the time of the Viking invasions, these youth initiations turned into regular warrior initiations. Going berserk became, just as knighthood did later, a regular "profession."[3] These wild, young warriors would often have metal rings forged around their joints and swore to only remove them after they had smashed in the skull of an enemy. Tribal chieftains and kings surrounded themselves with such young warriors clothed in bearskins. Even Harold Fair Hair (around CE 900), under whose rule Norway became Christian, had such warriors in his service. Those who had been part of such a confederacy and lived to tell about it were held in high esteem. Often such a daredevil became the founder of an entire clan.

Were-bear

Another probable instance of berserkers being recognized in society comes from the Alemannic tribes of olden times who gave tribal founders of a clan and farmstead owners the honorific title *Bero* (bear). These were probably men who had been berserkers, and the practice was based on the assumption that only he who knows well his own wild nature can comprehend the need to preserve the foundations of a peaceful, civilized society. But there are also reports about berserkers who completely gave in to the devil (Odin) and never returned from the wilderness. Ostracized by everyone, they developed into dangerous cannibals, werewolves, or were-bears, and it was believed they became real bears or wolves when they died.

In particular, the Alemannic tribes that conquered and settled the Swiss Alpine valleys and bordering areas in the course of the Migration Period regarded the berserkers as fighting bears. In Alpine winter festivals and carnivals, much "going berserk," though fairly watered down, naturally still lives on. During Alemannic Fasnet (carnival) in southern Europe today, a lot of rather rough—but playful—tomfoolery goes on, and people dressed up as bears are hardly a rare sight.

In pre-Reformation Berne, Switzerland, where carnival days and nights were celebrated in excess, it was rumored that a bear once broke out of the bear pit and mixed in with the drinking, brawling crowd. The grumbling guest that grabbed a grilled fish and some fresh bread here and there and slapped this or that partying citizen on the back did not attract any particular attention. To the contrary, if he even stood out, it was only because he was politer than the other "bears"!

Bernese flag bearer (painting by Humbert Mareschet, 1585–1586)

More echoes of going berserk can be found into the modern era. Into the sixteenth century, when the Bernese went to war under their proud banner, the strongest warrior, wearing a bearskin, led the marching troop. The high bearskin hats of the palace guards in London, Stockholm, and Copenhagen originate from the tradition of bearskin warriors.[4]

The mountain men and rangers of the Wild West, who fought especially ferociously with the Native Americans, also tie into this tradition—possibly without being conscious of it; they liked to wear bearskins, and the legends of frontiersmen Davy Crockett and Daniel Boone tell that they had single-handedly slain a bear as children, armed with only a knife.

American frontiersman fighting a grizzly

FYLGIA, THE FOLLOWER SPIRIT

For primitive peoples, it is not uncommon for a human being—or a god—to sometimes take on the shape of an animal. For them, it is absolutely comprehensible that a human being can have an animal second soul, or totem soul, and that this soul shows itself in dreams or in trances. A bearskin has an especially strong animal soul—a bear soul. When such a person gets into a battle rage, the animal soul can completely take over the body. Then the fighter is no longer a human but a veritable bear.

Ethnologists and Carlos Castaneda readers know the animal doppelganger as a *nagual*. The Scandinavians called it a fylgia, a follower soul, and they believed it was a personification of the person's power. In Norse mythology, a fylgja is a spirit who accompanies a person in connection to their fate or fortune. This soul helps the person have premonitions and warns of danger—nowadays, one would probably call it instinct. But this animal soul also leads its own life and occasionally roams through the forest as an incarnate animal. It can be inherited by the person's children through the generations and protect the family.

This story from Scandinavia about Bodwar Bjarki (Bodwar Little Bear) tells about the fylgia:

Bodwar Bjarki was a warrior in King Hrolf Kraki's entourage. Once, when riding out, the king was attacked by enemies not far from his hall. His accompanying warriors held up well against the superior power. Only Bodwar Bjarki was missing as he had missed the riding out.

Suddenly, in the midst of the raging battle, a huge bear appeared. It lunged into the battle. Protecting the king, it clawed and bit the attackers and tossed them from their horses and mauled them. Neither sword swipes nor spear jabs seemed to even faze the animal.

Hjalti, one of the king's warriors, got angry when he noticed that Bjarki was not there. Because each sword was necessary, he hurried back to the king's hall to see what was going on with Bjarki. It was not possible that Bjarki did not hear the ruckus and the yelling. When Hjalti jerked the door open, he saw Bjarki in a deep sleep on his bearskin. He roughly shook his lazy comrade awake.

"How can you lie here idly when your king is in dire straits!" he yelled. Bjarki only yawned, shook himself, and got up.

At that very moment, the fighting bear disappeared from the battlefield, and the situation got worse for King Hrolf. In the end, he lost the battle. The strange bear had been none other than the strong fylgia of Bodwar Bjarki. While sleeping on the bearskin in the king's castle, his animal soul was fighting as a bear right next to the king.

As the new religion tried to replace Odin, Thor, and the other Aesir (gods), the belief in the animal doppelganger also dwindled. The bear fylgia only lives on in the lower mythology as a bear-shaped, spooky being.

THE WAR OF THE ANIMALS

The bear is the king of the animals. The northern peoples were convinced of that. In the southern countries, the Near East, and northern Africa, however, it was the lion. It was only much later in northern Europe and through the influence of antique Roman culture and Christianity that the lion challenged the status of the bear as the heraldic animal on various coats of arms. But in the northern woodlands, the bear remained king for a very long time. Some tribal leaders kept forest bears in their halls for this very reason, and many a king added the byname "bear" or "sacred bear" (Old High German *Haleebern*, Old Nordic *Hallbioern*) to his name.[5] In any case, they surrounded themselves with bear warriors whether during feasts or in battle.

The lion questions the rank of the bear: François I as the lion king to whom the Swiss bear must bow (French miniature, sixteenth century).

But the bear was the king of only the four-footed animals. The birds had their own king—it was not the eagle as one would think but the plain and simple wren.[6] The amphibians, saurians, and other reptiles also had their own king: the white serpent that lived under the ancient elderberry bush of the homestead. The Grimm brothers recorded a tale that tells about a war between the king of the animals and the king of the birds:

Once when a bear and a wolf were meandering through the forest, they heard a bird chirping a lovely melody. The bear wanted to know what kind of a feathered creature it was that sang so beautifully. The wolf told him it was the wren, the king of the sky, and that one had to show him due respect.

The bear definitely wanted to see the palace of the other sovereign and took a peek through the branches. When he saw the tiny nest, he could only laugh contemptuously. The skinny, naked royal children seemed pitiful to him. He did not even acknowledge them with a bow. "This is not a palace and you are not royal children, you are unworthy children!" he commented and left. The children were so upset that they did not even eat the worms that their parents brought in their beaks for them later.

The wren and his wife flew right away to the bear's den and called out to him, "Hey, grouchy old bear, why did you chide our children? You will pay for that! We will fight it out in a bloody war." The angry bird king called on all the animals that fly—birds, bees, mosquitoes, hornets, gadflies, and bugs. They formed a mighty summing, screeching army.

The bear and the wren children

The bear also called upon all of his vassals and allies, the elk, wild boars, and others that walk on four legs. Because he was so clever, the fox was made a general. The general decided he should first go spy on the enemy and size up the situation. He was supposed to signal to the others with his red tail: If he put his tail up high, the order was "Attack!" But if he lowered his tail, danger was lurking and they should retreat.

However, their clever plan did not remain a secret. A tiny mosquito had hidden under a leaf at headquarters and heard everything. When the fox went off to scout out the situation, the wren sent out a platoon of hornets. They stung the fox so aggressively in the hindquarters that he had to tuck his tail and clear out. This signal started a panic with the animals. They thought all was lost, and they all ran in various directions as far away as possible.

The wren had won the war and the haughty bear had to eat humble pie. After he had apologized to the wren children, they began to eat again and were in good spirits.

The bear retreats in defeat.

THE CHIEFTAIN OF THE ANIMALS

For the North American forest peoples, the bear is the chief of all the animals. It is the strongest and quietest animal. It can even easily take already slain prey away from pumas and wolves. For the bear, this procedure is easier than the actual hunting—though for any other animal, it is an impossible endeavor.

Sioux medicine man Lame Deer highlights the bear's status with a story from his childhood: His father, who had just gotten a handful of "green frog skins" (dollar bills) went into a saloon to try his luck at poker. The white owner of the joint had a pitiful bear cub chained onto the bar. The cowboys and gamblers were having a great time teasing the bear so that it would stand up on its back legs. A big, cigar-smoking white man came into the bar with a Great Dane. "Nice pet," he said to the barkeeper, "but be careful that my dog doesn't make him into mincemeat."

"The bear can manage the dog," said the barkeeper.

"I'll bet fifty dollars that my dog will tear up your pet," the man bragged. "Let's have them fight!"

By now everyone in the bar, whites and Native Americans, was interested in the bet. The whites all dug into their pockets and bet that the clumsy, slobbering Great Dane would win. The Native Americans, including Lame Deer's father, bet on the bear because he is the chief of the animals. They made a ring of chairs and blankets outside and put the two animals in the middle. The little bear just sat there like an infant and paid no attention to the snarling, growling dog. It clawed some soil and rubbed it onto its head. The dog seemed to be smarter than its owner because, though it growled and

The white bear (drawing by Theodor Kittelsen)

154

barked like crazy, it did not dare attack the young bear. Only when its owner cussed and kicked him into getting serious did it lunge at the bear. With one blow of his paw that came as fast as lightning, the bear ripped the dog's throat so that it fell down dead on the spot. "The bear made a sound, just a 'hrmmpf' like a Sioux does when he is angry," Lame Deer commented (Lame Deer and Erdoes 1972, 116).

When the forest animals have a council meeting, a powwow, the bear takes the seat of honor at the west end of the teepee, or wigwam, so that the rising sun shines on its face. The chief of the bears is an albino bear because white is considered a sacred color.[7]

As already discussed, the Cherokee see bears as transformed humans. The chief of the bears lives in a "mulberry grove" on a high mountain peak in the Smokey Mountains. A magical lake is there, where wounded bears go to heal. In this wild, mountainous region, the bears gather in the fall and dance before they go into winter hibernation (Mooney 2011, 47). The following story is told in many variations in both the entire forested area and the bordering prairie. The story, "About the Origin of Disease," tells of a white bear that leads the meetings of all the animal nations. This is the Cherokee version:

In earlier, long-forgotten times, human folk lived peacefully and harmoniously with all of the animal folk. But at some point, the humans invented bows and arrows and spears and knives. They began to slaughter animals, took their flesh and skin without thanking them, took the feathers from the birds, and stepped on and squashed small living beings, bugs, and worms out of pure carelessness. As it became ever more unbearable, the animal folk complained to the chief of the animals, the old white bear.

White Bear called all of the bears together in the mulberry grove. After they had heard enough about the outrageous doings of the humans, they decided to go on the warpath. Because they knew how effective the human weapons were, they decided to also fight with bows and arrows.

"What are bows and arrows made of?" asked the chief. One of the bears that had observed the humans very intently answered, "The bow is made from the young branches of the Osage orange tree and the bowstring is made of our intestines!"

So the bears gathered the wood and one of the bears offered himself so that bow-strings could be made of his intestines. It was very difficult for them to make the bows because the Osage orange tree is very thorny, but they finally succeeded. When they wanted to practice shooting, some problems came up. When they tried to shoot the arrows, their long claws got caught in the bowstrings.

"We should cut off our claws!" one of the bears suggested. But White Bear objected, "One of us has already died for the bowstring. If we cut our claws, we will all die. How will we be able to climb trees in danger, how will we dig up roots and larvae? These human weapons are unnatural and not for us to use!"

None of the other bears could think of anything else so the old chief ended the meeting. The bears meandered off into various directions and forgot the matter. Eating sweet forest fruits, licking wild honey, and cozily meandering through the woods was much more to their liking, anyway, than political business.

The story continues but now without bears:

The elk chief, Little Elk, took the bear's place and led the council meeting of the forest dwellers. He was also angry, "Deer, elk, and other wild animals give their flesh and skins to the humans," he explained, "but one never hears words of thanks, words asking for pardon! They murder us, but they neither cover up our bones, as would be proper, nor do they leave gifts and tobacco for the ones who remain. As long as I hear no words of thanks, I will punish the humans. I will send them rheumatism and pain in their limbs so that they will become helpless cripples."

The snake spoke for the reptiles, the amphibians, and the saurians: "The humans disregard us, too, and treat us badly. We will appear to them in night-mares and wind around their bodies until they can't breathe. We will breathe poisonous breath upon them and will paralyze them with our piercing look so that they lose their appetite, waste away, and die of starvation."

The insects, worms, and other tiny beings were even angrier. "These cruel humans step on us and crush us. We wish they were all dead," said their speaker. Thereupon they invented all of the horrible diseases and plagues that even still afflict humans today—and if they had had their way, humanity would surely have completely died out and become extinct.

Only the chipmunk that humans left in peace for the most part, tried to put in a good word for the two-legged creatures. But the other animals were so furious that they attacked the chipmunk and clawed him down the back, which is the reason that these tree rodents still have a stripe down their back.

The dog that liked to roam around the locations of the humans and enjoy leftovers, bones, and excrement found there was the only animal that liked humans. It was sad and stealthily left the council, going to the human settlement where it has remained to this day. The rest of the animals declared the dog crazy and excluded it from their community.

The trees, bushes, and wild plants, which were silently present during the council, had heard everything. They did not agree; they had compassion for the humans. Besides, they had not always had good experiences with the animals—too many of them had gnawed on their sprouting parts, clawed their bark, destroyed seeds, or destroyed young trees by rubbing their horns on them. So they held their own powwow and decided to help the humans. For each disease the animals sent, one of them would provide a healing medicine. One plant after another told what disease it could heal. They sent a dream to a medicine man in which they declared, "We, the green folk, will help you with any disease. But we are shy, you have to come to us and ask us for help when you are sick. You can also ask the bear because he best knows our qualities."

CHAPTER 14
Bear Saints and Devils

From there Elisha went up to Bethel. As he was walking along the road, some boys came out of the town and jeered at him. "Get out of here, baldy!" they said. "Get out of here, baldy!" He turned around, looked at them and called down a curse on them in the name of the Lord. Then two bears came out of the woods and mauled forty-two of the boys.

2 KINGS 2:23–24

Around CE 590, Saint Columba took twelve companions and left Ireland and Wales for continental Europe (it is rumored he had to leave because he found the Irish women too beautiful, making it hard for him to keep his vows). In the name of Christ, these descendants of Celtic magicians walked through the realm of the Franks (more or less today's France) with the front of their heads shaved in the Druid fashion and wearing white gowns; they were burdened with books and had bone relics of holy martyrs in bundles tied to their walking sticks. Steeled by severe asceticism, they advocated morals and good manners in the princely courts—so much so that these courts usually very much encouraged them to move on soon after the customary obligatory rights toward guests had been observed. As they roamed the countryside in southerly direction, they came to the Alemannic lands. Only the unswerving belief in their God and mission kept them from being afraid of the wilderness, wild animals, and evil pagans. The Alemannic tribes had berserkers into the seventh century.

When the holy men, fasting and praying, were walking along the banks of Lake Constance, they happened upon a loud, boisterous *blót* ritual, a festival in honor of Wotan and other pagan gods where beer flowed like water. The pious men were appalled at this devilish carrying on. Especially young *Gailleach*—known as Saint Gall—the son of an Irish king, was outraged. He turned over the beer vat, smashed the idols against a cliff, and threw the pieces into the lake. The fearlessness of the monks puzzled and impressed some of the pagans so that they let themselves be converted. Most of them reacted with hostility, however, and battered some of the monks to death.

THE MESSENGER OF THE AGE OF PISCES

Saint Columba felt compelled to move on across the Alps, but Gailleach preferred Lake Constance—he loved to fish. Shamelessly naked Alemannic girls who occasionally happily splashed and bathed in the lake disturbed him; but he was able to drive them off with prayer and a ban.

As Columba was preparing to travel on, a temporary fever befell his friend Gailleach, who then stayed on the lakeside with his friend, Hiltibold. They were not afraid of the wolves, wild boars, and bears that populated the subalpine territory; after all, they were men of God and nothing had happened to the prophet Daniel in the lion's den. They strayed through the wilderness for weeks until, weak from fasting, Gailleach fell near a waterfall on the Steinach River. When the bundle of sacred relics tied to the knob of his walking stick touched the earth, the monks saw this as a sign to stay at that place and build a monastery.

Gailleach went fishing to regain some strength by eating and got enough fish for the two of them. After they had eaten, a bear came roaming through and ate the leftovers. Gailleach crossed himself, talked to the bear in a brotherly way, and then commanded the bear to bring wood for the fire and logs to build the cloister. In the name of Christ, he asked the thick-skulled bear to drive the other wild animals off and then retreat into the mountain. As a token of thanks, he gave the vanquished bear consecrated bread and pulled a thorn out of its paw.

The bear that Saint Gall (Gailleach) subjugated also stands symbolically for the ancestral soul of the Alemannic peoples. The bear was the totem animal of the Alemannic warriors and was connected to the two main gods of the tribes, along with Woutis (Odin) and Donar (Thor). When the bear accepted the consecrated bread, it accepted communion with the spirit of the new Piscean Age that was coming into its time. Simultaneously, the bear gives the new spirit warmth, protection, and shelter by bringing wood for fire and building. In old representations, the bear comes from the left side, from the heart side. This indicates that the Alemannic soul had accepted the Christian message (Burri 1982, 86).

The Abbey of Saint Gall (Switzerland) developed out of the hermitage that was founded in this way—an incubator cell for the new Christian culture. The conversion of the wild Alemannic tribes pushed forward from here. An iconic design portrays this meeting, which depicts how Gailleach blesses a bear and gives it consecrated bread while the bear walks upright and gives him a log.

Saint Gall subjugates a bear (left: seal of the monastery library in St. Gallen, Switzerland).

Between the bear and Saint Gall in the illustration, a cross signifies their meeting and conciliation. The bears that help and protect him are not necessarily wild forest bears, however. It is more likely that they are genuine bearskins, dressed in bear furs and acting on the orders of their chieftain, Duke Kunzo, who told them to be hospitable to the stranger. Earlier, pagan chieftain Kunzo had called the monk, this unusual magician, to his daughter's sickbed. Saint Gall was able to heal her with holy water and prayer, and from then on he stood under the Duke's protection, of which he was much in need—he still had to fear the pagans' revenge for insulting them and smashing their idols.

The festival of Saint Gall is held on October 16th, the time of year when the bears get tired and start to long for the quiet feeling of security in their earthen dens. By sending the bear away, Saint Gall also dismisses the old heathen heritage out of the realm of consciousness. It dwindles away from everyday consciousness and sinks into the cave of the unconscious. Some day—in the twilight time of a new age—this bear will emerge from the dark depths again. Maybe now, the beginning of the Age of Aquarius, the time has come?

THE BEAR AS A PORTER AND PLOWMAN

Not only Saint Gall but also other holy men and missionaries had to deal with the Germanic totem animal. Saint Mang, who legend says founded three cloisters in Allgaeu (in southern Germany) with Gailleach and Columba, also had to come to terms with bears. When he caught one nibbling on apples in the cloister garden, he successfully commanded it to stop and forced it to shake the tree so that the monks could gather up the fallen apples. Another bear scratched around on the root of an ancient pine tree and revealed a vein of iron ore. The discovery of the iron ore brought a financial boon to the cloister near Fuessen (where King Ludwig's famous castle Neuschwanstein is) as well as to the surrounding area. Saint Mang rewarded the bear with consecrated bread and the promise that no harm would come to it. On another occasion, the holy man tamed a whole pack of bears and trained them to fight against the demon of Lechtal. He drove them like a pack of docile dogs to attack a lindworm that was terrorizing the area of Ronsberg (Germany). The united bears destroyed the dragon that had eaten many cattle and humans (Endroes and Weitnauer 1990, 526).

Other holy men were not impressed with the bear's wildness either—for example, Saint Corbinian, missionary of Bavaria. When the devil appeared to him in the shape of a bear and slashed his packhorse, the man of God commanded the evildoer to carry the baggage in the horse's place. And Saint Maximin was on a pilgrimage to Rome when a hungry bear also attacked his pack animal and devoured it. This bear also had to obey the holy man in the same manner. Not until it had carried his baggage to Rome and back to the German countries was it relieved of its compulsory labor.

Under the circumstances of the times, the "pilgrimage to the Holy See" seems to be a euphemism for a dangerous undertaking, and the inhabitants of the canton Valais in Switzerland tell a similar story to those of Saints Corbinian and Maximin: In the vicinity of the San Bernardino Pass, Saint Martin was attacked by a wild bear that clawed his pack mule. This bear, too, then bowed down to the spiritual superiority and carried the holy man's baggage to Rome and back. The site of this event was named after the bear, Urseris (from Latin *ursus* = bear), and is today known as Osières. In another place, the tale is told of a severe bishop who made a bear plow for him after it had tore into his ox. And yet another similar tale tells of Saint Lucius who made a bear help him plow and carry firewood for a poor widow.

The story of the hermit Gerold, who turned his back on the sinful world and retreated into the Vorarlberg forest, shows a friendlier side to the erstwhile king of the forest. A bear that was being chased by a count and his dogs and nearly dead from exhaustion fled into the hermitage and laid his head subserviently into the hermit's lap. The hermit blessed the animal and commanded the hounds to be quiet. Deeply moved by this miracle, the hunter jumped from his horse and took a knee in front of the holy man. He gave him the piece of land and the wood to build a cloister.

What is being expressed in these saints' legends that are often almost interchangeably similar? Clearly, the new cloister culture was competing for the bear's habitat because it was seen as pleasing to God to clear the dark forest and expand the area of cultivation where wheat and vineyards could grow. The legends also show the power of the new Christian moralism that was replacing the old natural, instinctive native way of life. The bear, which in this case represents the old heathen ways, learns to obey and do good deeds. Likewise, the heathen peoples are being wrested away from the devil and subjugated by the Church. It is highly probable that the bears in these stories are again not real bears but either heathen bearskins or feral people who had retreated into the forests. Besides incorrigible animists, the forest sheltered outcasts, escaped servants and vassals, and others who lived a bear-like and wild life in caves.[1] They were seen as fair game, and the nobles sometimes made a sport of hunting them down and killing them like any other wild animals—bears, wolves, wild boars, and other game.

Saint Columba and Saint Gall with bears (L. Auers, Heiligenlegende, 1962)

According to legend, wild people were naked or dressed in furs, had matted hair, and gathered or stole their food—fruit, roots, sheaves, and animals—at night. They loved music and dancing, carried clubs, and were shy but willing enough to be of service when captured. A subject of fascination all throughout the Middle Ages, they live on even today in carnival customs and costumes in Alpine countries in Europe. They were believed to have similar abilities as bears, such as being able to foresee the weather, find iron ore, and know the secrets of all the healing plants. But especially their alleged sexual instinct excited the imagination of the pious Christians. In the legend of Wolf-Dietrich of Berne, we hear about the wild woman who desired the knight:

When the master fell asleep, the wild woman came
To the fire and saw the prince's body.
Walking on all fours, she looked like a bear;
Are you quite of this world, which devil brought you here?
Because the young knight rejected her she put a spell on him, so that he

had to stray through the woods for half a year and eat roots and herbs.
After Wolf-Dietrich gave in and slept with her, the story ended happily.
She accepted his faith and a miracle happened.
She was baptized, until then called Rough Ilse,
she was now called Siegesminne, the most beautiful far and wide.

Feral man and woman

THE BEAR GODDESS IN NUN'S ATTIRE

Rather than become fully bedeviled and banned, many of the gods of the Mediterranean region simply changed their form. Suddenly, they appeared as saints and still populate Christian calendars as well as altars and niches in the walls of the churches. In this way, virginal Artemis, the bear goddess, made her way into the Christian era as a Christian virgin. She appeared as Columba the Virgin, who lived at the time of Christian persecution under emperor Aurelius. After her pursuers had put her in a dungeon because of her beliefs, coarse henchmen aimed to amuse themselves by raping her, but a bear that happened to live in the back of the dungeon defended her. She was later put to death as a martyr—tied up, slashed and torn with a hook, and beheaded—but, thanks to the bear, she had remained a virgin.

The cult of the goddess Artemis used to be celebrated in a bear's den on the peninsula Akrotiri, on the island of Crete. The bear goddess transformed into "the sacred Virgin Mary of the Bear," and her festival is held, significantly, on Candlemas Day. A bear-shaped dripstone that used to be the centerpiece of the heathen cult is now interpreted to be a bear that, upon disturbing Mary when she was drinking some water, was turned into stone.

The bear also appears in the legend of the arch martyr Thecla, an attractive maiden from a distinguished household who did not want to succumb to fleshly pleasures and refused to marry. So she dressed as a man, followed the apostle Paul, and was baptized by him. Her family was so upset with her that her own mother reported her to the governor who was a notorious Christian persecutor. She was arrested and thrown to the wild animals. When a bear was about to maul her, a lion, in answer to her prayer for aid, lunged and saved her. After then living to ninety-one years old despite much persecution and castigation, the saint left this world by entering a cave that closed behind her forever.

In the form of Saint Richardis we find another bear saint—this time, once again, in the Alemannic region. This daughter of an Alsatian prince

Killing a wild man (Pieter Brueghel the Elder, sixteenth century)

was the wife of Emperor Charles the Fat. Accused of adultery, she took the test of fire and passed it. But afterward, she had had enough of the world and its ungodly doings and decided to devote her life to religious service in the name of the Lord. She retreated into the forest to live as a recluse, and there she met a bear that showed her a cave where she could set up a hermitage. A cloister was eventually built above this bear den at the foot of the Vosges Mountains in Alsace. Soon, it was discovered that the cave had healing power, especially for leg ailments. From the eleventh century onward, a bear was kept in the crypt and each pilgrim who came in the hope of being healed was required to give the bear trainer three coins (*guldens*) and a loaf of bread to the bear.

FOREST DEMONS AND MALICIOUS WILD ANIMALS

The Christians did away with animal worship; especially magical, sacred animals such as the bear, the wolf, and the raven were stripped of their divine nimbus. The bear, as the totem of warriors, ancestral spirits, bringer of fertility, and companion of the great goddess (by then degraded to a witch) now had to do compulsory service for the Church at the command of the saints (a similar punishment as given to the cheated devil). The bear had to haul heavy rocks to build churches and bridges, plow fields, gather wood, or even herd sheep, as for Saint Eutychius, for instance. However, the bear remained an ominous animal that possessed magical power. The more the animal was bedeviled, the more the fear of it grew.

The same courtesies the bear bestowed on the Christian saints it had actually bestowed on magicians and shamans in earlier times. The bear was their companion and animal of power. In medieval times, the bear was believed to serve non-baptized beings by, for example, watching over the devil's treasures or pulling the

Bear in a monk's cloak (unknown artist)

wagon for the mythological mountain spirit, Ruebezahl. People continued to only whisper its name because, just like the devil, the bear would come when called. People also believed that bears, like forest devils do, steal the colors from ferns and play other tricks.

The Church forbade contact with bears just like it forbade contact with evil spirits. The ecumenical council not only banned belief in astrology, interpretation of signs, reverence of nature, and other heathen practices but also the practices of keeping tame bears, wearing bear claws, and selling bear hair as medicine. The Quinisext Council decreed that former pagans who committed such crimes be sent to prison for six years. However, ninth-century artists were allowed to depict dancing bears.

The bear as a mount for a demon (from Jean Wier, Pseudomonarchia daemonum, sixteenth century)

Here and there, such as in Norway, for instance, farmers believed that bears protected their sheep, cattle, and goats from wolves. As a reward, they granted a bear one of the farm animals in the fall simply by turning a blind eye when a bear took one. In some communities in Allgaeu, Germany, farmers would put out the first calf born in the spring in the hopes that the bear would then leave the rest of the animals in peace on the summer pastures. But generally, people tried to avoid the bear, crossing themselves when they met the shaggy beast and reciting the traditional bear blessing from Saint Gall: "*In nomini domini* [in God's name] *my Jesu Christi*, move on and retreat from our valley, you forest beast! Your territory is on the mountain and in the gorges. Leave us and our pasture animals in peace!"

An Alpine blessing, which is part of a larger blessing that used to be called out at night high up in the Alps for protection, goes like this:

Saint Peter, take your keys in the right hand.
Lock away the bear's gait,
the wolf's teeth,

the lynx's claws,
the raven's beak,
the dragon's tail,
the vulture's flight.
Protect us Lord from such dreadful hour,
that such animals bite or claw . . ."

One can see that the more these Christians tried to ban their own "sinful" animal nature, the more they began to fear wild animals in the forest. Bears became increasingly demonized as the incarnation of unruly powers. Saint Peter's keys locked it away from the communities of good people. To meet up with the king of the animals was no longer awe-inspiring; instead, it only caused fear in humans and thus defensive reactions in bears. Nothing makes bears more aggressive than panicky people; or can they perhaps read thoughts as the Siberians and Native Americans claim?

Rigid medieval imagination divided the entire creation into good and evil, into creatures that were pleasing to God and those that had been ruined by Satan. Bruin found himself ever more on the wrong side in this kind of scheme. Believing they were doing deeds pleasing to God, people hunted

Traveling artists with dancing bear (woodcut by Hans Weiditz, Augsburg, 1513)

down bears and wolves with almost fanatical determination—with poison, lances, crossbows, brutal traps, pitfalls, and nets. Accompanied by drums, trumpets, screeching women, and barking dogs, hundreds of hunters swarmed to drive out from their hiding places the "thrashing beasts" and "ferocious wild animals." Bears were lured with honey, doused with brandy, and killed or taken into cruel captivity. (A liquor made from honey has its origin in eastern Prussia, in Germany, and is called *Baerenfang,* or bear trap.) It was not a rare sight to see a bear tied to a pole in the village square, eyes blinded, beaten until it had open wounds, and desperately trying to defend itself from the whipping and the dogs that were tormenting it. For the masses, the spectacle was less a gruesome form of entertainment than a moral edification. The bear incorporated sin and the devil, and the display showed how it had met up with its just fate.[2]

Animal researchers believe that bears actually did become more aggressive in the Middle Ages. The more often people intruded into their habitat so that they could not search for acorns, roots, and berries in peace, the more often they—driven by hunger—killed tame animals. Once the inhibition threshold has been crossed, a bear can turn into a habitual thief.

In the following tale about the mill bear, we can see how the once sacred animal had become a demonized being:

A spirit bear haunted a mill near Niederbronn in Alsace. The miller became desperate, fearing poverty and the ruin of his mill. No handworkers were willing to fix anything there and no apprentice stayed longer than one night. However, one day a perky young fellow showed up and offered his services. He had heard a bear spirit haunted the mill, but he was not afraid of it.

That night the wind was favorable, and the windmill blades turned at a good pace. The young man set to work. Toward midnight, he stretched out on some bags of flour to rest up. Just as he was about to nod off, a creaking could be heard. A black bear trotted in and sniffed the cases and bags. When it saw the apprentice, it lifted its paw.

But the apprentice was prepared. He had a freshly sharpened axe right next to him. He defended himself with the axe and cut off the paw of the attacker. The bear left the mill howling loudly.

Parading a captured bear in Valais, Switzerland (eighteenth century)

The master was happy to see the apprentice in good shape and content the next morning when he came in for breakfast. But there was no porridge—the miller's wife was not there. They found her moaning and feverish in bed. And her lower arm was missing! She was exposed as a wicked witch and arrested.

Who is this black witch who appears as a bear? Knowers of mythology will recognize the grain goddess, the grain mother, who appeared in pagan times as a bear or accompanied by a bear. Now, having been banned from consciousness, she has become an evil nocturnal spook—so it happens to all gods and goddesses who are no longer honored and are pushed into the unconscious. They become black demons of the night.

BROTHER KLAUS'S BEAR OF LIGHT

The visions of Swiss saint Nicolaus von Fluee show a pleasant picture by comparison. Brother Klaus was a poor mountain peasant but had shown himself to be a courageous warrior and councilman. One day—it happened to be October 16th, the patron day of Saint Gall—he left his wife and ten children and retreated into the forest as a hermit. It is said that he lived for twenty years from nothing but the sacrament, from bread and wine. Princes and rulers made pilgrimages to his hermitage to ask him for advice, and, thanks to his clear spirit, he was even able to hinder a civil war in Switzerland. He also had interesting dreams and visions while he was living in his hermitage.

In one of his visions that shook him to the core, a magnificent wayfarer appeared to him. He had a wide-brimmed hat, a walking stick, and a large cloak. The wayfarer began to sing and it seemed like the entire creation sang along. The Pilatus Mountain (near Lucerne, Switzerland) sank down to the level of the earth and the blessed ones—the dead—appeared. In the midst of this overwhelming scene, the clothes of the wayfarer changed, and suddenly he stood in front of the monk dressed in bear's fur. The fur was sprinkled with a radiant gold color. Brother Klaus felt that the stranger had communicated to him the mysteries of heaven and earth.

Nicolas von Fluee, 1417–1487

It was surely "Woutis" (Wotan), the god of his Alemannic ancestors, who had entered his subconscious and taken shape in his vision. (Wotan, the wayfarer, is known to appear with a wide-brimmed hat, staff or spear, and a wide cloak). Brother Klaus had been able to recognize this old god and not see him as a devil—as was usually the case in the Middle Ages; he had united the vision with his steadfast Christian faith and had seen the radiant divine bear, the chieftain of the dead spirits that lived in the mountain (Burri 1982, 97).

In another vision, three noble-looking men appeared to him. They asked him whether he would put himself with body and soul into their hands. The hermit answered, "I will not give myself to anyone but almighty God." After hearing this, the three men laughed merrily and prophesied that goodly God would free him of his earthly burden in his seventieth year of life, and then they gave him "a bear claw and the banner of the mighty army."

Who may the three men have been? They were probably the ancestral gods, Wotan, Donar, and Tyr. They could laugh merrily with this saint because he did not ban them back into darkness. His Christianity was not exclusive, narrow, and dogmatic. So they blessed him with the power of the bear, as well as his ancestors, the Alemannic warriors. In this way, Brother Klaus helped the Alemannic soul reconcile with the inflexible beliefs that the Irish-Scottish monks had brought to his country.

CHAPTER 15
Bear Plants, Bear Medicine

In the forest a leaf falls from a tree:
The eagle can see it,
the coyote can hear it,
but the bear can smell the falling leaf.

NATIVE AMERICAN PROVERB

When spring thunderstorms clash and the godly bear, Thor, smashes the bones of the cantankerous ice giants with his lightning hammer until their icy stronghold turns into thaw water, it is time for the terrestrial bear to leave its paradise of sweet dreams and come out of its den. After the long winter, Bruin does not look as mighty as usual. The bear has lost a lot of weight—about one third of its normal bulk—and its fur looks like a worn-out coat dangling around its bones. During the long winter sleep, the bear does not urinate or defecate. It has a terrible thirst—it is as thirsty as a bear!—so the first thing it does is quench it. Then it begins to eat purgative herbs, mainly looking for spicy hellebore, a strongly purgative and circulation-accelerating plant. The natural plug of excrement that has closed off the lower intestine over the winter is excreted, and then the proverbial hunger—"hungry as a bear"—comes into play.

Brooklime, watercress, wild onions, chickweed, young nettles, sour dock, and many other edible spring plants that make up the bear's first meals and reactivate its metabolism and circulation also fire up its glands and inhibit anaerobic fermentation and putrefactive agents in the intestines. They are the same herbs that our ancestors ate as blood-cleansing cures—usually also in the spring after a long winter without fresh greens.

Willow bark, willow buds, and meadowsweet shoots (*Filipendula*) that contain natural aspirin (salicylic acid) flush excess uric acid out of blood and tissue (for bears as well as for humans) and free the bear of the back pain that usually comes from lying for so long in the cold. Bears like to eat the young shoots of hogweed as much as traditional European farmers will make a soup of them as a stimulating and digestive spring meal. Bears also like young dandelions, a traditional addition to a spring salad that humans also enjoy. Dandelion increases gall secretion, is diuretic, clears out slag, and tones the intestines. Bears clear winter catarrh and phlegm out of their lungs by eating plantain and colt's foot leaves. As one can see, in the bear's apothecary we find the Celtic-Germanic "nine herbs" that people also traditionally ate during spring festivals and are still occasionally found in cleansing Maundy Thursday or Good Friday soups.[1]

PLANTS THAT INDUCE SLEEP

Just as Bruin looks for fresh greens in the spring, he also finds sleep-inducing herbs in the fall that help him go into hibernation. Humans of olden times, as well as early scholars, were certain that Bruin knew these plants very well. A Swiss legend tells of a cattle herder in the high Alps who saw a bear greedily eating a certain herb. It made him curious, and he tasted the plant himself. His eyelids became so heavy that he lay down under the upside-down cheese vat to take a nap. When he woke up, it was spring; he had slept soundly over the winter despite bitter cold.

Another story tells about a poor, old widow who lived alone in a drafty cottage on the edge of the forest. She was weak, and it was hard for her to gather enough wood for the winter. One day, when she was gathering brush-wood, she noticed a bear in a meadow. She observed how the bear carefully dug up a creeping plant and ate it while grumbling happily. Afterward, the bear did some somersaults and then trotted off happily on its way.

The old woman was curious and tried some leaves of the plant, too. On the way back home, she got so tired that it was all she could do to make it to her bed of straw before falling asleep. In her dreams, she floated up into heavenly realms with blossoming meadows where happy people were dancing in rounds and singing songs. She also saw a beautiful woman with billowing hair and big pearly white teeth and thought it must be the goddess herself. At the feet of the goddess, the same bear lay that she had seen earlier in the forest. He let her pet his furry coat and grunted happily as if he were licking honey. When the old woman awoke, she thought she was still dreaming because a mild spring wind blew through the window and outside in the greening trees she heard spring birds singing. Though it seemed to her she had only slept for a few hours, she had actually slept the whole winter and the frost giants were long gone into the high glacial mountains. When she saw her reflection in the water, she was shocked. In the reflection, she saw a young woman with rosy cheeks and full hair without any gray streaks looking back at her. The "sleeping plant" had rejuvenated her.

A MASTER OF BOTANY

When the famous American grizzly bear researcher and wilderness expert Ernest Thompson Seton wrote that the bear knows more about plants and roots than a whole college of botanists, he was not telling us anything new. The bear's incredible herbal knowledge has impressed many observers. But what else could one expect of the wise king of the forest? A bear's nose is at least as good as that of a bloodhound. Researchers debate about how many hundred times better a bear's nose can smell than a human's modest olfactory organ. A bear can already smell from a great distance very exact nuances regarding what it can eat and what it cannot eat. For this reason, especially old bears with a lot of life experience can hardly be fooled by poisoned bait.

Even in antiquity, the bear was considered the doctor among the animals. For the hunting peoples of olden times, it was always the bear spirit that showed the healers which healing plants to use for lack of appetite, for fertility, or to drive off bad spirits in general. It is not by chance that an old Celtic coin shows a bear with a root in its mouth. For the Native Americans across the board, medicine is not medication like we understand it to be. A medicine being—whether a healing plant, peace pipe, medicine man, medicine woman, or medicine animal—is a being with power, a being with *mana*, that can be tapped into under certain circumstances. Hardly another among the animals has as much "medicine" (mana) as a bear does. Accordingly, the strongest healing plants, especially roots, were known as "bear medicine." The Midewiwin, the grand medicine society of the Ojibwa, carved the strongest healing roots to look like bear claws and wore them as a necklace, just like a genuine bear claw necklace.

So that medical plants do not lose their power, they are not to be dug out with metal tools but with wooden or horn tools, or even like a bear itself would do—with bear claws. Such rules for gathering herbs are universal amid native peoples and can be traced back to the Stone Age—that is, to the time before metal was ever used. According to medicine man Bill Tallbull, bear medicine is so strong that it should not be kept in the house or even in the cab of a pickup truck as one could be overwhelmed by it.

The "doctors" of the Californian Native Americans often wore bearskins or mountain lion skins and lived, similar to the berserkers, away from the rest of the tribe in the wilderness. They were considered so full of power that they could not be tolerated in the villages; their power could be dangerous for normal people. Their medicine had the power to heal but also to kill. One would find bear claw tracks on whomever had been their victim.

Native American bear images from the northwestern coast. Left: Tsimshian; right: Kwakiutl.

Among the Iroquois, the bear mask society followed the instructions of the bear spirit and had the shamanic medicine power (*orenda*) to heal gout and rheumatic ailments. Long ago, the bear spirit had appeared to a half-starved hunter who was lost in the forest. Out of pity, the bear gave the suffering human medicine songs and taught him dance steps. With these, humans could conquer the plagues brought on by the cold, moist weather.

The Celtic, Germanic, and Slavic ancestors of the northern Europeans also knew about potent bear plants. Contrary to wolf plants like baneberry, daphne, stinking hellebore, or spurges that are caustic or highly poisonous, or useless, foul-smelling "dog" plants, they saw bear plants as motherly, protective, and refreshing. They called especially big and vital plants "bear plants," such as hogweed, burdock, angelica, or lovage. They saw a bear character in such tough plants as bearbind. Plants with especially strong magic—for instance, club moss, bear's garlic, burdock, and maidenhair moss, or bear's bed—were known to drive off witches, demons, and nightmares, just as bear teeth, claws, and hair do. Bear's bed is also known in German as *Widerton*, meaning "opposing magic," because, usually worn in the hair or on a hat, it was used to counter black magic.

Bear and elk with fly agaric (Siberian drawing, author unknown)

Plants that encourage hair and beard growth, such as stinging nettle, burdock, or Alsatian broomrape, were also categorized as bear plants. Furthermore, the plants that make milk rich and sweet (in animals and in humans), increase potency, and strengthen or protect the uterus were seen as bear plants provided they were not put directly under the protection of the great vegetation goddess herself, Freya or Mother Holle, or later on under the Virgin Mary. And finally, also classified as veritable bear plants were the consciousness-altering, magical plants that allowed the berserkers to get to know their own animal nature.

BEAR'S GARLIC, BEAR LEEK, OR RAMSONS

Anyone who has been in the Alps in the spring has noticed how bear's garlic (*Allium ursinum*) still has the status of a somewhat sacred plant. In the spring, no mountain farmer would go without blood-cleansing bear's garlic soup (made of the leaves before the plant flowers) even though in modern times the winters are not like they used to be as far as a lack of vitamins go. Just like the bear's appearance drives old man winter away from the countryside, this delicate green soup drives winter weariness—scurvy, scrofula, iron-deficient anemia—out of the limbs and entire body. The sulfuric mustard oils of this plant that is related to the onion clean out the stomach and intestines, regenerate intestinal flora, release tension, and give a warm, fuzzy feeling like that of a bear hug.[2] It is said one should eat bear's garlic on Walpurgis Eve (April 31st) to avoid harm from the witches who fly around especially throughout that night.

Otherwise quite sober-natured herbal pastor Johann Kuenzle could not help but grow effusive when he wrote about bear's garlic: "People who are chronically

Blossoming bear's garlic

sick," he writes, "people with eczema, rashes, scrofula and anemia should revere bear's garlic like gold. . . . Young people will blossom like a rose arbor and open up like pinecones in the sun," and "people who are full of rashes and eczema, their whole bodies scrofulitic, as pale as if they had already been lying in their graves and the chickens had scratched them back out, will look completely refreshed and healthy after a good, long cure of this goodly gift from God" (Kuenzle, 1977, 30). Bears also enjoy this liliaceous plant, which smells like garlic, as a purifying cure in the spring. Kuenzle proclaims "our ancestors learned about this plant by observing bears" (Kuenzle 1977, 31).

CLUBMOSS

Common clubmoss (*Lycopodium clavatum*) is even more "beary" than bear's garlic. In ancient times, it was believed that this dark green forest floor plant had the same kind of magical power as a bear's paw. Indeed, the word "lapp" on the end of the German word for the plant (*Baerlapp*) goes back to a Celtic word meaning "paw." The plant sprouts really do look like shaggy animal paws. The botanical name *Lycopodium* means "wolf's paw."

Other names of clubmoss are stag's-horn clubmoss, wolf-paw clubmoss, foxtail clubmoss, running clubmoss, running ground-pine, running pine, running moss, and princess pine. In German, it is also called devil's claw (*Teufelsklaue*), witches moss (*Hexenmoos*), and Drude plant (*Drudenkraut*). The last one most likely refers to Druids because, for Celtic magicians, the plant was shrouded in legend. A sacred plant for them—they called it *selago*—they were very careful about how they picked it. Barefoot and robed in unstitched white gowns, they sought the plant in new moon nights. After a long incantation, they picked the twigs with the left hand. No iron could touch the plant because it would drive away its

Common clubmoss

spirit. They offered the plant mead (honey wine) and bread in reconciliation and used it for amulets to protect from all kinds of harm, from "the evil eye," bad magic, and bewitchment.

Even today clubmoss still has a reputation. An old neighbor of mine would stick a twig on his hatband on occasion, claiming it would help him when having to deal with officials and higher authorities. Young girls who want to get married used to be advised to sew some clubmoss onto their dresses so that they would be irresistible. The sick were advised to put some of it in the Saint John's belt (a garland of various plants woven and worn as a garland or around the waist at midsummer) and toss it into the Saint John's fire (the traditional midsummer fire) so that all their suffering would burn there. To a certain degree, some of these customs even still live on in rural areas in Europe.

The yellow pollen of the spores are called lycopodium powder (German *Hexenmehl* = witch's flour, *Blitzpulver* = lightening powder, *Erdschwefel* = earth sulfur, *Drudenmehl* = Drude [Druid] powder). When these oil-emulsifying and aluminum-containing spores are tossed into an open fire, lycopodium powder sizzles and pops as if Asbjørn (the godly bear) himself were striking with his mighty paws. Stone Age shamans used this dramatic light-explosive effect as did theater directors in past centuries. The powder was also used as the flash in early photography.

Just as the Europeans of long ago did, wherever it grew, Native Americans also used the spores as wound powder that absorbed moisture and accelerated healing. It was sprinkled on the navel of newborn babies to accelerate healing and used as powder for baby bottoms. Pastor Kuenzle prescribed the plant, or baths of the cooked plant, for cramps and varicose veins; he also recommended the plant cooked in wine and taken as a cure for gall and bladder stones. Maria Treben, who brought the natural "God's Pharmacy" (herbal healing) back to modern people, recommends it for cirrhosis, cramps, high blood pressure, shortness of breath, and other ailments (Treben 1982, 9).[3]

BEARBERRY

Anyone who has suffered from a painful bladder or kidney infection and been lucky enough to cure it with bearberry tea (*Arctostaphylos uva-ursi*) has learned to appreciate the healing power of this plant. A decoction of the leaves disinfects the urine. However, one should avoid eating meat when taking bearberry tea because its effect is dependent upon an alkaline reaction in the urine.

Bearberry is a creeping dwarf shrub from the heather family that is part of the bear biotope from Europe to Siberia and North America. It is guaranteed that no hungry bear will amble past these berries with indifference in the fall. Wherever it grows, for the Native Americans bearberry is one of the most important "medicine plants" (powerful plants). The berries were threaded for necklaces or roasted in bear fat or fish oil in a pan where they puff up and pop like popcorn (Moermann 1999, 88). But mainly the leathery leaves were added to a mixture of tobacco, staghorn sumac leaves, and the inside bark of common dogwood. This mixture was known as *kinnikinnik* (Algonquian = smoke mixture). According to Bill Tallbull, this smoke attracts the spirits and makes it possible to contact talking coyotes, thunderbirds, and the bear spirit, as well as distant chiefs of other tribes.

Bearberry

BURDOCK

Another bear plant worth mentioning is burdock. Burdock radiates a bear-like vitality with its huge, elephant ear–like leaves, mighty taproot, and a flower head with many scratchy hooks (miniature bear claws). The botanical name *Arctium lappa*, means, "bear paw" (Greek *arktos* = bear; Celtic *lapp* = paw). As a genuine bear plant, it also promotes hair growth. In apothecaries in Europe, one may still find burdock hair oil made from the roots or seeds. One can make the hair oil by macerating the crushed root in oil for three weeks in a warm place. The oil is also used to treat rheumatism and joint and skin ailments.

The Germanic tribes dedicated this composite to mighty Thor, the godly bear, whose lighting strikes could drive off dragons and other creepy, crawly creatures. It follows that Germanic folk medicine had a tea made of the roots for any "worms" that can nestle into the body and rob people of their strength. The tea does indeed stimulate liver and gall bladder functions, is sudorific, and flushes toxins out of tissue and organs. The root also has bacteriostatic and fungicidal attributes and can be used externally for acne and infected wounds. Burdock is definitely a bear of a plant. It is even claimed that the plant can be used to counter bad magic: Burdocks in the hair keep the devil away; burdocks in cows' tails keep away witches who like to sneak up and drink the milk; and a burdock leaf under the sole of her shoes was believed to help a woman with a prolapsed uterus.

BEAR'S MILK, LICORICE, AND HOGWEED

As has already been mentioned, a bear's milk is very rich (30 percent fat) and very sweet. Legends tell that anyone who drinks bear's milk will become a hero. A Russian tale tells of one such hero who had to get milk from a forest bear to heal his ailing sister.

"Bear's milk makes us strong!"—the slogan of the Bernese Alpine milk producers.
Left: original print; right: present version.

Understandably, Alpine meadow flowers that give cows' milk an especially aromatic flavor are also connected to bears. One of these milk herbs is bear wort (*Meum athamanticum*), which is also called baldmoney or spignel.

The signature of this aromatic umbelliferous herb is very distinct: It has a thick brown bunch of "hair" on the rootstock that looks similar to bear fur. Wherever this native of northern Europe grows, it is a highly respected plant in folk medicine. It is known to strengthen the stomach and heart and is usually taken in the form of schnapps (it can be macerated in clear alcohol, such as vodka, for a couple of weeks).

Alpine lovage, or mountain lovage (*Ligusticum mutellina*), is equally cherished as a milk herb. An Alpine saying goes:

Panicle, mountain lovage and Alpine plantain
are the best things our little cow did eat.

According to legend, long ago a lazy, disrespectful female Alpine herder cursed mountain lovage because the cows had so much milk from eating it that she was forced to milk three times a day, and it was very hard work to get the cheese wheels down the mountain. The curse went into effect, and the milk-giving power of the plant receded. The prayers of an old man canceled the curse—but only to a degree.

Native Americans recognize a warrior plant with bear power in *osha* (from *osa* in Spanish, meaning "female bear"), also known as bear medicine or wild lovage, which grows in the southern Rocky Mountains. Regarded as a cure-all, the warming, sudorific root is chewed for flu, viral diseases, and stomach and intestinal ailments; women use it to activate menstruation; and the dry root is used for incensing to purify the atmosphere. The Crow mix it with kinnikinnik. Warriors chewed on the root when they had to run long distances because it had a good effect on the lungs, and an amulet made of osha helps protect from rattlesnake bites. When asked about the plant by anthropologist (animal behaviorist) Shawn Sigstead, the Navajos he was interviewing claimed, "We learned about the healing power of this plant from the bear." The skeptical Harvard scholar, however, wanted to find out for himself if bears were really interested in the plant. When he tossed the plant into a bear cage, the bears pounced on it like cats do on catnip or valerian and chewed it with obvious delight, spread the chewed-up plant matter onto their paws, and then rubbed it onto sores and areas where they had fungus. Follow-up research done with grizzlies in Alaska showed that they reacted just as "crazily" when they happened upon the plant. In the wild, they ate it as a means against intestinal parasites, chewed the root, and washed wounds with it or even washed their faces with it. A male bear in love will also dig it out and bring it to the female bear he is wooing (Storl 2001, 203).

Wild licorice (*Astragalus glycyrrhiza*), closely related to licorice (*Glycyrrhiza glabra*), is another bear plant that grows in sparse forests or as a cover after clear cutting. In the Middle Ages, the juice from the root was cooked into a syrup and made into a medicament with some honey, blood, various herbs, and a good amount of opium. It was then used to remedy poisoning, wild animal bites, and the pestilence. For Native Americans, licorice was also considered a strong bear medicine. Indigenous prairie tribes chewed on the root while in the sweat lodge because it helped them withstand the last nearly unbearable rounds of heat while sweating. For them, the sweating that drives out impurities of the body and soul serves as a preparation for contacting mighty spiritual entities.

A common plant called hogweed (*Heracleum sphondylium*) dominates over all the other plants and grasses in the meadows with its mighty, juicy stems and big, lobed, hairy leaves. The bear nature of this giant becomes evident with the seeds' aphrodisiacal effect. After all, the bear was known since earliest times as a veritable fertility beast. Hogweed should not be confused with giant hogweed, or giant cow parsnip (*Heracleum mantegazzianum*), from the Caucasus, which has recently become an invasive plant in Europe and North America and should be avoided as much as an angry grizzly bear. Just to touch the plant—especially when the sun is shining—will cause an inflammation with a blister as big as a hot iron would leave.[4]

Hogweed

CHAPTER 16
Bear Fat and Bear Gall

*Bear fat is a healing means that has a solid place in the medicine chest
of shamans until this day and comes from "bear cultures."*

NANA NAUWALD,
BAERENKRAFT UND JAGUARMEDIZIN
(AUTHOR'S TRANSLATION)

The living bear is cherished even more as an apothecary itself than
are all the bear plants put together. All of its body parts are laden
with healing energy. In China and East Asia, only ginseng can compare to
the mighty healing power of the bear. Ginseng (Chinese = man-root) is the
"emperor of the plants" just as the bear is the "king of the forest." They both
have in common a human-like form, and, according to the oldest healing
principle—head to head, heart to heart, kidneys to kidneys (i.e., like cures
like, *similia similibus curentur*)—both the human-like root and the "forest
human bear" cure the entire human being. As alchemists would say, both
have a human signature. Tungusic peoples in Siberia avow that both ginseng
and the bear have a human soul and speak to both the plant and the bear,
as to a human being. In ancient China, it was even believed that an exceptionally gifted herbal practitioner could marry the ginseng plant and that it
would appear to him as a radiant virgin. It was believed to even be possible
that he could sire children with her. Likewise, a shaman can marry the bear
spirit, or the bear spirit can sire children with women it visits at night. The
human relationship to these two carriers of potent medicinal power is loaded
with energy and surrounded by numerous taboos and rules.

In other parts of the world, the bear—its fur, teeth, gall, fat, flesh, and blood—was also seen as a reservoir of the strongest of healing means against which the worst demons of disease and black magic had no chance. In the Artemis temples of antiquity, living bears were kept for therapeutic reasons. The priestesses cured hair loss and gout with bear fat and a chronic cough with a drop of bear gall stirred into honey water. Bear testicles were prescribed against "falling sickness" (epilepsy).

THE BEAR'S CHARISMA

Surely one could analyze the bear's fat, gall, kidneys, and testicles for the molecular active ingredients and find out very interesting things. After all, have healing plants not also been analyzed and freed of the undergrowth of superstitious imaginations? Bill Tallbull could only shake his head as I discussed such ideas with him: "The bear has medicine power, but it is not a substance. It is more like a charisma that surrounds him. Each hair, the claws, and all parts of the bear have this power!" Was he telling me another of his tall tales that he had on hand for curious tourists? Like so often, he read my thoughts even before I had finished thinking them and added with a whimsical smile: "This charisma can change a human's consciousness. If the bear did not have this power, the white people would have wiped it out by now."

The bear's charisma! Even until the beginning of the twentieth century people would invite traveling artists who had dancing bears with them to come to their barns or the local mill. The very presence of a bear was enough to drive away bad moods, spooks, and bad magic. In the Carpathian Mountains, a bear claw is still hung over a child's crib for protection. According to the principle that like can deal with like, these dangerous, murderous weapons of the carnivore will keep anything threatening away from the helpless little one. The Inuit also hang a bear tooth around the neck of a baby so that it will have a good appetite and good digestion and especially so that it will grow strong teeth. Good teeth were historically vitally important for the Inuit, not only to eat, but also because they spent hours chewing dried animal skins to make them soft, malleable, and easy to sew. The Inuit still believe that an amulet made from bear parts will make them invincible, as long as the bear did not die by human hands. Knut Rasmussen, the famous polar researcher, adds: "It is not the amulet itself but the soul of the animal from which the amulet is made that has helping and healing power" (Nana Nauwald 2002, 107).

Traveling artists with a dancing bear

It is a universal, archaic belief that the power, the "soul" of a living being, can live on for a long time in the bones and especially in the skull, the teeth, and the claws. This belief also applies to human remains and explains many of the burial rites in the old and new world. Christians also believe in the radiating power of the bones of the martyrs and saints and cement them into altars. In the entire northern hemisphere of yore, dead bears were handled with as much respect as dead humans were. In Siberia, the entire bear skeleton was carefully buried or, as done by many Native Americans as well, carefully placed on a platform or in a tree. The bear's skull, which is where the reincarnating soul resides, was often painted, just as human skulls also often were (Schlesier 2013, 57). Shamans stay in contact with the helpful spirit of the bear that is now residing in the otherworld by wearing its claws and teeth.

Bear tooth amulet

Bear claw and bear tooth amulets for pregnant women were used until recently, and Roma peoples still use them today. In the Mediterranean, a bear claw on a necklace is believed to ward off the evil eye. Old Norwegian peasants would put dried bear eyes on the beds of children to ward off nightmares that not only frighten them but also sometimes cause cramps. In many places, newborn babies, as well as sick and old people and people who had rheumatism, were lain on a bearskin. This practice was done not only because of the warmth that a bearskin offers but also mainly for the vitality, the energy, that the shaggy fur radiates. A bearskin was even believed to heal those bitten by a rabid animal when such victims were wrapped in one. Bridal couples of the Sami people would sit on a bearskin during the wedding so that they would profit from the bear's strong vitality and fertility. For the same reason, in ancient Prussia, the couple was served fried bear testicles; later on, roasted bear innards were placed under the bridal bed instead.

Everywhere blood is believed to be a magical, strengthening substance. What blood could be stronger than that of a bear? Only chiefs, shamans, warriors, or the best hunters were strong enough to take it, and the bear's heart, inner organs, and fresh, warm blood were reserved for such people to consume ceremoniously. The berserkers also ritually charged themselves up with bear blood, brain, and bone marrow. It is said of legendary Achilles that he got his heroic courage from sucking out bear bone marrow as a child.

In this same spirit, the proud councilmen of Berne, Switzerland, used to claim the meat of a slain bear for themselves. For example, in 1891, when the town celebrated its seven-hundred-year anniversary, they strengthened themselves and their authority with a tasty dish of bear—accompanied by festive brass music. The meat was chased down with a hearty stream of special dark beer. In addition, even into the middle of the 1990s, at an annual bear feast for the most important councilmen of the city, the bear warden of the ancient bear pit in Berne and the mayor were the first ones to be served the best parts—the paws and the liver. Anthropologists speak quite openly of a ceremonial, totemic meal in this case as well as any other. The bear fat was sold to the apothecaries, and the furs decorated the offices. A legend of an old Bernese who was downright addicted to bear meat tells how the more he ate, the more hair he had on his body and the stronger he became. Instead of speaking, he evermore only grumbled. Such a case sounds highly unlikely, but why are the Ainu, who became ethnologically famous for their totemic bear feasts, the hairiest people known to anthropologists? They are stocky, have round faces with deep-set eyes (no epicanthic fold), are extremely hairy, and the men have extremely full beards. By chance?

"No, most certainly not by chance," argued Bill Tallbull as we discussed the subject one day. "One does become what one eats," he explained plainly and justified his preference for the meat of wild animals and his rejection of calf meat and milk. "Just look at the soft white people with their everlasting milk drinking. They have become like dumb calves," he said with a dismissive gesture.

The eastern Siberian nomads, who have a highly ritualized bear meal, do not go so far as to suck the marrow out of the bones and would not dream of it. The bear spirit could revenge itself in a horrific way, and the potency in the bear could turn into a negative power causing disease, accidents, or severe weather. Each bone should remain intact. The bones are carefully rearranged in exact anatomical order just as one would do with a deceased human being and then put carefully into the earth or wrapped in birch bark and placed in a tree. Only in this way can the bear wake up into a new life.

Wooden healing amulets with bear motifs (Siberia, Museum of Ethnology, Berlin; above left: Golden, the others Gilyak). Ailments treated, from top to bottom: back pain (2x), disease, and chest pain.

For some of the hunting peoples, the ancient Finnish hunters for example, the bear's brain was considered the best part. Medieval Europeans did not eat it, though—perhaps memories of wild berserkers and their non-Christian customs were too strong. Even the Romans were convinced that a bear's brain had a strong influence on a person's spirit. Plinius warned it would make a person go crazy; the bear's fantasies and delusions would transfer to the person who would begin to believe he or she was a bear. Repugnant stories of noblemen, mainly, who ate bear brain and turned into vicious were-bears made the rounds in Europe.[1]

THE CURE-ALL

Bear gall plays a special role in healing lore. It is said to be good for anything and everything—a veritable cure-all. In Finland, the bitter liquid is given to sick people as a sudorific. In Central Europe, frostbitten limbs used to be bathed in water with some bear gall in it. Bear gall was also used to treat skin and eye ailments, jaundice, cancer, and animal bites. It was put into the vagina in the form of a suppository shortly before intercourse to increase the ability to conceive. And some knights tied a bear gallbladder around the right hip before mounting an enamored damsel in order to "be a man as often as he wished." Universal scholar Conrad Gessner (1516–1565) at the University of Zurich, inspired by traditional Swiss lore, claimed that bear gall, bear fat, and bear blood drive off nasty fleas and blood-sucking vermin that nest in beds and that it suffices to merely put a saucer of it under the bed (Schmitz 1998, 145).

Macabre statistics indicate that bear gall is still a much-coveted item in East Asian medicine. From 1980 to 1990 alone, sixty thousand bear gallbladders were imported from China to Japan. During the same timespan, bear gallbladders brought in big money in India: 4,300 gallbladders were sold to Japan for the incredible price of $64,000 for 1 kilogram (approximately 2.2 pounds). Bear paws in the amount of 600 kilograms (approximately 1,300 pounds) were also imported to Japan during this time and sold for a price of around $850 per plate in special restaurants. Obviously, being able to afford a bear paw meal is regarded as a status symbol. In 1980s South Korea, a poacher killed one of the last Asiatic black bears even though these animals were, theoretically at least, under strict protection. After the poacher was arrested, the government sold the bear's gallbladder for $64,000 at a public auction (Mills 2002, 179). In 1990, one could still order roasted bear paws in the Hilton Hotel in Seoul, South Korea (Savage 1990, 118).

Vancouver, British Columbia, where many East Asian people have settled in the last few decades, has become a major trafficking hub for bear gall and bear meat. Bear gallbladders can be bought for approximately $1,000 and sold in Korea for up to $55,000 apiece—as much as a human kidney for a transplant! That is an enormous profit, comparable to illegal drugs such as heroin, for example. Business with the bear's anatomy worldwide adds up to $100 million a year, which is incentive for unscrupulous poachers and mafia-like criminals (Busch 2000, 163). Fortunately, British Columbia authorities became aware and it is increasingly difficult to pursue these nefarious activities. In 1991, a Korean man, who had a bear gallbladder in his possession, was found murdered in his New York apartment. Up to forty thousand bears are shot illegally every year in North America. Sometimes, the cadavers are just left in the forest after the gall bladder has been cut out.

Mercilessly hunted, just as the whales as a source of raw materials, the rhinoceroses for their powdered horn that supposedly gives aging men their virile youth back, or elephants for their tusks that turn a big profit, the Asiatic bears—the Asiatic black bears, sun bears, sloth bears in the Himalayas, as well as the Siberian brown bears—are seriously endangered. In bear farms in China, the animals are kept in tiny cages and "milked," that is, a catheter is rammed into their belly and the gall bladder is tapped. Half of the bears do not survive this procedure. Bear gall (Chinese *yu dan*, *xioung dan*, or *dong dan*), which contains the active ingredient ursodeoxycholic acid, is used for fever, hemorrhoids, conjunctivitis, diabetes, liver disease, and epilepsy; but, contrary to some claims, it is ineffective as an aphrodisiac or as a healing means for cancer. In Traditional Chinese Medicine, bear gall is considered "cold"; that is, its effects are "cooling" for such symptoms as dry throat, reddish face, constipation, high pulse, fever, and headaches. Ursodeoxycholic acid can be made synthetically nowadays, or out of cattle bladders. In addition, some fifty-four different herbal preparations can effectively replace bear gall.

Japanese healing lore differentiates three different qualities of bear gall: yellow gall, amber gall, and black gall. Amber gall (*kama-no-i*) comes from a bear in the snowy season and is considered one hundred times more valuable than that from a bear killed in the summer. Before a bear retreats into its den, it busily gathers ants and rubs them into a sour-tasting paste between its paws. It keeps the paste, which helps the bear maintain its strength during hibernation, on the inside of its paws and licks them from time to time. It is this ant paste that makes the winter gall especially valuable; hunters in search of this amber gall head out before the spring equinox, lodge rocks and a crossbeam over the entryway to the bear's den, and then smoke the bear out with tobacco and hot peppers. When it storms out of its den in anger, it trips over a taut strategically placed rope. The beam and rocks fall on the bear; it is best if the bear dies with little or no loss of blood. The Japanese say that, whenever a bear is killed like this, a mighty storm begins, which they call *kama-are*, raging bear.

BEAR FAT

Bear fat is almost in more demand than bear gall and also has the reputation of being a perfect cure-all. Since antiquity, it is believed to be unbeatable for making hair grow and healing rheumatism. It alleviates internal pain and heals battered skin, abscesses, and gout. It was recommended to women for a prolapsed womb. Not surprisingly, corrupt druggists often sold simple pig fat as expensive bear fat. Even in the nineteenth century, a druggist from northern Germany is reported to have sold fifteen to twenty hundredweights (approximately 100 pounds) of American pig fat yearly as bear fat.

In the times of long ago, when there were still bears in European forests, people barely distinguished between scientific facts and magical effects, between "reality" and miracles. Sickness was not seen as a functional disturbance of biological processes or damage done by microorganisms; instead, it was seen as the result of evil magic or the wicked doings of invisible, evil spirits. Bear fat would protect not only from cold, raw winter weather but also—and even mainly—from black magic, bad spells, and other invisible wicked doings. According to the principle that one must fight fire with fire and demons with demonic power, the accumulated bear power in bear fat was used as an apotropaic (from Greek *atropopaios* = evil averting) against various diseases. Fearful people still saw the bear itself as a forest demon and ogre.

Bear trainers rubbed themselves down with bear fat to protect themselves from their dancing bears—which was surely effective as they then smelled like a fellow bear. For similar reasons, Roman wine producers oiled their pruning knives with bear fat to keep vine fretters and other visible and invisible vermin out of the vineyards. Warriors and hunters applied bear fat to their knives less for keeping them rust free than for making them seem like the lightning-fast strike of a bear's paw. The smashes and sparks of swords and battle-axes were always associated with the thunder and lightning of Asbjørn, the bear in the heavens. The Kamchadals and Ainu still call thunder the divine bear's roaring, and in the ancient Indian Vedas, storm and thunder gods, the warrior-like *Maruts,* are also often referred to as bears in the sky. This association was transferred to modern firearms that also spark and rumble. It is also not so very long ago that European hunters and troopers oiled their weapons with bear fat salves.

Bear fat is also supposed to magically help a failing memory; after one rubs it into the temples, thoughts and memories shoot through the head like wildfire. Conrad Gessner, renowned scientist of his time, claimed in his book about animals, *Thierbouch* (Zurich, 1563), that rubbing bear fat onto one's face will ensure a keen understanding of everything read and heard. This practice was probably a remnant of an old heathen custom. Shamans and berserkers rubbed bear fat enhanced with psychedelic plants into their skin before falling into trance-like states. Thus, worlds opened up that otherwise remained closed. They were then able to communicate with otherworldly beings, nature spirits, ghosts, kobolds, and other spirits, or they were able to roam the forest in the body of a wild animal. Nightshade plants, such as dangerous henbane or belladonna, and poisonous plants, such as monkshood or poison hemlock, were sometimes used as well, in appropriate minimal dosage. Bear fat is easily absorbed into the skin and releases such plant substances in an easily controlled way.

For Christian monks, these kinds of salves were understandably anathema. There was no doubt in their minds that the devil himself had created these wicked plants and that not only bear fat was used to produce these devilish salves but also the fat of assassinated infants or secretly exhumed corpses. But not all the pagans let themselves be scared away from such salves, and the knowledge regarding these "flying ointments" went underground. However, it was criminalized to the degree that ultimately hundreds of thousands who dared use them, and got caught doing so, were publicly burned as witches. Even as late as 1749, Maria Singer, a second abbess in Unterzell, Germany, was beheaded as a sorceress for the simple fact that she had planted belladonna in the garden.

The flight (Ulricus Molitoris, 1489)

Many Native Americans did not hunt the sacred medicine animal at all. But when they did, it was mainly for its valuable fat. They believed that the magical medicine power of the animal was stored there and that almost all ailments could be healed with it—from abscesses, eczema, epilepsy, and rheumatic pain to worms. Healing plants, especially tobacco, were cooked in bear fat, and the resulting salve was applied to the ailing body parts. A typical recipe from Virginia made from bear fat and mashed angelica and pokeweed was used to "strengthen the body" and to keep fleas and lice away (Vogel 1982, 218). Mixing color into bear fat also intensified the magical power of war paint.

AMBER

The magical medicine power that was ascribed to all of the bear's body parts, especially the teeth and claws, was also transferred to honey-colored amber, which is petrified, fossil pine tree resin. In German, amber is called *Bernstein; Bern* comes from *Brennen* ("burn"), that is, a stone that can be burned, but folk-etymologically, it is "bear-stone" because the German word for bear, *Baer,* sounds similar to *Bern.* Just as a necklace made of bear claws or an amulet made of bear tooth, an amber amulet can also protect from disease and demons. An amber necklace is said to help infants grow strong, healthy teeth. Like bear fat, this "electric" stone is said to protect against enchantment and treat rheumatic pain. Pregnant women who wear an amber necklace will have an easier birth. It is as if some bear spirit lives in the honey-colored stone.

A bear carved into amber (Mesolithic; Resen Mose, Denmark, 9000 BCE)

CHAPTER 17
Rituals of Departure:
Reconciliation with the Bear Spirit

snare a bear: call him out
honey eater
forest apple
light-foot
Old man in the fur coat, Bear! Come out!
Die of your own choice!
Grandfather black food!

GARY SNYDER, *MYTHS & TEXTS*

Of course, the bear does not let his strength, his gall, and his fat be taken easily. The bear's spirit is very dangerous, and a bear hunter must beware of its revenge. Not unlike the shamanistic ritual that warriors performed before heading out on a warpath, Native American bear hunters would gather first in a body-and-soul purifying sweat lodge. They incensed themselves with tobacco and sage, painted their faces with magical color, and left early in the morning, unfed, to find the bear's den while carrying medicine pouches and singing medicine songs. Through these ritually prescribed measures, they left behind everyday consciousness and entered a magical state, thus being in the right state of mind to approach the mighty animal.

The Sioux, as well as some other tribes, danced grizzly bear dances in preparation for meeting the bear. "Striding and jumping, accompanied by drums and songs, they mimicked the movements of a bear, dancing in a circle. The leading role fell to the shaman, as was common for most religious dances, and he wore a bearskin. The other dancers had bear masks over their heads and were painted colorfully. At the end of the dance the women started yelling and cheering them on, and then the hunt could begin" (Mauer 2002, 28).

Native Americans of the prairie performing a bear dance (drawing by George Catlin, 1848)

The bear dance or the right medicine song—the bear song that could bring the hunters into contact with the bear spirit and let their honorable intentions be known—was of crucial significance. A legend of the Haida people of British Columbia tells how human beings received the bear songs:

There was once a young girl who went with her girlfriends to pick berries in the forest. But instead of singing the berry songs as she should, she chatted and laughed foolishly all day long. In the evening on the way home, the strap of her full berry basket tore. Her girlfriends were all too far away for her to call them. Two young men in bearskins came along and asked her in a friendly way if they could help.

"Come with us. It is getting dark. Our camp is near here," they said and took her with them. Soon they came to a campfire around which other figures, also in bearskins, were sitting.

It is nice here, but tomorrow I will go back to my people, the girl thought. Just then a mouse tugged at the bottom of her skirt. "Psst, little daughter," the mouse whispered, *"do you even realize that you are amid bears? It will be hard for you to leave here!"*

And so it came to pass. The days and months went by, and the bears showed no sign of bringing her back home. One of the spirit bears was especially friendly to her and invited her to sleep next to him. As time passed, she became his wife. Soon after she bore twins that were half human, half bear.

The girl's brothers had sought to find her as soon as she had not come home. One day, they appeared in front of the bear's den. Before the young lady could say a word, arrows flew and wounded her bear husband mortally. As he was dying, he called his two sons and taught them the sacred bear song that human beings should sing to every killed bear. This was the only way that his soul could be comforted and the only way he would be able to come back to the world.

Bear shaman of the Black Foot (George Catlin, 1848)

How the Cheyenne learned to treat a slain bear in the right way is told in the following story:

Once very long ago even before there were horses, a Cheyenne was walking with his wife in the prairie. He shot a bison. Just as they were skinning it, a bunch of hostile Crow came along. They killed the man and forced the woman to go with them. The leader of the group took her as his third wife. The other two wives did not like her because she was much prettier than they were. They beat on her and gave her the hardest work to do. She had to fetch wood and water, scrape hides, and sew moccasins.

A young Crow who often watched her fell in love with the beautiful woman. He had heard her crying often and had ever more compassion for her. One day when the men were out hunting bison and the women were digging roots, he brought her a fast horse. "Flee from here as fast as you can," he told her.

She rode and rode until she was sure no Crow would be able to follow her. She was exhausted and lay down to sleep for a short time. While she was sleeping, the horse got free and ran off. She had no choice but to continue on foot. As she was walking, she saw a shadow that seemed to be following her from a distance. Though she started to walk faster, the shadow caught up with her. It was a bear.

"Do not be afraid," it spoke with a human voice, "I am walking in your footsteps so that your pursuers will not find you. I will show you the way to your people, dear daughter."

They continued through the wild countryside, and the bear was fast on her tracks. When she slept at night, the bear watched over her. Every day it hunted down a buffalo calf or an antelope so that she had enough to eat. The bear only ate what she left over. When they came to the wide Platte River, the bear carried her across.

Finally, they saw smoke from campfires in the distance. "There are your people," the bear grumbled in a friendly manner. "Go to them and tell them that I brought you home safely. I will wait here. Bring me a bison back divided into four pieces."

When the family members saw the girl they believed to be dead, they were overjoyed and began to celebrate. They put a bowl with buffalo meat right in front of the snout of the bear and decorated its head with feathers and colorful ribbons. They put a necklace of river pearls around his neck and blankets on his back. Finally, they offered the bear the peace pipe, blew smoke in his face, and put tobacco in front of his nostrils.

Even today, Cheyenne treat bears as guests when they appear out of nowhere, and the ones their hunters have killed are also honored with respectful rituals. Reconciliation with the bear spirit was no less elaborate in the Old World. For example, the Mansi people, a hunting and reindeer-rearing people from the upper Ob River area in Russia, would ask the still sleepy bear for forgiveness before their hunters lured it from its den. The hunters would then wear masks made of birch bark and alter their voices so that the bear would think it was Russians or Tatars who dared commit such an atrocity. After killing it, they immediately spoke to the slain animal while sprinkling water or snow over it to refresh it, "Surely, grandfather, it was a Russian axe that struck you. By chance, we happened upon you and found you so badly battered, noble bear. We will celebrate a merry feast with you! You will be wined and dined at a golden table!" As they skinned the precious fur from the animal, they sang about its life, its descent to earth, its roaming through the forest, its occasional meeting with women and children when the berries were ripe, the feast it was soon to attend, and its ascent to divine realms.

When they were back in the village, they did not carry the bear's furry carcass through the normal entrance, but, as with dead bodies, through a hole made solely for this purpose, or through a window. The bear was then placed on a seat of honor, and silver coins were put over its eyes and beautiful rings on its paws. Each person at the festive meal bowed before the bear and kissed its snout. A bear dance followed, which portrayed scenes out of its life. Women covered their faces, and men wore wooden phalli that they strapped on with hip belts.

The bear feast is a dismembering and reassembling that mirrors a shamanic initiation. A new shaman also experiences, in a trance, his own death, the dismemberment of his bones, his consumption by hungry demons, the reassembling of his bones, and his rebirth into a higher state of being. The bear's bones were all bundled together and buried on a wooden platform just like one of the Mansi's own dead.

When the Tungusic peoples in Siberia celebrate a bear feast, the process is similar. During the festival, they crow like ravens so that the bear's spirit, which can still hear everything, will think that black vulture-like birds are feasting on its flesh instead of humans. The ancient Finnish and Lapland peoples also woke up the bear they planned to slay with friendly words. "Poor grandfather, surely you had an accident," they lamented after slaying it. They also sang sacred songs as they carried the slain bear home. They removed the clothes they had on while hunting, changed to something else, and painted their faces red with alder sap. For three days, they did not return to their living quarters while they skinned, gutted, butchered, and cooked the animal in a separate hut far from the settlement. To fool the bear spirit, they did not enter the hut through the door but through a hole made specifically for this purpose. The women, believed to be especially susceptible to the powerful bear spirit and thus easily possessed by it, were not allowed to show themselves during the preparation and so did not help butcher and cook the bear. When the hunters would bring the meat to the women's quarters, they would act like strangers and pretend to be

Siberian Nanei tribe bear idols (Shimkyavitch)

speaking another language. They also did not carry the meat through the normal entrance here, using another specifically designed opening. Pregnant women were not even allowed to touch the meat, and, for a whole year, women were not to touch or feed the reindeer that had pulled the bear carcass to the settlement.

The attempt was made to convince the bear that a gala festival was being held in its honor in a brightly lit palace. During the festival, the bear would be given a sixteen-year-old maiden as its bride. If it was a female bear, a youth would be given as a groom. A wild, erotic festival followed, and, at the end, the bear's skull was hung in a pine tree on a hill while people sang consoling songs for the departing bear soul. "We will not hang you too low, so that the black ants cannot eat you and the wild boars cannot gnaw on your bones. We will not hang you too high, so that the birds of prey will not harm you and the wind does not dry you out too much." The bear was admonished to remember all the good deeds that were done for it and to tell the lord of the animals about them. The bear's skeleton was rearranged anatomically correct and bedded on birch branches. It was put into a grave out of the reach of dogs and rodents. At the very end of the ritual, the hunters would jump through a purifying fire.

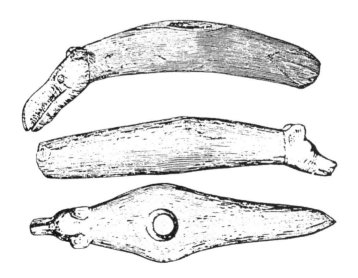

Finnish bear idols from Keralia

205

Gilyak people during a bear festival

Siberian Khanty people would similarly wake a bear out of hibernation, asking for forgiveness according to exactly prescribed rules before slaying the "furry human being." The lungs, stomach, and intestines were immediately buried, and the ribs, backbone, and limbs were dismembered without damaging them. Wearing birch masks over their faces, they would perform a bear dance around the skull and the fur and mimic the movements of the "four-legged forest human." While dancing, they would take the soul of the bear into their souls and become ecstatic. The stripped-down body along with the skull and the pelt were brought into the village on a sled. After an extensive celebration that lasted for several days, selected tribal members hung the bones, which were wrapped in birch bark, up in a juniper tree. Ritual images were carved into another piece of birch bark that was hung up with the bone bundle. When this bark carving fell out of the tree after some time, the Khanty knew that the bear had been reborn and had started a new life.

These kinds of bear festivals that culminate in a sending-the-bear-away ceremony were celebrated in numerous variations from the Sami of northern Scandinavia throughout Eurasia and the northern half of America to the

Inuit of Greenland (Schlesier 2013, 57). They belong to the oldest rituals of the circumpolar peoples and have their roots in the shamanic culture of the Old Stone Age.

A BEAR IS A LOVE-HUNGRY WOMAN

Not only for the Sami but also for numerous hunting peoples, the ritual marriage of a male or female bear, as well as sexuality in general, plays a major role at the bear festival. In this context, cultural anthropologist Hans Peter Duerr writes (Duerr 1987, 85), "Not only was the 'Lady of the Animals' a bear for many peoples, but the bear itself was often seen as a furry and very libidinous 'woman' and it appears that often after the hunters had slain a bear they either actually performed or imitated performing coitus with it. For example, a Yakut who participated on a bear hunt with Evenks, tells that after the hunters had killed a bear they imitated the act of sex with the body. When the Evenks prompted him to do the same, he declined; then 'the two Evenks pulled him by the ears over to the bear and he complied.' Also according to the Dolgans,[1] the bear is basically 'a woman,' and after killing a bear they also imitate the act of coitus with the bear's body to provide it pleasure." When the Karelian Finns went out to hunt a bear, it was said they are going out "to woo the forest virgin." A female bear looks very much like a young woman when skinned, especially the breasts—the Estonians, the Sami people, Siberian tribes, and many Native American tribes claim this to be true.

Carved bone from La Magdeleine

The erotic relationship to the female bear being seems to be very old. Duerr, for example, assumes this from the example of a bone carving from La Magdeleine (Dordogne, France; early Old Stone Age) that depicts a penis directed toward a bear's head. Or is it the case, as some prehistorians claim, that the penis is ejaculating into a bear's mouth? Or is the bear breathing on the penis to strengthen it? During a genuine shamanistic trance, or "astral trip," the penis (or clitoris) always has an erection. Could it be that the soul animal that is seen or contacted in trance is shown here? We just simply do not know; many interpretations are possible.

In the cave of Le Mas d'Azil, in Ariège, France, a broken scapula was found depicting a shaman or an "animal man" who seems to be approaching a bear with sexual intention (one can see the paw).

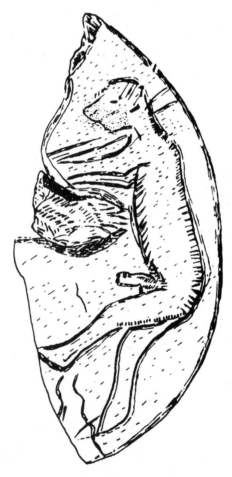

Fragment of a bone carving from Mas d'Azil

Greetings from the Bernese "Mutz" (Bruin)

She thumbed through the written pages, reading a bit here and there. "Bear fat, bear hair . . ." my wife murmured. "It seems to me that in order to write about bears it would be good to have some real contact with a bear."

"I am in contact . . ." I protested.

"I mean wear something that is connected to a real bear. What was once connected remains connected. You need a tooth or a claw, or some hair. You yourself write about the inherent power in such things!"

"I am just telling about it. It is superstition." I waved my hand. "It is a matter of 'sympathetic magic,' like anthropologist James Frazer called it. I am only telling about it. After all, we are modern, enlightened people."

"The Enlightenment seems to be crumbling," she commented, "you yourself claim often enough that shamans of simple native peoples know more about such matters than all of the researchers put together with their reductionist distortions."

"Well, maybe . . . but where am I supposed to find bear paraphernalia?"

"I'll go look for something. I'll go to Berne and visit my friend, Susanne. We can at least go to the bear pit and ask the warden for some of Bruin's hair."

She took a train to Berne and stayed with her friend who, like an atavistic Helvetic mountain spirit, knows about herbs, rocks, and spirits—and little else. They made some hazelnut-honey cookies—made from indigenous hazelnuts and honey.

When the Mani—this is the respectful name of the chief male bear in Berne— saw them, it came close and stood on its back legs. It ignored the carrots the other spectators were tossing and opened its mouth wide to catch the cookies. It had been fed so many carrots that even its excrement was orange. It smelled something special would come from the two women. Or was it that it read their thoughts like the hunting peoples believe? It playfully caught the cookies and then roared loudly. Primeval memories were surely awakened in the depth of the bear's soul, memories of times when the hazelnuts ripened in the fall and whole hives of wild honey were to be found in the forest. It looked up and must have seen the bear goddess, the Dea Artio, whose sanctuary has been in the river loop of the Aare in Berne since time immemorial. Susanne decided to visit the bear pit more often. A primeval memory was surely also awakened in her soul.

Shortly afterward, the two women asked to speak to the bear warden. They were allowed to come along down a flight of stairs where they saw a man who looked "as wild and untamable" as the bears. Without a word and with a friendly but wild, mildly curious glance, he handed them the bear hair they had asked for, wrapped in cellophane and labeled "bear hair."

"When we first saw the hair, it kind of seemed to radiate," she told me when she brought it home. After noticing my puzzled face, she continued, ". . . with a golden glow! That was our first impression."

And that is how it came to be that, as I sit here writing this, I have a tuft of real bear hair on my desk.

CHAPTER 18
Places of Bear Power

When the bear feast was over,
the sacred bear dance was danced.
I [the bear] was clothed in a wooly cloak with long down,
I was decorated with chinking silver.
When the sacred bear festival was over,
I raised up to the seven maws of the heaven bear, my father,
On the dearest end of the sounding—like the silver—iron chain.

FROM A SONG OF THE SIBERIAN KHANTY
PEOPLE AT THE END OF A BEAR FESTIVAL

There are certain places on earth where we can sense unknown energy. In these places, we may feel awestruck, terrified, or deeply moved— they are places that primitive people believe to be the abodes of gods and spirits. There are also bear places, not just bear habitats but places where the bear spirit takes possession of human consciousness. In these places, people can dream bear dreams, sensitive people can perceive the bear's spirit, some native peoples can experience themselves as the bear's relatives, and gods can appear in the form of bears.

Some of these bear places have only lived on in the form of legends and tales: the Arcadia of antiquity, the Pyrenees over the healing springs of Lourdes, the forests around Mount Shasta, and the canton Appenzell in northern Switzerland. There are other places that until only recently—or even continuing on today—have been sacred places for living bears: the forested islands of northern Japan, Yellowstone National Park, Bear Butte, the

McNeil River, the Abruzzi Apennine Mountains in Italy, and the town of Berne, Switzerland.

According to the Native Americans of the prairie, magical animals taught the first human beings in caves found near Bear Butte—a butte that looks like a sleeping bear from a distance. For this reason, medicine people are still drawn to these caves. My friend Bill Tallbull also went there often to reconnect with the origins of his tribe while fasting and meditating.

SMOKEY BEAR AND YELLOWSTONE

The Yellowstone area is uncanny. Local Native Americans avoided it until the arrival of white people who later made a national park that boasts over a thousand hot geysers shooting upward toward the azure-blue sky; lukewarm rivers; basins of hot, bubbling mud; an entire mountain of obsidian; a petrified forest; red, yellow, and black basalt formations that look like a crazy sculptor was at work; considerable wild animal herds; and a barely touched Alpine-like wilderness for guests to enjoy. One of the main attractions is—or used to be—the bears.

Since the production of the Ford Model T, the stream of visitors has not abated. The grizzlies and the black bears soon learned to expect treats from these visitors, and hundreds of them, young and old, left their fish and berry paradise to waylay the motorized guests. "Bears are wild animals. They are dangerous. Do not feed them!" One can see these signs throughout the park. But who sticks to these bureaucratic rules when there is a mother with cute cubs right near the car looking with puppy dog eyes and hoping for some treats? In no time, the brakes squeak, whole packages of cookies, chocolate, potato chips, and hamburger leftovers are dumped out the window for the bears. Like living teddy bears, rambunctious young bears sniff the car with great curiosity and play around on the hood. What does it matter if an antenna breaks off or the windshield wipers get bent . . . it is a great show! Cameras click and whir. City people who have never been near any animals other than spoiled house pets get excited and actually get out of the car to have a picture taken near the darling animals. One tries to put his four-year-old on a bear's back, another offers a bear, buddy-like, a can of beer.

Another car stops. A poodle barks like crazy through the window that is open just a crack. The brown giants—there are more of them there in the meantime—run away from the tiny barking dog. A worried bear mother shoos her cubs up a pine tree—it could be a hungry wolf. Everyone laughs. The family will have great pictures to show at home in Baltimore or Boston. The park rangers are not pleased with this ado, but the bear fans are not impressed with tickets or reasoning. They should know that they are not doing the bears any favors by giving them white flour, white sugar, and greasy chips. With junk food (and even good human food), they cannot fatten themselves up enough to live through the long winter. If they eat too much of this kind of food, they go into hibernation in a weak and undernourished condition—and it is very well possible they will die before spring comes. When they have no more reserves to live from, they just never wake up again.

Beware of the bears.

Besides, just like humans, bears get bad teeth from such soft, refined food. A bear with a toothache is as grumpy as a human being with a toothache and is very unpredictable. But once bears get a taste for junk food, they get downright addicted. The cubs already learn from their mother what tastes good and how to beg for it. Because the bears in the park have mainly only positive experiences with their bare-skinned, two-legged fellow animals, they no longer avoid them. They sniff and paw around in the garbage bins behind hotels and do not let themselves be shooed off. They break into tents and vacation houses, steal provisions, rip up backpacks, bite tin cans—and if anyone interrupts them, they are not exactly compliant.

This is how it went on for years. With several million visitors each summer season, there were constant incidents. Despite all the warnings and security measures, bears wounded or even killed people again and again. Either a tourist wanting to have a picture taken holding a cute teddy bear was struck down dead by its angry mother, or a child gave a bear a cookie from the car window and the bear bit off his hand along with it, or another car wreck with several cars happened because everyone was watching the bears instead of the road. There was just no cure for the bears' cravings and the tourists' stupidity.

Cartoon by Gary Larson, 1993

In the early 1970s, the park administration decided to remove bears that bothered tourists and were notorious garbage scavengers. They were not killed (at first), but, if the tagged bear appeared again at the same garbage pit and annoyed tourists again, it was shot without hesitation. To catch the bears, some food was placed inside a culvert, and, when the bear went in to eat it, a trap door snapped shut after the bear touched the food. The bear was then drugged and brought to a remote area some two to three hundred miles farther away. It was an ingenious plan, but it did not work. Before long, nearly all of the deported bears were soon at their usual stomping grounds. One ranger told me jokingly, when I was working in Yellowstone, "Sometimes these bastards are back here sooner than we are! Deporting them is just an empty ritual staged for the old ladies from the animal protection. We could save a lot of time and money if we would just shoot them in the first place."

Animal behavior researchers who studied this problem discovered that bears have a distinct sense of home. They become disturbed when they are set out in a strange area and are especially afraid of other bears that are complete strangers with whom they have not yet established a relationship. They long for their home area, the bears with whom they already have friendly relations, and familiar smells even if that means the smell of junk food and garbage bins. Without even taking a break to rest, they head back to their home area with a speed of about twenty miles per hour not knowing they will be shot when they get there.

In the early 1960s, forty to fifty bears a year were shot in Yellowstone. Because a female bear needs five or six years to become sexually mature and only has one to three cubs every three to four years, and only one third of the cubs survive the first year, shooting so many bears a year is a definite guarantee for extermination. Not until 1975 was the attempt even made to protect the approximately two hundred bears that had survived, by closing down dumps and covering them with plenty of dirt. Up to fifteen years later, bears were still seen sniffing around where the dumps had been, longingly remembering all the good things they had found there to eat.

Guests in Yellowstone today will see many bison, elk, antelope, deer, and maybe a wolf but will rarely see a real bear. The only bear the guests will be sure to see is that on a Smokey Bear poster. The mascot of the park, with a shovel and a bucket and in a neat ranger uniform, warns campers to be sure to completely put out their campfires and not throw their cigarettes out of their car windows with his famous warning, "Only you can prevent wildfires!"

Smokey Bear poster

SALMON GOURMETS ON THE MCNEIL RIVER

The bears that gather once a year on the McNeil River at Alaska's McNeil State Game Sanctuary, far away from civilization, have a much better lot. In the last week of July, hundreds of bears come to feast on fat salmon swimming upstream to spawn where they hatched. Defying the torrent and jumping over any hindrance, the ones that make it all the way back are completely exhausted and can finally spawn. For many others, the journey ends where they get jammed up in swirling pools under waterfalls. The fish take a rest in these pools, but this is also where the grizzlies wait for them. Each bear has developed its own individual expertise at fishing. Some of them plunge into the water and grab a fish with their mouth. Most of them elegantly flick the salmon out of the water with a paw. The old patriarchs have the best places. Young bears and mothers have to settle for places that are not as good, and the smaller black bears are forced to try their luck farther downstream.

Soon the grizzlies are so full that they only catch female fish and cut open their undersides with a claw to slurp the eggs like a dessert. They leave the disemboweled carcasses for the seagulls, or, if they float downstream, the black bears can have them. Only 150 select nature lovers, equipped with cameras and tripods, are allowed to be present at this feast. No culvert traps, no hunting guns, no tempting garbage smells endanger the harmony between bears and humans. The grizzlies that are otherwise so feared barely acknowledge the intruders here. All they want to do is eat their fill in peace with no disturbances. The annual event proves zoologist professor Bernhard Grzimek's statement that "bears can very easily live peacefully with human beings."

A GUEST FROM HEAVEN

Bears that live with humans? Maybe my friend, the "garbage dump bear" Carlo, was right when he claimed that Neanderthals kept bears as guests in their caves, or more likely that primeval humans were the guests of cave bears, each living in a separate part of the cave. Behaviorists say that bears remember every human that they have ever met by that person's smell. Presumably, the cave bears knew "their" humans and left them—in mutual agreement—in peace. Supposedly, it occasionally happens that different kinds of animals share a shelter, such as a fox and badger in a den.

Mighty kings in times of antiquity held bears in their palaces. If one can believe the reports of early Christians, some cruel Roman emperors spoiled their bears with human flesh. The poor animals were more involuntary prisoners than guests, however. The Romans imported them from the primeval forests of Germania—along with slaves, cheese wheels, soaps, furs, amber, smoked ham, and blonde female hair. The bears served mainly as replacement fighters in the arenas where they were sent to the slaughter in brutal fights against gladiators, dogs, and other predators. Emperor Caligula, for example, is said to have let four hundred bears fight against an entire company of gladiators.

Roman ivory carving from the fourth century showing Consul Areobindus, the sponsor of a circus performance with bears

Many medieval castles also held bears. But in these cases, too, they could hardly be described as contented guests. They mainly served to support the sovereign's self-aggrandizement, symbolizing his power, prowess, and invincibility. The bears in the Abbeys of Saint Gall or Andlau were also not held as honored guests but served as examples of the lower drives and the importance of overcoming them through the almighty power of the spirit.

Even today in Thailand and other South Asian countries, sun bears, of which the supply is furnished by a black market, are kept in cloisters and in private households on chains. The Buddhists believe that they receive karmic merits by being friendly to the animals and spoiling them with food. Through the pity shown to them, these poor souls imprisoned in an animal's fur will be shown the way of true dharma. But when the bears grow up and become a burden to their caretakers, they are usually sold to merchants who furnish the market with bear paws and gallbladders (Mills 2002, 176).

The bear guests of the Siberian aboriginals had the best lot as captives. Even into the twentieth century, the Ainu, Orogen people, Gilyaks, and other tribes that still lived as hunters, fishers, and gatherers similar to the Stone Age peoples kept bears as honored, spoiled guests in their villages. The Ainu once lived in large areas of northeastern Asia but can now only be found on the island Hokkaido, the Kurils, and southern Sakhalin in Russia. Similar to Native Americans on reservations, the times are over when they could live as free hunters. The clash with industrial society destroyed their way of life, and they fell to drink. These days, they sell bear carvings and bast fiber cloth (from which they used to make clothing) to tourists who come to their impoverished villages to see something exotic.

Anthropologists took notice of the Ainu because of their very hairy bodies, the lip tattoos of the women, and their bear feasts. Scientists assume that the Ainu were once the aboriginals of all of Japan and that many of the Shinto nature gods, called *kami*, go back to these aboriginals. In the Shinto religion, higher beings that humans should respect are called *kami*.[1] *Kamui* is the Ainu word for bear.

In earlier times, when Ainu hunters found a lost bear cub, they brought it home with great joy. The arrival of "the divine" was an occasion for a drinking festival. A family that had nursing children adopted the cub, and it lived in their house with them. If it whined in the night, it was allowed to sleep next to its adoptive parents. The children loved to play with the little fur ball, and nursing mothers suckled it as was necessary. For example, as late as the beginning of the twentieth century, an anthropologist witnessed how a bear cub was passed around in a circle of women and each suckled it. If the little bear plundered the pantry and ate the millet porridge, it was seen as very cute, like "an undisciplined, spoiled kid." When the guest became big enough that it could unintentionally hurt its hosts, its teeth were filed down and it got its own hut. But even while penned up, it remained tame and trusting. It was still fed with delicacies, bathed, and taken for walks with a chain while its cage was kept very clean.

Eventually, though, one day in the fall, it was time to "send him back home." Preparations began for a big festival called Iomante (Sending-Away-Festival). The entire area was incensed with mugwort, large amounts of millet beer were brewed, and mountains of millet dumplings were prepared. Now the gods were invited to come and dance, feast, and drink along with the tribe. Then one of the men went to the bear and explained to it that it would now return to its ancestors. He said, "Oh, divine bear, you came into this world to visit us. Please do not be angry with us. Tell your father and mother how we treated you well. We will make many carved sticks as offerings, and we will send lots of beer, cakes, and other delicacies with you. If you are a good bear, you will come back to us soon. We will be good hosts to you again."

The unsuspecting animal was then tied between two large posts. Now the martyrdom of the sacred guest began. A hail of dull arrows rained down upon the bear, and it had to take countless whiplashes. The bear fought until it was exhausted. The women cried and pitied the guest that had been with them for two or three years as their son. The Ainu say the torture is necessary because it helps the soul loosen itself from the body. When the torture session was over, the sacrifice was "sent to heaven" loaded down with prayers and litanies. In the early dawn, the bear's head was fastened between two posts, one behind the neck and one under the chin, while the bear bit into a piece of wood as it was strangled; the two wooden posts hindered it from shrieking, which would have been a bad omen. Immediately afterward, with the first ray of the sun, a specifically chosen archer shot the sacred bear with one single arrow through the heart.[2] They were very careful that not one drop of blood was spilled on the ground, which would also have been taken as a bad omen. The men drank the warm blood from the heart and smeared it into their long beards.

Then, the dead bear was taken through a door on the east side of the lodge where it was skinned. The head and fur (still connected) were then let down into the house through the chimney—the spirit entrance. Like a rug in front of a fireplace, it was placed on a mat and decorated with earrings, pearl necklaces, and other ornaments. Sacrificial staves, dried fish, millet dumplings, bowls of millet beer, and also even a plate of its own cooked meat were placed in front of the snout. In Sakhalin, a pipe with tobacco and matches were put in front of it. An old man spoke to the bear once more: "Dear, young bear. We offer all of this to you. Bring it to your parents. Tell them that your Ainu father and Ainu mother raised you with many sacrifices [and so on]."

Hedge of sacrificial posts with bear skulls

For the Ainu who follow their ancestry back to a bear ancestor, this sacrifice is a sacrament. The sacrificed animal is the messenger to the god that lives in the mountain forests and simultaneously radiates down from the constellation Ursa Major. The bear feast is no less a meal of communion than

221

the Last Supper of the Christians. (During the ritual, each tribe member takes a swig from the cup that the sacrificed animal also used to drink from.) Just as a Christian shows himself or herself to be a Christian by partaking of the Holy Communion, so does an Ainu show himself or herself to be a genuine Ainu by partaking of the bear feast. (The word Ainu means "human.")

The bear as a divinity: procession to the fishing holes. The women in the background beat a drum made out of a tree trunk (L. v. Schrenck, Reisen und Forschungen im Amurlande, Petersburg, 1881).

Each part of the sacrificial animal was taken in the ritual. The guts were salted, cut up into small pieces, and eaten raw. The men drank the still warm blood and rubbed it into their long beards to partake of the power, courage, and virtue of the one that was sent from heaven. The hunters moistened their clothes with the blood for good luck in hunting. At the end, the skinned skull was put up on a forked pole, called the "pole of sending away," in front of the house. The pole was carved and decorated—similar to the Christian cross—and remained there as an object of worship.

The Gilyaks, another Paleo-Siberian tribe that is at home in the Amur River delta, had a similar bear festival. They also kept a bear in the village as an honored guest. The welcome guest was seen as a kind of higher human and a delegate of the forest god; they believed its presence brought blessings and drove off bad spirits. After the villagers had fed it for a couple of years, the time came for it, too, to be sent back home during the time of the winter solstice. Before it was sacrificed, it was brought to the fishing holes on the frozen river to bring blessings. Then, it was taken through the settlement and brought from house to house. Everywhere the bear was greeted with joy and laughter and was fed with delicacies. Courageous young men jumped up onto it to give it a kiss on the cheek. If they got an ear cuff from one of its paws, they were considered blessed and would be proud of the scars left by the sacred bear for their entire lives. Just as with the Ainu, after this round came the lashing on the stake and death through a shot in the heart. The bear's head and fur, left connected as well, were pulled over a frame and worshiped.

Bear festival of the Gilyaks; the dead bear participates in the festival
(L. v. Schrenck, Reisen und Forschungen im Amurlande, Petersburg, 1881).

A bowl of its own meat and that of a dog that had been sacrificed for it were put in front of its head. The women wrapped cloth around its cheeks and nose to dry its tears. Its brain, the seat of magical power, was stirred into rice wine and consumed. In the wild orgy that followed the sacrifice, the power of life was unleashed and nature was charged up with new fertility.

The Tlingit, Kwakiutl, and Nukta on the West Coast of North America (Washington and British Columbia) practiced bear sacrifices similar to those of the Siberian aboriginals. The Algonquian tribes also knew these bear rituals (Lissner 1979, 22).

VISITING THE KING OF THE FOREST

For Siberian and North American hunting peoples, a bear is not just an animal that is hunted and utilized. For these forest peoples, "grandfather" or "grandmother" bear has a human soul. A bear is a hidden relative that is only wrapped up in a lot of thick fur and has the same ancestors as humans do. A story of the Gilyaks gives us a glimpse into the way that these peoples feel about the nature of bears (Findeisen 1956, 22, author's translation).

Once in the deep winter, a fisherman from the Gilyak tribe walked up river to see about some fish that he had caught in the fall and had stored on a platform. The snow was deep and he couldn't find the path, so he began to go in circles in the endless forest. Days and weeks went by, and it turned into spring before he finally found the scaffold where he had stored the fish. But a stranger was sitting next to it.

He spoke to the fisherman, "Come with me. Let us go to my village; it is not far from here. You will be our guest."

It was not long before they came to a big winter house and were greeted by many barking dogs. The Gilyak fisherman was quite surprised that he knew all of the dogs. They were the dogs that his people had sacrificed during former bear feasts. In the first room, he saw many bearskins on the floor. The warm inside room was full of women, and an old man sat in the seat of honor.

"You are a person from the lower end of the river, I see," said the old man. "We ourselves are forest people. You used to kill dogs for us and send us salmon

skin, fish blubber, and cranberries. We would be happy if you would live with us for a while."

After saying this, the old man fell asleep. He slept for three days and three nights. Then he got up and spoke again, "Today your people will celebrate a festival. Many good foods will come to us from the lower river." Turning to the women, he added, "Clean the floors and benches!" The women began to clean everywhere and put down pine boughs on the last sleeping place.

In the evening, when the sun went down, the old man opened the door of the house. Ten bowls with different sumptuous meals and berries floated through the door and found their place on the decorated sleeping place. The fisherman was invited to try some, and after the old man had also eaten some, he spoke, "We old people still observe this custom. You know, we acknowledged you and we will let you return to your village. Now you have experienced something new and have something to tell your people."

After three days of feasting, during which the Gilyak fisherman feasted well, too, the old man fell into a deep sleep again. When he finally woke up again after three days and three nights, he spoke to his people, "The people from the lower end of the river will go out looking for a bear again today. My children, please think about that!"

Most of them had worried faces. One of them said, "My heart hurts!"

Another said, "My throat hurts!"

The old man spoke again, "My dear ones, think about it. One of you must go!"

Now a man got up who had been lying on a bench quietly. Without a word, he took off his cloak; then he said, "If no one else is willing to go, then send me."

Hereupon the old man went into the first room and took one of the many bear-skins. "Here, my son, take the bearskin and put it on. And now be on your way to my children that live on the lower end of the river."

When the quiet, good-natured man put on the bearskin, he turned into a bear. Grumbling as bears do, he walked around the fire in the middle of the room before he went outside. The old man accompanied him to the river; then, the bear stomped on alone through the snow in a downriver direction and disappeared.

Many months passed; then, the bear returned. He brought a sled along with him that was full with various foods and was pulled by many dogs. The delicacies were bedded in moss. There were also onions. The bear took off his bearskin and turned back into a man. He told the old man how well the people downriver had treated him and how well he had eaten there. He also told the old man, who was none other than the lord of the forest, about the worries and wishes the people had and how they wished for luck when hunting, many salmon, an abundant berry harvest, health, and peace with their neighbors.

And then, after the Gilyak fisherman had seen and heard all of this, he was sent back to his people downriver. He lived there for one more month and told about what he had experienced, and then he died.

The kind of bear ceremonies that Paleo-Siberian hunters and gatherers celebrate must be very old. They must be as old as hunting techniques and shamanism with songs and chants, frame drum and spirit flights, as old as the knowledge of a "lord of the forest," or "mother of the animals," as old as the cone-shaped, teepee-like leather summer tents and the half-subterranean winter houses with a fire in the middle. These cultural elements go back to the early Paleolithic and the Paleolithic peoples who brought them over the Bering Strait some twenty to thirty thousand years ago into the New World.

A bear cult with bear sacrifices in Paleolithic Europe was previously described in Chapter 2. Further such evidence was found in Montespan Cave (Haute-Garonne, France), deep inside the mountain, in which a life-sized clay model of a bear with only its head missing was found next to wall drawings of horses, deer, and bison. On the floor, between the front paws of the clay figure, the man who discovered it, Comte Bégouen, found the skull of a real bear. The back of the clay figure is smoothly polished, and a triangular cavity is located at the neck. It can surely be concluded, from this evidence, that the Paleolithic hunters must have pulled the fur, with the head still attached, over the clay figure and fastened it with a wedge at the neck. Comte Bégouen explained, "We can assume that we found the skull that was left there from the last ceremony" (Lissner 1979, 282). That was over twenty thousand years ago. Was that also a "ceremony to send the bear away"?

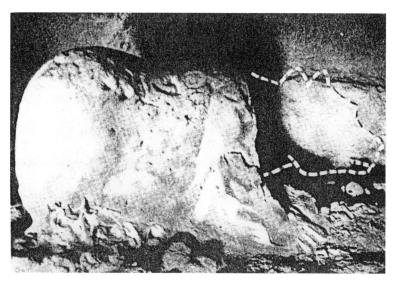

Paleolithic clay figure of a bear without a head (Montespan Cave, France)

But that is not yet all. The clay figure shows some thirty round holes, as if—as with the Siberian sacrifice—dull arrows had been shot at it. In the famous Trois-Frères Cave (Ariège), a drawing shows a bear spewing blood out of its mouth. The body is covered with small round circles, and the arrows that hit the bear are also drawn. A stab wound to the lungs must have killed it, the only explanation for a stream of blood from the mouth (Lissner 1979, 284).

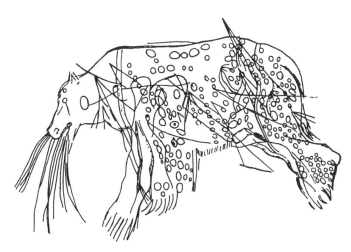

Bleeding bear (Trois-Frères Cave)

Prehistorians found the fossilized skull of a young brown bear in Silesia with the incisors and canine teeth removed or filed by people of the Aurignacian culture—also from the early Stone Age. As we have seen, this ritual also happens to the "divine guest" when it is "visiting" the Ainu or other native peoples (Eliade 1981, Vol. I, 26).

Of course, that which the prehistorian's shovel and the cave researcher's studies reveal can be interpreted in various ways. Nevertheless, these definite traces of a prehistoric bear cult remind us of the bear sacrifice and bear cult of the last primitive peoples of Siberia and North America. There is no coercive reason to doubt a continuation of these cultural practices. The traditional tales of bears, bearskins, or women espoused with bears are probably just as old.

The last Iomante, sending-the-bear-away ceremony, of the Ainu took place in the early 1930s. No divine guest comes anymore; no one calls him and hosts him. For that reason, according to the Ainu, the bear is disappearing from the mountains and forests of the northern Japanese islands and Sakhalin. The people who honored him are being absorbed by Japanese mass society, and their culture is dying out.

CHAPTER 19

Bear-opolis—Berne
(City of Bears), Switzerland

The bear, seen from the outside, was always the same! However,
the ones who wore its fur were often replaced, so that the city mascot
could always start up with new strength with its joyful or threatening
gestures.

SERGIUS GOLOWIN TELLING ABOUT
THE BEARSKINS OF THE BERNE CARNIVAL (1986)

One need not travel to Hokkaido or Alaska to meet up with the bear spirit and experience a living-bear cult. One can discover it in the middle of Europe. Bears, everywhere bears! Brown bears with a long red tongue hanging out can be seen everywhere—painted on walls, carved into wooden gables, printed on labels as a trademark, chiseled into stone, as sentinels for public buildings, or as a guardian of a well. As an animal of power, illustrated bears can be seen playing "Hornussen,"[1] wrestling (*Schwingen*[2]), or drumming troops into battle. Signs on inns, flags, and crests show a bear lumbering down a golden, honey-colored path in a red field. Newspaper kiosks sell the *Berner Baer* daily, plastic or wooden bear souvenirs for tourists, and chocolates sweetened with honey boasting a bear on its label.

As an American exchange student, I spent the first few days in amazement of the picturesque, old streets of Berne. The bear spirit is present everywhere, and I would not have been surprised to happen upon a pile of bear droppings, as I would have seen in the Rocky Mountains, on some dark side street or under a huge tree along the Aare River. Not far from the entrance to the anthropology department that I frequented daily, a bear stands in full armor over a well in the medieval-looking street called Kramgasse. On the other end of the street, above the arch of the Zytglogge Tower (Clock Tower), an armored troop of bears marches out of a small door and disappears again at the top of each hour. Today, if one continues down the cobblestone street to the Nydegg Bridge, living bears can be viewed at the Bear Pit—a spacious enclosure that opened on the Aare in 2009. Here, constantly surrounded by admirers, the big *Mani* (male alpha bear) reigns. He is the patriarch and the incarnation of the city totem. Next to him, younger bears and mother bears romp around with cute cubs. Otherwise taciturn Bernese talk to the bears as one would talk to grandchildren or old folks. They carry on conversations with them as if no one else were around, affectionately talking to them as if with their innermost selves.

Bernese flag

"Chum Baerli," ("come, dear bear") says an old grandmother standing next to me, kindly tossing a carrot as she would give her beloved grandchild a cookie. Across from me, a corpulent park employee looks at the *Mani* with admiration and says, "Mol, mol, du bisch e Guete" ("Yes, indeed, you are a fine fellow"). It is not the kind of normal gawking one would see in a zoo.

BEARS WHO HAVE BECOME HUMAN

There is no doubt that one can experience a living-bear cult in this city on the Aare. The Bernese bear cannot be compared to its cousin, the rather skinny Berlin bear that is a mere heraldic animal and is awarded as a film prize but no longer corresponds to the soul mood of the population. The more time I spent in the bear city and bear surroundings of Berne, the more the population seemed to be made up of bears who had become human. Their earthy appearance, the strong, sturdy stature of not only the farmers in the Emmental (Berne surroundings) but also many city Bernese, accredited the comparison. Their expression seldom changes much more than that of a brown bear. And the obstinacy! This thick, round skull, this *Baeren Gring* ("bear skull") of which they are so proud! As an example of the quality of this thick skull, a story is told of a Bernese who was weary of life and jumped from the tower of the cathedral. On impact with his skull, the only damage was a smashed cobblestone road.

Someone with such a thick skull is about as easy to push around as a grizzly that happens to be snooping around in a garbage bin in Yellowstone National Park. Such a character neither needs to be talkative, like the businessman from Zurich, nor demonstrate affected citizen-of-the-world sophistication, such as a cultured Geneva resident. He is, like the bear, slow and deliberate. But if he becomes convinced that his point of view is right, neither death nor the devil can argue him out of it. He remains steadfast with both feet firmly planted on the ground and is by no means gullible; like a bear, he remains skeptical when confronted with unusual, outlandish thoughts. Indeed, bold, high-flying thoughts were never for the Bernese. Just like their totem, they remain steadfast and matter of fact and never leave down-to-earth reality out of the equation no matter what kind of ideals are presented. Because the bear is an earthy animal, it follows that the Bernese could not be enthused by the flying imperial eagle, which they removed from their crest as early as two hundred years ago.

Seal of the city Berne, from 1470

The favorite sport of the Bernese, *Schwingen*, says a lot about their bear-like character. *Schwingen* is an old Alemannic wrestling sport in which— originally played by local farmers—one of the stout, colossal hulks will try to grab the other by his belt or rolled up pant leg, move him from the spot, and finally pin him to the ground. It is often the well-placed "bear grip" that decides the match, and the winner is awarded a bull (*Muni*). The sport reminds one of sumo wrestling in Japan, but also of how befriended male bears greet each other. The winner is celebrated as an alpha bear, the strongest among the bears.

Swiss wrestling, "Schwingen"

A typical Bernese is never mean, but, like a playful bear, might not know his own strength. Friedrich Volmar describes him quite well in his classic book on bears: "A bear that was disturbed in its winter hibernation went up to the house and gave the oaf a couple of ear cuffs. Unfortunately, the well-punished fellow never got up again" (Volmar 1940, 243). A Bernese, by nature reserved and easygoing, is not easily provoked. But when he has had enough, the apparently sluggish, grumbly bear becomes wild and fearless. He is tough and will not give up.

It may be the case that in Celtic-Roman times in the Berne area the motherly, caring, and nourishing aspect of the bear was in the foreground—as the bronze figure of a bear goddess (Dea Artio, first mentioned in Chapter 9) found in Muri, near Berne, seems to indicate—but the brown bear portrayed on the coat of arms after the founding of the city was the Alemannic warrior bear, the fighting alpha bear that had struck fear into the founders and always guaranteed the city its independence.

The French king, the emperor, and the pope were glad to enlist fearless Bernese warriors into their service as mercenaries. Thus, it may be concluded that the Bernese Alpine bears have not died out but have only changed their appearance by taking on human form. In today's times, in which there is no more wildernesses in Central Europe, the bear spirit has found its only way to incarnate. It would seem the true Bernese are the bears.

Even their favorite dogs, the Saint Bernard and the Bernese mountain dogs, look like bears and are often named *Baeri, Bari, Baerli* (variations on "bear"). The huge Saint Bernards, with their bear-like snouts, long fur, stout legs, and massive bodies, have been kept by the Swiss for some two thousand years. The Bernese in particular do not seek typical dog-like characteristics, yappers with a crooked back, gabbers, opportunists, and similar common mutts. This is the only way for them to have dogs because, after all, why would a bear want a dog anyway?

DUKE BERCHTOLD AND NOBLE LADY MECHTHILDIS

Duke Berchtold V. of Zaehringen founded the city of Berne. Etymologists would be quick to recognize that the name Berchtold, which comes from Berthold—in which both the words "bear" and "ruler" are combined—means "bear ruler." In some areas in Swabia and Switzerland, a legendary figure, a wild hunter called "Berchtold" or "Bertholt," haunts the land during the winter solstice. He takes Odin's (Wotan's) place as the leader of the wild horde *(Woutisheeres)* that sweeps over the countryside in late fall and winter.

Berchtold's Day, on the second of January, is celebrated here and there in southern Baden (Germany) and in northern Switzerland. It is celebrated with loud parades and much feasting and dancing. For the farmers and peasants, Berchtold's Day marks the start of regular rigorous farm work once the festivities of Christmas and New Year's have been thoroughly celebrated.

Even though Duke Berchtold is best known as the historical figure who built the city in 1191 as a bulwark against the expansion of Burgundy, we find his warrior bears, the bearskins associatively, in the legendary world of the wild hunter Wotan. The Duke decided that the tongue of land completely covered with a thick oak forest and surrounded on three sides by a river was an ideal site to build a fortified city. He named the town after the first animal he saw in the forest in accordance with ancient custom that says such an animal appearing at the beginning of an important undertaking is a sign pregnant with meaning. Surely a good omen, a bear came ambling along! The ancient totem animal of the Alemannic warriors would surely overcome the Burgundians and other enemies!

The Duke stalked the bear and slayed it, and a bear meat feast was held in the castle, Nydegg. Now the city had its name and its heraldic animal. The spirit of the slain animal went into the citizens and continues to live on in them—a genuine totemic legend of origin that can hold up to any anthropological comparison. But not only the bear hunting hero and founder is mentioned in this legend—the bear goddess is also included. She appears in the form of Noble Lady Mechtildis.[3]

Not far from the place where the Duke had slain the bear, a young noblewoman with her baby daughter in her arms was trying to find her way through the undergrowth in the forest. A harsh stroke of fate had rendered her homeless. Suddenly, she heard loud crashing in the undergrowth. She was frightened to the core as she saw a huge female bear ambling her way—but the animal passed by the two of them grumbling in a friendly manner.

They had just barely recovered from the shock when a snarling wolf appeared right in front of them. There was no doubt the wolf would devour them. When they screamed in terror, the bear appeared again. Who knows, maybe the wolf had once struck one of her cubs—in any case, the bear attacked the wolf. But the wolf bit the bear, leaving dangerous wounds. Finally, the bear broke the wolf's neck with one of her paw swipes and it fell down dead. The screaming, growling, and bellowing attracted the hunters from Castle Nydegg. When they saw the bear was still alive, one of the hunters nocked an arrow and prepared to shoot, but Mechtildis jumped in between the two. "Spare the bear that has saved me!" she called out.

The bear dragged itself off, bleeding from many wounds. But it stopped several times and looked at Mechtildis and grumbled. Finally, the noble woman understood. The bear wanted her to follow. Soon after, they came to a bear's den. Two cubs that had been waiting for their mother to return came running to meet her. She was just able to lick the cubs' little faces and look once more into Mechtildis' eyes and then she died. The surprised hunters captured the two cubs and took them along with the woman and her small daughter back to the castle. When Duke Berchtold heard what had happened, he was deeply moved. He had his horse saddled immediately and rode to the den. When he saw the courageous bear lying there in a pool of blood, he was silent for a moment. Then he pledged: "You died here because you defended innocents with your own life. I wish to be your successor. I will build a city here where the hard-pressed may find refuge. It shall be called Berne and a brown bear shall be on the city crest."

The building of the city with a bear on its crest went quickly. A city council was built above the bear's den. The den itself was made into the treasury. The two cubs were kept in the castle and always treated well. The city bakery was commissioned to bake tasty bread for them. Young warriors enjoyed wrestling with them to test their courage and strength.

When Christmas came around, noble Mechtildis baked the first Bernese gingerbread. An image of the bear and her cubs decorated the gingerbread.

Anthropology of comparative religions shows us that the baker symbolizes the corn (grain) goddess and that gingerbread is a typical sacred bread, often formed into an icon, which is eaten at sacred times such as the winter solstice (Christmas) or Easter. It is eaten as a substitute sacrifice—in this case, a bear—and is believed to bless and strengthen those who eat it. Bread symbolizes focused life strength, and, combined with the bear, it is especially potent. Even today, many Bernese believe that their gingerbread is especially healthy.

Long before they converted to Christianity, the heathen Alemannic tribes had many such iconic breads that were consecrated to the thunder bear/god Thor. There were also breads shaped like boars, consecrated to the vegetation god, Freyr; breads shaped like horses, consecrated to Wotan; and other animal-shaped yuletide baked goods. Such breads are also substitutes for archaic animal sacrifices[4] (Baechtold-Staeubli and Hoffmann-Krayer 1987, 3:373). Special Christmas breads that we still enjoy go far back to such sacral traditions.

THE PATRON SAINT

Each occidental Christian city was assigned a patron saint, and the protection of the city of Berne fell to Saint Christopher. This fearless giant with the strength of a bear who had once carried the Christ child across a raging river, fit well to a city built on a ford in the Aare River.

In 1498, shortly before the Reformation, a ten-meter-high (approximately thirty-three feet) "Christoffel" (Saint Christopher) was erected on the upper city gate. With long hair, a beard, and piercing eyes, he looked down upon the city. The Christ child that sat on his shoulders was soon removed, and a sword and halberd were put into his hands. From that point on, Christopher was only a giant, a guardian of the threshold. When, in the middle of the nineteenth century, the railway was built near the upper city gate, the "idol" became nothing but a hindrance and was torn down in the name of progress. All that was left was his stern face—which one can see in the underground passage in the Berne railway station—and a few fragments, such as, for example, his thumbs. The latter can be seen exhibited as souvenirs with bear decoration in the museum.

The Bernese were never really enthused about a Christian patron saint. The real patron had always been—since having saved Mechtildis—a bear. The city symbol, the bear, has been kept and honored for at least five hundred years in the bear pit. Around the time that the railway came and giant Christopher had to resign, a completely new and bigger—the fourth official— bear pit was built on the other side of the Nydegg Bridge not far from the place Duke Berchtold is said to have slain the first bear. Thus, in May 1857, accompanied by uniformed cadets, a brass band, two cannons, and horsemen in black-and-red uniforms, the cult animals were moved from their old enclosure in cages and on a wagon decorated with flower garlands. With fanfares, drum rolls, cannon balls, and jubilation from the onlookers, the true regents of the city rumbled on to their new residence. There, a large tree, decorated with delicious fruit and baked goods, like a Christmas tree, was waiting for them.

A similar procession took place many years later on the city's seven-hundredth anniversary. On this occasion, the patricians, honored citizens, and honored guests ate one of the bears ceremoniously, symbolically consuming the bear that the Duke had slain. An Ainu or Gilyak would surely have nodded approvingly in the face of such a feast.

Just as with the Ainu, it has always been important for the Bernese that the bears fare well. If the bears are doing well, things are well for the city; if they are not well, it is a bad omen. And woe to any scoundrel who harms the bears! It has been said that enemies have tried to bribe the bear custodians to poison the bears in an effort to demoralize the Bernese.

In 1575, two white bear cubs were born, and the population was convinced that their birth was a sign that much would change for the better in the world. (In eastern Asia, a white bear is also seen as an omen for enduring good luck over generations.) However, it was a source of great concern when in 1712 almost all the bears died. Further, the worst event for the Bernese was in 1798 when the French kidnapped the alpha bear and his mate and brought them to Paris where they died soon afterward. In addition, the French had left a dead cub in the bear pit. What an evil omen! Twelve dark years passed before a new bear couple could be greeted with music, flower garlands, and waving flags.

Hunting down a bear in the Canton of Waadt (woodcut, early nineteenth century)

On this note, one might think that the Bernese met wild bears in the forest with similar sympathy and respect. But that was unfortunately not the case. In the city, the bear was held in high honor as a symbol of power and fearlessness; however, wherever it was found in the surrounding countryside, it was pursued mercilessly. The wild bear was feared as if it were spawn of the devil. Bears tore up cattle and goats and scared the daylights out of many a wayfarer.[5] Like today in Alaska or Canada, many hair-raising stories regarding meeting up with bears made the rounds. A recurring theme was the duel: a lumberjack or cow herder in the high Alps is attacked by a bear and a wrestling match ensues. The human tries in vain to drive a knife into the beast. Then the bear trips and falls backward over a cliff with the human on top of him. The animal breaks its back when it lands; the human gets away unscathed.

The last wild bear in Switzerland, slain in 1904 in Val S-charl

Regular hunts with hundreds of people, swarming dogs, screeching women, drums, and trumpets were organized by the authorities for the amusement of the population, and monetary rewards were promised for shooting or capturing a bear. The hunter was a hero, and the dead bear was paraded through the town or village in a triumphant march with drums and ceremony. The killing of the beast was always an occasion for festivity, for a noisy feast with plenty of alcohol and singing. The bear was stuffed with straw, or only the head was taken with glass eyes in the eye cavities and a long red tongue made of cloth in the mouth; then, it was nailed onto a nobleman's house or the town hall. The last living bear in the Bernese surroundings, together with a wolf, was slain in the beginning of the nineteenth century after which it was stuffed and mounted on the gable of an inn. The last wild bear in Switzerland—a small six-year-old female weighing only 116 kilograms (approximately 255 pounds)—was shot in Lower Engadine, east of Davos, in 1904.[6] The two hunters were rewarded with a bounty, and the meat was served to the spa guests of the largest hotel (Volmar 1940, 64).

The last word has not been spoken, however. Who knows, maybe bears will return to the Helvetian mountains. Now and then a wolf crosses the high mountain passes from Italy into Valise, where it is usually shot. There are habitats suitable for bears in the southern Alpine valleys, in Ticino and in the Jura Mountains. In Trentino, not very far from the Swiss border, there are still a handful of wild bears. Maybe Bruin will be able to transcend the human-devised border. Until then, the Bernese bear will remain the lineage holders of the Swiss totem animal and held in high honors: A new ten-thousand-square-meter (approximately 32,800 feet) outdoor enclosure extends to the Aare River so that the bears may not only climb trees but also splash around in fresh, flowing water.

One bear that has returned is the "Fasnacht" (carnival) bear. After one hundred years of being banned by Christianity, the Bernese Fasnacht was resurrected in 1982. In February, the time when bears wake up from their winter hibernation and smell the air, the "bear from the bear forest" is let out of his cage and announces the time of tomfoolery (in other areas known as carnival). Along with the traditional bearskin wearer—in whom the Bernese bear spirit is incorporated—many of the long-forgotten mythological bear forms have come back to life: the wild man who wears a bearskin (*Mieschmaa*); the fool and harlequin (*Hurispiegel*); the forest devil; the donkey-doctor (crazy doctor); the devil's grandmother (*Hutte Frau*); the blackened man; the child eater; Queen Bertha, who represents a Burgundian duchess but, in reality, is ancient Celtic Brigit, or Bertha, who is "full of light," the god-like female companion of the bear; Noble Wilhelm Tell and his son; the evil reeve, Gessler; whole troops of warriors; artisans; and many, many fools.

Bernese Fasnacht figures, from left to right: bearskin, Mieschmaa in bearskin, and Hurispiegel in pompous women's clothes and with a bear face

In the olden times during the time of Fasnacht, wooden tables were set up in the old city center under the eaves and ham and bread were served so that bearskins and their comrades could eat their fill. "We took enough forest away from the bears in order to build our solid city. It is only right that, in the beginning of the year, we give the bears enough to eat until they and their friends can eat no more" (Sergius Golowin 1986, 13). And, as is fitting for the bear as the incarnation of virile life energy, he also chases the girls, grumbles at them, whirls them for a few rounds of dancing, and would most likely mate with them if he were not constantly distracted by honey cakes and cool drinks.

CHAPTER 20
Teddy Bear and Winnie-the-Pooh

The many roles of the bear—father figure; protective mother; ances-
tor; hairy, grumbly relative; seducer; courageous warrior, simultane-
ously animal and human—are combined in the cherished teddy bear.

CLEMENS ZERLING AND
WOLFGANG BAUER,
LEXIKON DER TIERSYMBOLIK

Although we modern humans eliminated this animal with precision
from our forests, we left it in the children's rooms of our descendants.
It seems that we somehow did not want to break off completely from
our roots.

REGULA MAYER, *TIERISCH GUT*

Hardly any other animal has left such a strong and lasting impression on
the people of the northern half of the globe as the bear has. Its archetypal image has engraved itself deeply into their souls. Contrary to many wild
animals that populate the world of fairy tales and fables, furry Bruin—with
a few exceptions—appears as a good-natured, snuggly, and contented being.
From a safe distance, he is seen more as a friend than a threat. One likes him
and would like to be close to him. How else can one explain the behavior of
visitors in national parks who sometimes even try to put one of their children
on his back, or the Bernese who sometimes spend hours near their beloved
bears as if they have a healing aura? One tends to forget that bears can hardly
be tamed and can be very dangerous. Legends told to youths are full of forest

rangers, Native American youths, young girls, and young boys who have befriended bears. Novels by Jean M. Auel tell about a Stone Age girl named Ayla who belongs to the bear clan and later, as a shaman, calls upon the spirit of the cave bear. Other stories tell of bears, similar to those of dolphins saving humans from drowning, who save human lives. For example, a grizzly bear protects a Native American child from the wolves that have surrounded it, or a Japanese farmer falls into a canyon in the middle of the winter and is saved by a bear that fed him a paste made of ants and kept him warm enough until someone found and saved him.

Friendly, clumsy bears romp through comics, children's television programs, and books, and they can also be seen on various cereal boxes. Baloo, the bear from Kipling's *The Jungle Book,* is as loving and kind as children wish all adults were. In comic books in Germany, the bear Petzi (Barnaby, in English) invites children to join him in many adventures, and Paddington Bear parodies the British way of life. In Germany, *Gummibaerchen* (gummy bears—jelly bears originally made of boiled-down fruit juice) are practically a currency for children and can be traded for toys or given as a token of friendship. Teddy bears reign sovereignly over most other toys or other stuffed animals. And bear hugs are the best hugs.

For a psychoanalyst, bears are symbols of positive anima, life, and plenty; motherliness, fertility, coziness, good-naturedness, and good food are also associated with bears. The opposite is the wolf (though not rightly so), as a negative animal symbol associated with hunger and hardship in winter, a potential killer, a Little-Red-Riding-Hood-eater, and, for righteous Christians, a symbol of the devil and false prophets. Giving a child a stuffed toy of a wolf instead of a bear is hardly imaginable. The sly, devious fox also stands in opposition to the good-natured, gullible bear. The fox represents low, instinctive intelligence, as opposed to the primeval, innocent, and pristine nature of the bear. In Nordic mythology, the bear is associated with the thunder god, Donar, who is a friend of humanity; the wolf is associated with Odin, or Wotan, god of the dead and high magician; the fox is associated with the clever god of fire and trickster, Loki. Thus, the animals and the mythological figures represent various aspects of the human soul.

THE DUMB BEAR

In many fables, a bear is often outsmarted by a clever fox or a cunning peasant. The bear is not familiar with the smooth ways of the world and is regarded as naïve or even foolish. The following story from Lapland tells how he gets fooled once again by the clever fox.

A hungry fox that had not caught even one single mouse all day long saw a Laplander approaching with a sled. The sled was full of freshly caught fish. The fox lay down on the road and played dead. When the fisherman saw the apparently frozen animal, he thought it would make a nice fur hat—so he stopped and loaded it onto the sled. As he drove on and paid no attention to the fox, it became quite alive again, grabbed the biggest fish, and disappeared.

Just as the fox was about to devour the fish, a bear came trotting along and asked him where he had found such a nice, fat fish.

"From the well in the village," the fox lied unabashedly. "I hung my tail in it and the fish bit. But it is not so easy. You probably wouldn't be able to take the pain."

The bear, who very much liked to eat fish himself, thought it couldn't be all that bad. When the people had gone to sleep, he trotted into the village, lowered his tail into the well, and waited patiently until a big fish would bite. It seemed that the fox was right as the waiting was quite uncomfortable. His poor tail got ever colder. His deceitful advisor who had been observing him the whole time started up a raspy bark so that the villagers would wake up.

"Grab your bows and spears! A bear is sitting near your well and is pissing in your water!" he yelled. The villagers came running, and the poor bear had no choice but to jump away and flee, ripping his frozen tail right off. Since then, bears only have a short stub instead of the proud tail they once had.

The bear caught the fox later on and wanted to rip him into a thousand pieces, but the red-haired scoundrel outsmarted him once again.

The sly fox and the naïve bear (drawing by Theodor Kittelsen)

Again and again, the bear gets the short end of the stick whenever he has to deal with the clever fox. A Norwegian story tells about a happy bear who had caught a fat pig (Asbjoernson and Moe 1960, 120).

> *"This will be a delicious feast," the bear thought on his way to his den with a pig under his arm. A fox, whose stomach was growling for hunger, saw the bear with his prey.*
>
> *"Grandfather bear," he asked, "what do you have there?"*
>
> *"Pig meat," said the bear.*
>
> *"I have something, too, that tastes especially good," said the fox.*
>
> *"What's that?" the bear asked.*
>
> *"Honey—from the biggest hive I have ever seen," answered the fox.*
>
> *"Really?" the bear asked, who started to slobber at the mere thought of the sweet stuff. Honey was heaven on earth for him. "Do you want to trade?" he asked.*
>
> *"No, no way," the fox answered, "but maybe we can make a bet. Whoever can name three different kinds of trees the fastest gets a bite of meat or a lick of honey."*

The bear thought the idea sounded not bad. He would lick up the whole beehive with one try. His mouth was already watering. On the word "go," they each named three kinds of trees as fast as they could:

"Fir, red pine, Christmas tree," the bear grunted in one breath.

"Ash, aspen, oak," the fox barked.

The fox was faster; besides fir, red pine, and Christmas tree are all the same kind of tree. So the fox got to take a bite of the pig. He bit out the best part, the heart. The bear was outraged and grabbed the fox by the tail.

"Please let me go!" the fox pleaded. "If you let me go, I will show you where the beehive is and you can have all of the honey!"

They went to the tree where the beehive was. But the hive was not a beehive; it was a hive of hornets. When the bear put its lips on the hive to get at the honey, an angry swarm of hornets stung him viciously on the nose and face. The bear could only barely save himself from them. He ran away as fast as he could, completely forgetting his pig and the clever fox.

Fox and bear make a bet (drawing by Theodor Kittelsen).

Even the simple peasant is able to outsmart the naïve bear as we can see in the following story from Finland.

A bear who was so hungry his stomach was growling watched from the edge of the forest as a peasant harvested beets.

"That must be something very special if the peasant is spending so much time and effort about it," the bear thought and went over to the peasant. "Give me your harvest or I will eat you!" the bear growled. The peasant, who was not easily scared, was somewhat startled but composed himself quickly.

"Go ahead, brother bear, take the harvest. But leave some for me so that I will not die of hunger. Who would plant the field next year in that case? Come, let's share the harvest fairly. You can take that which grows above the ground and I will content myself with the roots."

The bear liked this suggestion. The peasant loaded the beets into his wagon in next to no time and left the shaggy bear alone with the leaves. The bear's mouth watered, but after the first bite he realized that the peasant had outsmarted him.

The next year the peasant was harvesting grain from the same field. Suddenly, the cheated bear was standing in front of him with fletched teeth and growled threateningly, "Give me the harvest, peasant! This time you will not cheat me!"

"All right, have it your way, brother bear. Serve yourself and eat it all. But what good will it do you if I starve over the winter? Will you be able to crop the field in the spring? I give you the friendly advice that we should share. But this time, take what you will so that I must not be accused of cheating again."

The bear was happy, "Good," he grumbled, "this time you take what is above the ground and I take what is below!"

The peasant secretly laughed up his sleeve, harvested, and brought the grain into his barn. The poor bear got a bloody tongue and nose from trying to eat the stubble. He found absolutely nothing to eat.

"The next time I will pay him back," he swore to himself.

The next year the peasant was felling wood in the forest. He had brought an old billy goat and tethered it to eat in the bushes. Then the bear appeared.

"Peasant, your final hour has struck!" the bear growled. At that moment, the billy goat stuck his head out of the bushes and bleated loudly. The bear was shocked.

"What kind of a strange creature is this?" he asked. He had never seen a goat before.

"Oh, that is just my friend, the terrible bear hunter," the sly peasant answered. "He just asked what kind of a strange, hairy tree is standing there and why I don't fell it and tie it up in the wagon."

"Be quick, peasant, and do what he says so that he doesn't notice that I am a bear!" the bear begged of him, wide-eyed with fear.

"As you wish," said the peasant and knocked the bear down with the axe then pulled him onto the wagon and tied him up. In the village, the other peasants beat the bear up so badly that he never again dared bother any of them.

THE PRESIDENT AND THE FIRST TEDDY BEAR

Where does the general positive image of the bear come from? How was he able to secure his place in the hearts of so many people? Could this affection even have its roots in the Stone Age? Could it be that the mighty cave bear, by his very presence, really did protect early humans from wolves, huge cats of prey, giant hyenas, and other fiery-eyed meat eaters with killer teeth? Was that the reason he was cultishly honored? Of course, the cave bear was dangerous and treated with much respect, but he was never a man eater. The cave bear's dull, wide molars reveal that it was a plant eater. It was definitely not interested in humans as food (Dehm 1976, 21).

Surely, the humans of the Paleolithic era saw the bear as an incarnation of the numinous power that gives all beings life and protects them but can also take that very life. Could it be that the interspecific relationship that developed is stamped deeply in the human psyche and lives on as a primeval memory? At least for the peoples of the northern hemisphere, who most likely also have at least some Neanderthal genes, this seems to be the case, especially among children, who, in some ways, go through the same developmental stages throughout childhood that snuggly, grumbly bears do. They feel protected while holding their teddy bear in the "dark cave" of their room. When a nightmare jolts them out of their sleep, a door creaks, or the wind howls, their teddy bear is their best friend. Rescue services often have teddy bears as part of their equipment to give to children traumatized by accidents or fire. Psychological studies have shown that they can calm children best. But this little bear fixation is not the only reliable source of comfort; in many countries, it is still a custom to protect children with bear teeth or bear claws hung over their beds or put in the cradle.

The teddy bear as a comfort and companion for children in the hospital
(Dutch illustration in a children's book by Rotraud S. Berner, 1985)

Folklore researchers have often observed that children's games and rhymes are full of old cultural lore that is otherwise believed to have been lost. Hopping games, riddles, rhymes, and ring-around-the-rosy chants are as much relics of past cultural epochs as are bows and arrows, spears, hoops, or tops the remnants of former adult hunting and magic practices. Memories of older times live on while playing "Indians" or sitting around campfires, times in which humans lived as wild hunters. So it must be that the joyful acceptance of the teddy bear echoes times when humans were closer to wild animals and their souls could communicate with the souls of the animals. How else can one explain the enormous success of teddy bears?

Child and teddy bear (Swedish children's book illustration by Olaf Landstroem)

However, the teddy bear in its present form is not very old at all. It is, like jet airplanes and computers, a product and also a symbol of the twentieth century. But it is a symbol of hope, a counterweight to all the technological monstrosities that this unnatural century has produced. The teddy bear came into existence in the year 1902. In November of that year, President Theodore "Teddy" Roosevelt drove to Mississippi to settle a border dispute. During a break in the drawn-out negotiations, the president, an enthusiastic big game hunter, grabbed his rifle and went hunting. After a long wait, no game showed and a worried lackey went ahead with a plan. He put a pitiful, small bear on the road knowing that the president would be coming that way. When Teddy Roosevelt saw the pitiful creature, he said, "This is where I draw the line! If I would shoot this small creature, I wouldn't be able to look my sons in the eyes."

The *Washington Post* then published a tongue-in-cheek political cartoon that referred to the original reason for his trip—however, the political aspect was soon forgotten, and the little bear from the cartoon became a public darling. The toy business saw its chance, and soon a stuffed bear was marketed as a good-luck mascot. The teddy bear was, thus, named after this president whose image is chiseled into the rock at Mount Rushmore in the Black Hills, not far from Bear Butte.

Caricature of Teddy Roosevelt (Washington Post, November 10, 1902)

That same year in Germany, Margarete Steiff, who had been in a wheel-chair since she was two years old, got the idea to sew a small bear and stuff it with wood shavings. Her nephew, Richard Steiff, who wanted to become a painter and spent a lot of time drawing bears in zoos, made the pattern for her. She continued making the stuffed animals for many years with much devotion and enthusiasm.

Mrs. Steiff's bear became an international hit, and the Steiff family soon had to build a factory to meet the demand. Between the years of 1903 and 1908, the so-called "bear years," the time was ripe for the teddy bear, and the number produced during that time period went from 12,000 to about 975,000—a phenomenal number that was not reached again (Cockrill 1992, 12). Even President Roosevelt got teddy bear fever; he ordered one of the Steiff bears dressed in hunter's garb for the table decoration at his daughter's wedding. Today, Steiff teddy bears have become a collector's item: In September 1989, an original Steiff teddy bear from the year 1926 was sold to an American collector at Sotheby's for 168,000 German marks (roughly 80,000 dollars). In 2007, one was sold at Christie's in London for well over 50,000 dollars.

Mother of the stuffed teddy bear, Margarete Steiff

The original Steiff teddy bear with its pattern

THE WISE BEAR OF LITTLE UNDERSTANDING

The teddy bear was soon found in the world of children's books. One of the most famous stuffed bears belonged to a boy named Christopher Robin and must have been the inspiration for his father, A. A. Milne, as the main character in the stories of *Winnie-the-Pooh*. The first story of Pooh, a sweet tooth whose head occasionally gets stuck in a honey jar, was written in 1926. Since that time, *Winnie-the-Pooh* has become a million-times-over best seller. A regular cult developed around the story, and adults were taken with it, too. The American sinologist, Benjamin Hoff, even took up his pen to show that the snuggle bear is actually a master of the Tao. The Tao (the path) is the foundation of the oldest Chinese teaching of wisdom. According to Hoff, Pooh incorporates the key thought of *wu wei*. He stands for the ability to live effortlessly in harmony with everything, completely and naturally like water that flows over all hindrances and is clear and selfless like a perfect mirror. He answers like an echo—without trimmings, straight up, uncomplicated, and without calculation. In this spirit, what is necessary is done effortlessly and spontaneously. And because this "doing without doing" is in harmony with nature, no mistakes are made; there is no misbehavior. Taking one's time, enjoying things, being natural: that is the nature of a bear and is the Pooh way—the Tao of Pooh.

Pooh's philosophy is certainly worthy of a Chinese Tao master, such as the following dialog with his friend Piglet[1]:

Later on, when they had all said "Good-bye" and "Thank-you" to Christopher Robin, Pooh and Piglet walked home thoughtfully together in the golden evening, and for a long time they were silent.

"When you wake up in the morning, Pooh," said Piglet at last, "what's the first thing you say to yourself?"

"What's for breakfast?" said Pooh. "What do you say, Piglet?"

"I say, I wonder what's going to happen exciting to-day?" said Piglet.

Pooh nodded thoughtfully. "It's the same thing," he said.

Once Pooh visited his friend Rabbit and ate his full of honey and condensed milk until his belly was as round as a balloon. When he wanted to leave, he got stuck in the rabbit hole and had to wait until he had lost some weight. Though he was sorry that he could not eat for a time, he took it in stride. A fat bear, he admitted, is always a happy bear.

Pooh is just simple, spontaneous, and uncomplicated. His name fits—he can definitely be compared to the Tao concept of *p'u*, meaning "an unhewn clump" or something cloddish, natural, honest, something close to the Tao, to the origin. Pooh is the "bear of little understanding," the bear without intellect. His head is empty, his mind is clear and uncluttered, and his action is refreshingly unconventional.

Pooh is not the only animal in the Hundred-Acre Forest of Milne's stories. Others represent the feelings that fill our soul: the donkey's spirit is always clouded by worries; Piglet is fearful and hesitant; the kangaroo is nervous and fidgety; Rabbit is brainy; and the owl is always lecturing and has its head full of book learning yet still does not know anything. They all pretend to be special—only Pooh is just simply as he is. He lives in the here and now. He ambles happily along the forest path—symbolic for life's path—without having to think about a reason or goal, without complaining about the time wasted while ambling or calculating the rewards for his efforts.

Not the scholarliness of the owl, not Piglet's caution, not Rabbit's cleverness, but Pooh's simple, spontaneous ideas are the right answers to the problems that present themselves in the Hundred-Acre Forest. Seen in this light, even this bear is also the king of the forest. And like all bears, he is full of zest for life. Pooh can only shake his head at his busy friends who are constantly hustling in the name of progress instead of spending time humming their own melodies as bears do.

Pooh with honey pots in the rain (illustrated by Ernest H. Shepard, 1926)

CHAPTER 21
Encyclopedia of Famous Bears

I'm a very special Collector's bear . . .
So handle me with extra care!
I need someone who knows to treasure
me more than money can ever measure . . .
Someone who's learned that life is love,
Someone who watches stars above!
A person who stops to smell the flowers . . .
A person who walks in April showers.
For I have so much love to share
that I'll go with you anywhere!

LINDA KATZOPOULOS, *TEDDY BEAR POEMS*

Humans just do not get over their fascination with bears, not even in the increasingly virtual world we live in. Bears can still be found everywhere. They are hardly seen anymore in the forest (i.e., modern, usually ailing, tree plantations that are called forests), but whole hordes of shrill, colorful, absurd, pathetically sentimental bear personalities can be seen in films, comics, advertisements, and cyber space. They have very little to do with nature but reflect the state of our civilization and its population. The following is an incomplete selection of some of these notorious bears.

ALOYSIUS

Aloysius is a teddy bear that became famous in films and whose paw was embedded in cement in front of the Chinese Theater in Hollywood for "his exceptional acting performance." Aloysius belonged to the eccentric British Lord Sebastian Flyte, who carried the stuffed bear everywhere he went. He treated him like a little brother. As is fitting for a blue-blooded bear, he had his own silverware, dishes, and even a hairbrush with the monogram "A" for Aloysius. The bear dined in fancy restaurants and went to the hairdresser regularly. Sebastian took him along on all his trips, traveling first class, naturally; the only exception was Venice. Sebastian did not want to take his teddy bear along because, so he wrote, "he would meet many terrible bears there and be exposed to bad influences."

Evelyn Waugh wrote about the eccentric nobleman and his teddy bear in the novel *Brideshead Revisited*. The book was adapted into a successful television series, with Aloysius as the main character. Aloysius had to have a double, though, because Sebastian feared that his teddy bear would not be able to take so much excitement. A double, named Delicatessen, was found in Maine, and, looking very much like the original Aloysius, was also christened as Aloysius; he also led a feudal lifestyle from then on. He flew first class with Concorde and sat in the most expensive restaurants with, for instance, Jackie Onassis at the neighboring table. After his film career, his excellency, Aloysius, retired to the biggest teddy bear museum in the United Kingdom in Witney (Oxfordshire).[1]

BALOO

Rudyard Kipling (1865–1936), Victorian author and enthusiastic advocate of the British empire and colonialism, knew India. He was born in Bombay and lived for a long time on the subcontinent. He became famous for his statements concerning the civil tasks of the colonial empire and the moral duty of the whites ("the white man's burden") to educate the "backward, colored peoples." But he became even more famous for writing *The Jungle Book*, which appeared in 1894 and tells the story of Mogli, a poor Indian wood cutter's child, who is kidnapped by a pack of wolves. Baloo, a good-natured, lovable bear, adopts the boy and becomes his protector and teacher (reminiscent of the old myth that tells of a human child who grows up with bears or other animals in the wild). The boy lives with the animals in the jungle, free of the rules and constraints of civilization. But Baloo also teaches him that the jungle has laws. In the end, Mogli returns to the world of humans and becomes a wise and experienced teacher for his compatriots.

The Jungle Book was a worldwide, Nobel Prize–winning success. But the Walt Disney animated film of 1967 was even more successful. Since then, the lovable, singing, dancing Baloo lives on in people's hearts. His song, *The Bare Necessities*, became a catchy tune for a society worn out from constant stress and lack of time. In 2016, Jon Favreau revived the story with another successful film.

Kipling gave his characters genuine Indian names. For example, in various northern Indian and Nepalese dialects, *baloo* means "bear." (*Mogli* means "frog"; humans have a smooth skin like frogs.) Also, since *ba* means "harvest" and *lu* means "bringer," Baloo is the harvest bringer, the protector of the harvest, a fact that brings us back to the "grain bear" of Indo-European folklore and the "vital force in vegetation" of the folklorists. Anthropologists Claudia Mueller-Ebeling and Christian Raetsch (Mueller-Ebeling, Raetsch, and Shahi 2000, 251) write about the Kirati, a shamanistic tribe of eastern Nepal: "The bear (baloo) is generally regarded as the protector and teacher of the shamans. The Kirati also call him the 'god of the threshold,' a sort of Stone Age *Ganesha*. The Kirati use bear paws, claws and/or teeth in healing ceremonies."

Mogli and Baloo

BARNABY BEAR (RASMUS KLUMP)

Barnaby Bear (known as Rasmus Klump in the original Danish version), a cute little brown bear that wears red pants with white polka dots, originated in Denmark. He and his merry crew sail all around the world on the boat that he built and named *Mary*, after his mother. The whole world is their playground, each desert a sand box and each ocean a pool to splash around in. Aboard the ship, happy anarchy rules. There are problems and catastrophes, but they are always resolved with humor, courage, and refreshing naiveté—and without violence. Even though the little bear travels around the world, he is always back home in time for pancakes.

Barnaby Bear's friends on his adventures are the plump penguin, Pingo, a pelican who always has any tool or whatever else could be of use in his large throat pouch, two little rascals, a turtle, a parrot, and an old seal named Seabear, who sleeps and eats a lot, always smokes a pipe, and tells sailor's yarns, but always has good advice when the crew is in a pinch.

The first Barnaby Bear comic appeared in 1951 and was created by Carla and Vilhelm Hansen. In 1952, it appeared in Germany with the little bear called "Petzi." A worldwide hit, there are some thirty-seven adventure comics that have sold millions of times over. The little bear was especially popular in Japan.

Barnaby visits King Ursus.

BART

Bart, a genuine Alaskan Kodiak bear, who was born on January 19, 1977, in a zoo and died of cancer on May 18, 2000, at the age of twenty-three, is surely the most famous film and television star among bears. Animal trainer Doug Seus adopted him when he was only five weeks old and brought him to his ranch in Utah. He was raised on a bottle in the house until he was one year old and weighed nearly three hundred pounds, at which time he got his own "house." After he was eight years old, his trainer drove him around in the back of his pickup truck, taking him to the car wash where he got his daily shower. On one of these outings, two tame deer happened to see him and fell down dead on the spot out of fear. Bart grew to nearly ten feet tall and ate almost forty pounds of food a day. His trainer never used force, violence, or tranquilizers to teach him; he only trained with loving attention. When Bart did something right, he got a reward such as an apple, a pear, or a carrot. His preference was, though, a hamburger or pineapple milkshake (Busch 2000, 120).

Bart appeared in a dozen or more Hollywood films. He was a regular "John Wayne" of bear actors and starred with the likes of Brad Pitt, Anthony Hopkins, Daryl Hannah, Jonathan Taylor Thomas, and others. For his role in *The Edge*, he was paid one million dollars. His most well-known film is *The Bear* in which he plays the leading role of a grumpy old bear that adopts an orphaned cub and outsmarts a trigger-happy hunter, converting him into a pacifist toward bears. In this classic film, this "hymn to nature," viewers were shown dangerous meetings with mountain lions, coupling bears, and a psychedelic trip when the cub stumbled upon fly agaric mushrooms. The films that Bart starred in were shot in the Alps, the Dolomites of Austria and Italy, and the North American wilderness.

BEN (BOZO)

Ben, whose real name was Bozo, was a female grizzly and the star in a popular TV series called *The Life and Times of Grizzly Adams* (NBC 1977–1978) with Dan Haggerty. The good-natured grizzly, who needed neither leash nor tranquilizers, gained one hundred pounds during the shooting because of the many jam sandwiches, hot dogs, and marshmallows given as rewards. She also appeared in films such as *The Adventures of Frontier Freemont* (1976) and

Grizzly Mountain (1998). In the latter film, ranger, gold digger, and adventurer James Capen "Grizzly" Adams (1812–1860) is portrayed as a friend and protector of wild animals, who prefers the loneliness of the wilderness to civilization. In reality, he was an obsessed trapper who greatly contributed to the decimation of the California grizzly, and the wild animals that he didn't kill (bears, wolves, pumas) he sold to zoos and circuses. He got his nickname "Grizzly" because he strolled through the streets of San Francisco with two nearly grown grizzlies without a leash; he had trained them with brutal methods.

"Grizzly" Adams (illustration from The Adventures of James Capen Adams, Mountaineer and Grizzly Bear Hunter of California *by Theodore Hittell, 1860)*

THE BERLINER BEAR

Though a bear is depicted in Berlin's coat of arms and the city is named after the bear (Berlin means "small bear"), compared to the Russian or Bernese bears (see the related entries), its role is not very convincing. Considering the history of the Prussian Berliner, one is inclined to say that the wolf, to give credit where credit is due, would be a more appropriate totem for the city. The nickname of Margrave Albrecht I, founder of the city, was *Bear*, which appears to be the origin of the animal's place on the coat of arms, on the seal, and within the city's name. Or was there maybe even a real bear involved that happened to be ambling along the Spree River through the alluvial forests?

The first Berlin coat of arms, from 1280

It was not until 1935, however, that the bear became the official totem of Berlin. And, in 1937, on the occasion of the seven-hundredth anniversary of the city, a bear pit, in response to the public request to have the totem animal in flesh and blood, was installed. Two years later, Urs, Vreni, and Purzel moved in as a gift from the city of Berne. The animals did not outlive the merciless bombings of the Second World War, unfortunately. However, in 1949, the Bernese sent two more brown bears, Jutte and Nante, to Berlin.

Contrary to the Bernese bear pit, the Berliner pit is practically unknown and is not listed in the city tourism guides. The Berliner bear only became known during the Cold War blockade of Berlin and as a result of the "Golden Bear" and "Silver Bear" prizes of the international film festival in Berlin. The secret mascot of Berlin, however, is a hippopotamus: Knautschke, a hippopotamus bull, was one of the few animals that survived the near-total destruction of the city's zoo during the World War II bomb attacks on Berlin as well as the fodder scarcity brought on by Stalin during the blockade. With his stubborn will to survive and his "big mouth and thick skin," it's no wonder he became a symbol of the Berliner and the first zoo animal to be on a postage stamp in Germany.

Berlin seal from 1460—a bear with the imperial eagle on its back

THE BERNESE BEAR

The Bernese soul is a bear soul. And living bears, which must always be called *Urs* (Latin = bear), live in the middle of the city. Chapter 19, Bearopolis, provides an in-depth look at this particular type of bear.

CARE BEARS

These colorful, cute, furry little bears that are always smiling live up above the clouds in Care-a-Lot, which sounds similar to the Celtic fairy realm of Camelot. Care-a-Lot is a wonderland, a bubble bath for the soul, a huge playground with rainbows, sparkling stars, and clouds of cotton candy. When the Care Bears notice that someone on Earth is sad or facing difficulties, they come down to help. As their names—Love-a-Lot Bear, Friend Bear, Tenderheart Bear, Good Luck Bear, Funshine Bear, Cheer Bear, Superstar Bear, Harmony Bear, and so on—suggest, they incorporate the purest of positive vibrations. They are the storm troopers of the "Love Ideology" of an infantile New Age.

Whether one is inclined to dismiss the Care Bears as kitsch, in the real world of stocks and dividends they are absolute winners. The Care Bears were developed by the greeting card corporation *American Greetings* and marketed aggressively. Between 1983 and 1987, more than forty million Care Bear toys were sold, several Care Bear films and TV series were produced, and over forty-five million Care Bear coloring books, comics, and children's books were sold—not to mention the over seventy million Care Bear greeting cards in the 1980s alone.

DANCING BEARS

Dancing bears existed in antiquity, but they can still be found in Turkey and parts of Asia. Training a dancing bear begins, in most cases, very early after the mother is killed to get to the young cubs. To lead the animal, the trainer pierces the lips, or the nasal bone, puts a ring through the hole, and attaches the ring to a leash. The poor beings learn to dance on hot plates or a heated floor so that they lift their paws alternately to relieve the pain. The trainer plays a drum or tambourine so that the bear learns to associate the tact of the music with the pain under its paws. Tourists who take pictures of themselves with dancing bears should know that they are supporting one of the worst kinds of animal torture (Ames 2002, 204). Dancing bears should not exist.

Training dancing bears (medieval woodcut)

EWOKS

Ewoks, a sort of caricature of Stone Age people, were introduced by the Star Wars Trilogy and appear as friendly, shy inhabitants of the moon forest Endor. Their language is made up of grunting, growling, and wheezing sounds. They live in huts high up in trees and are connected to other trees by ropes and hanging bridges. Chiefs, elder councils, and shamans are the leaders of the Ewok tribes. Their religion revolves around big, old trees, and a tree is planted at the birth of one of these bear-like creatures. They fight with Stone

Age–like weapons at the side of the Jedi warriors against a wicked empire. The hairy moon inhabitants were so popular that George Lucas made two successive films featuring them—*Caravan of Courage: An Ewok Adventure* (1984) and *Ewoks: The Battle for Endor* (1985).

FOZZIE BEAR

Fozzie Bear is a character from *The Muppet Show*. The brown bear with googly eyes, a small hat on his head, and a bow tie would like to be a comedian, but no one finds his jokes funny.

GENTLE BEN

Gentle Ben, an especially big black bear *(Baribal)*, is a fictional character most often portrayed by an American black bear named Bruno in the leading role, with Dennis Weaver and Clint Howard, in the TV series *Gentle Ben* (CBS 1967–1969) and later in various films, such as *Gentle Giant* (1967), *Gentle Ben* (2002), and *Danger on the Mountain* (2003). The popular TV series shows Ben as the clumsy pet of a game warden and his family in the Everglades in Florida.

In real life, Bruno began his career as an orphaned cub from the forest in Wisconsin. He was brought to an animal ranch in California, near Los Angeles, where wild animals were trained to play film roles. Before his eventual fame, a flash flood destroyed the ranch; however, Ben was found three days later a few miles away covered with crusted mud and starving. Another time, a diesel locomotive that had gone out of control hit his cage, but the lucky black bear survived again.

GOLDILOCKS AND THE THREE BEARS

The story of *Goldilocks and The Three Bears* is as much a part of standard fairy tale lore as are *The Nursery Rhymes of Mother Goose*. Every child knows Papa Bear, Mama Bear, and Baby Bear. The three bears lived in a small house in the forest, and each had their own porridge bowl, chair, and bed that were just the right size. One morning, after having made their beds and cooked their breakfast porridge, they stepped out of the house for a while—the porridge was still too hot, anyway, and needed to cool. The little girl with the golden curls ("locks")—in earlier versions, it was a wizened old woman from the forest—happened by and looked into the window. As it looked like no one was at home, she went in. Since she was hungry, she tried the porridge from the big bowl that was Papa Bear's bowl and found it too hot. Then she tried Mama Bear's porridge and found it too cold, but Baby Bear's porridge was just right and she ate it all. She decided to rest a bit and tried Papa Bear's chair, but it was too big. Mama Bear's chair was too big, too. Baby Bear's chair seemed just right, but when she settled into it, it broke into pieces. Then she decided she was so tired she needed a nap. She tried Papa Bear's bed, but it was too hard; then she tried Mama Bear's bed, but it was too soft. Baby Bear's bed was just right, and she fell fast asleep.

When the bears came back home, they were shocked to see that someone had eaten from their porridge bowls, sat in their chairs, and tried out their beds— and there she was still asleep in Baby Bear's bed! As Baby Bear exclaimed, "There she is!" Goldilocks woke up and ran away as fast as she could.

The story could describe a typical early morning dream in which, after the soul wanders in "the otherworld" during the night, the person wakes up and a change of consciousness occurs whereby the soul crosses the threshold and has to pass by the guardians—in this case, the three bears.

Papa Bear, Mama Bear, and Baby Bear (English children's book)

GUMMY BEARS

The little gelatin bears are not candy like any other kind of fruit candy in Germany. They are part of the German way of life. Two hundred thousand tons are consumed each year in Germany alone—lined up, they would go around the Earth three times. Thomas Gottschalk earns millions just advertising them. Gummy bears inspire all kinds of side products in Germany, including gummy bear puzzles, gummy bear tarot cards, and a gummy bear oracle.

Dietmar Bittrich's *Das Gummibaerchen Orakel* (as well as *Gummy Bear Tarot*, available in English) became a best seller in Germany after it was published in 1996. Its success is no wonder when one considers how many German women are interested in esoterica, horoscopes, and oracles, and how many eat gummy bears regularly. In this Dadaistic caricature, Bittrich tells how his mother set him out in the wilderness in Canada, and a grizzly bear family took him in. He lived with them until he was twelve years old and learned about the instincts and habits of the bears. He saw electric lights for the first time when he was thirteen, saw his first sink at fourteen, fell in love at fifteen, and saw his first gummy bear at sixteen. Since that fateful year of 1975, Bittrich lovingly and intensively studied the being and meaning of gummy bears. After twenty years of research, he presented the first and ultimate gummy bear oracle. In Germany, the book became the standard work on the subject from the first edition. Bittrich presently lives in Switzerland and works toward the resettlement of wild gummy bears in Alpine regions.

The creator of the bears themselves was confectioner Hans Riegel from Bonn (Ha-Ri-Bo, where the company name *Haribo* comes from), Germany, who, together with his wife Gertrud, in 1922, made the first of their kind by hand and poured them into molds; he personally delivered them to his customers on his bicycle. Called "dancing bears" back then, the bears certainly brought him luck. Since those humble beginnings, the company has grown to its present-day staff of six thousand and produces seventy million bears a day. Now, gummy bears are produced in France, England, Denmark, Austria, Spain, and the United States.

PADDINGTON BEAR

In a London subway station, the Brown family stumbles upon a small bear. Completely lost, the bear stands there in his duffel coat that is a bit too big and a wide-brimmed hat, such as only a British eccentric wears. He is holding a suitcase and has a note hung around his neck that reads, "Please look after this bear. Thank you." The good people are touched. They take the bear home, who claims to have come all the way from deepest Peru, and name their new house guest Paddington, after the station where they found him. What follows is the foreign bear's often funny attempts to comprehend the British way of life. He invariably sticks his foot in his mouth on occasion. Paddington's character is actually completely British and harmlessly eccentric. He is extremely polite and loves jam, which unfortunately drips and sticks everywhere; he enjoys perfumed bubble baths, likes to go shopping, reads books, drinks tea, decorates his room, and sleeps, as is proper, in pajamas; essentially, he is a parody of the English petty-bourgeoisie.

Michael Bond began to write the book, *A Bear Called Paddington*, after he bought a teddy bear in the London department store Selfridges. The book first appeared in 1958 and became the best children's book of that same year. More Paddington books followed, as well as a flood of Paddington stuffed bears, tapes, and animated films. The cash registers never stopped ringing at Paddington and Company, while, in the meantime, a large statue of the famous bear from Peru is installed in the London Paddington station.

THE RUSSIAN BEAR

A great many entries for "Russian Bear" can be found on the internet:

- a colorful kind of butterfly (*Euplagia quadripunctaria*)
- the popular Canadian free-style wrestler and twice-born Christian, Ivan Koloff
- an anabolic cocktail for body builders and muscle men, such as Arnold Schwarzenegger or Ivan Koloff
- the Russian Bear Schnauzer, a huge, shaggy schnauzer

- a delicious cocktail with lots of vodka, crème de cacao, and cream
- a fundamentalist Christian personification of Magog, the realm of evil, and the hordes of the Antichrist that will descend upon America and Israel in the last battles of the apocalypse
- the Russian folk soul that sees itself as a bear

The largest population of brown bears in the world lives in the taiga and tundra of Russia. Since time immemorial, the bear—Michail Ivanowitsch, Mischka, General Clumsy Foot, Honey Eater, the Wise Old One—has played an important role in the cultural cosmos of the eastern Slavs. As far back as heathen times, forest bears were seen as guardians of the threshold to the realm of Leschiy, or Lesovik, the one-eyed lord of the forest, who, even today, according to folk belief, protects wild animals and punishes offenses against the forest.

Russians identify with their totem animal as they see it—strong and down to earth, clumsy in vodka bliss, and endowed with a heart of gold.[2] He is not as charming, clever, and contentious (as the case may be) as the Gallic rooster, not as fanatically orderly and clean as the German "Michel," and does not bristle with merciless justice like the American eagle. He presents himself as smiling "Mischka," as could be seen in the mascot of the 1980 Olympics in Moscow.

The good-naturedness of the Russian bear should not be interpreted as weakness; if he is annoyed or driven into a corner, he is capable of unpredictable outbursts of violence. Many conquerors have felt the force of his angry paws—the Tatars, the Turks, Napoleon's Grande Armée, and most recently the proud German Armed Forces. A leading prominent journalist of a large newspaper recently warned about provoking the Russian bear—NATO and the EU must be careful not to get too close for comfort and thus appear interested in snacking on his honey pots (i.e., Russia's oil reserves).

Mischka, the mascot of the Olympic games in Moscow, 1980

SMOKEY BEAR

Smokey Bear, with his jeans, shovel, and ranger hat, is a forest ranger and an American icon. Similar to the campaign of Uncle Sam, during the second World War, who looked sternly, pointed his finger at onlookers, and declared, "I want you," Smokey looks condescendingly at the national park guests and commands, "Remember, only you can prevent forest fires!" When the strapping bear first appeared on posters in 1944, he had a military duty. There was a general fear that Nazi agents or shots fired from Japanese submarines might set the West Coast forests on fire. At first, the War-time Advertising Council proposed Walt Disney's Bambi as a symbol for the forest fire-fighting campaign, but in times of war a uniformed bear was more appropriate. Smokey was named after a successful firefighter named "Smokey" Joe Martin.

Smokey first came about during a huge forest fire in the spring of 1950 in the Capitan Mountains of New Mexico when rangers found a bear cub with badly burned paws. This cub that they first named "Hotfoot" became the official animal totem of the state of New Mexico and, at the same time, was declared the living mascot of the National Forest Service. After his burns

One of the first posters of Smokey Bear

healed, the living symbol was sent to Washington, DC, to live in the national zoo. Soon after, he became so popular that sending him all the mail from hordes of children and admirers grew into a difficult task, so the U.S. Postal Service was forced to give Smokey his own zip code.

In 1952, in order to avoid a merciless commercialization of Smokey, the U.S. Congress passed a bill against such exploitation of the popular bear. The living Smokey was given a female bear companion so that he could live as naturally as possible, but no cubs ensued. When Smokey died in 1976, he was buried ceremoniously in the presence of many spectators and prominent politicians in the "Smokey Bear Park" in New Mexico. (More about Smokey can be found in Chapter 18). In 1984, the U.S. Postal Service issued a stamp that depicted Smokey as a cub, clinging to a tree trunk, and surrounded by a charcoaled landscape.

WINNIE-THE-POOH

Winnie-the-Pooh, named after a genuine American black bear in the London Zoo, was the first teddy bear in literature. A. A. Milne, the well-to-do writer and editor of the satire magazine *Punch,* wrote the book *Winnie-the-Pooh,* in which the stuffed animal toys of his son, Christopher Robin, played the main roles. Ernest H. Shepard illustrated the book in addition to being the illustrator at *Punch. Winnie-the-Pooh* became a classic and the main character an icon of children's literature. (See more about Winnie-the-Pooh in Chapter 20).

YOGI BEAR

Yogi Bear, named after the popular baseball legend Yogi Berra, can be seen since 1959 on the *Huckleberry Hound Show.* He lives in the national park "Jellystone," somewhere between Wyoming and Montana, and specializes in searching rest area waste bins for something to eat, begging tourists for food or stealing their picnic baskets, and driving the park rangers up a wall. Yogi, who believes he is much more intelligent than the average bear, goes about his business in a clever way. Yogi and the little bear Boo-Boo—who are sponsored by Kellogg's Corn Flakes—have become very popular and have appeared in over one hundred newspapers, have earned over one hundred million dollars as toys, and are permanent stars on the Disney Channel. On summer vacation, parents can pack up the kids and dog and drive to a Yogi Bear's Jellystone Park Camp-Resort found in nearly every state.

AFTERWORD

Hope for the Bear's Return

Grandfather bear, Golden Paws,
King of the Forest, King of the Animals,
Anima's Lover, The Goddess's Lover,
Bearer of the Stars.
Your strength moves the wheels of the heavens,
the seasons, life itself.
May your place in the forests, dear wild brothers,
in the mountains, and in human hearts, be granted.
Heavenly bear! Do not desert us!"

AUTHOR'S POEM

Thoughts are energy. If one concentrates one's thoughts on an object, whether it be a rock, a plant, an animal, or a human, one touches it. Invariably, one will be rewarded with an answer. Not long after I finished this book, some bears—to be precise, it was the Bear Tribe Medicine Company—invited me to come to a medicine meeting in Schwangau, Germany. I had heard of Sun Bear, the Chippewa medicine man and visionary, and knew he had prophesied the end of the consumer society that is based on technocratic megalomania and had offered the traditional wisdom of the Native Americans for healing. Against the opposition of other Native American medicine people and shamans, he also shared his knowledge with the children of white people.

Emblem of the Bear Tribe Medicine Company

I expected a symposium at which environmental problems and those of peoples facing extinction would be discussed, so I prepared a lecture titled, "Bear herbs, the strongest healing plants." I was not prepared for what I saw at the meeting. I felt myself almost sent back in time, into the Stone Age Magdalenian when the people of Europe to North America lived as big game hunters and paid homage to a bear cult. Whole families were staying in tents at the foot of the snowy mountains. Bundled up in furs and knitted woolens, they sang songs for Mother Earth and Father Sun: "The Earth is our mother and with each step we touch sacred ground." They treated each other like brothers and sisters. They also sang for Grandfather and Grandmother Bear, accompanied by a genuine shaman drum. They summoned the bears to let our strength and wisdom return to us.

In the evening, the bear tribe people sweated in a traditional sweat lodge. They incensed their bodies with prairie sage, offered sweet grass and tobacco to the spirits, passed the sacred peace pipe around, and sent their prayers to the Great Spirit at the medicine wheel.

While I was talking about healing plants, a huge, long-haired young man with lots of amulets, crystals, and runes hanging around his neck came and stood in the door to the tent. This guardian of the threshold was called "Breitschaedel" (a German name that means "broad skull"). It was his real name and not a name he had given himself. He was as good-natured as he was wild—a berserker having difficulty with the times he was born into. It came to my mind that an incarnated bear spirit was there in front of me. Here, in the shadow of the Alps, where the Bavarian kings had built their castles, I had found a "place of power" where a bear vision could come to me.

The Earth, and our near relatives, the plants and animals, talk to us all the time—this was Sun Bear's message; we must only learn to listen again. They are not just objects that can arouse scientific interest but the expression of spiritual archetypes that live in us and outside of us in nature and can take on many shapes. Here, the bear archetype appeared to me, talked to me, and touched me.

But not only the bear's spirit can present itself in these historic times of change. Real bears, shaggy, grumbling bears, are also coming back to the sacred mountains of Europe, to the Alps. Thanks to the World Wildlife Fund (WWF), bears that migrate from the Balkans are no longer shot as a matter of course. And in 1989, a bear was set out near Oetscherberg, Austria. Against all expectations, she was seen in 1991 with three cubs. Since that time, the population has grown to twenty-five. More bears, coming from Slovenia and Croatia, are expected to be set out in South Tyrol and Lombardy. In Trentino, Italy, where some of the last Alpine bears live, no less than ten bears were sighted between 1999 and 2002. The bear population has increased at a natural rate since then but unfortunately the human population observes this with mixed feelings. Beekeepers have justified apprehensions about bears being around, but hikers should not be worried; the authorities reassure the public that the animals are rather shy and tend to be peaceful.

The crises of our civilization—the hole in the ozone, pollution, climate catastrophes, the extinction of species, etc.—seem absolute and unstoppable. However, as a Native American from the Klamath tribe assured me, scientists equipped with monitors and the most sophisticated computers do not know everything. Their perspective is ultimately only that of an ant. The Earth itself is a bear. Stinking factories and huge cities are like fleas and ticks on her. Soon, she will shake herself and scratch the parasites off, cleansing herself. Then humans and animals can live in harmony again and all can enjoy life.

"A nice dream," I said.

"Dreams and visions create realities," he answered.

That wild animals are returning—the bears in the Alps, the wolves in Saxony—is for those who read signs, a sign of hope. It is the hope that is expressed in the song of completing the medicine wheel:

The dawn of a new time is coming,
Golden light is flowing all over the earth.

NOTES

INTRODUCTION

1 *Bruin* is an old northern European endearment for the bear meaning "the brown, furry one."

CHAPTER 1

1 Western religious ethnology talks about "animal possession" of indigenous shamans. But this is a typical ethnocentric misunderstanding. These people are in unison with the animal spirit, not possessed by it.

2 For example, a panther warned Phoolan Devi, a modern female Robin Hood in India, that a gang of police was about to descend on her hideout (Devi 1997).

3 Henning Eichler, an independent shaman researcher, told me this in conversation.

4 *Satata-siddhi* (Sanskrit *satata* = continual, *siddhi* = supernatural powers) refers to unusual "shamanic" abilities, such as telepathy, levitation, mind reading, invisibility, bi-location, entering another body, and so on.

CHAPTER 2

1 For more information, see https://en.wikipedia.org/wiki/Bear_worship.

2 On the other hand, several prehistorians doubt that the small statue was even an intentionally created work of art. The "pseudo Venus" seemed more likely to have come to be through the chance wearing of a tool; besides, no one believed the Neanderthals possessed such craftsmanship

(Kuckenburg 1997, 296). The figure that was in the local museum of St. Gallen was unfortunately not handled properly and turned to dust. All that is left are some photographs of it.

3   The Neanderthals were a human species that had genetically adjusted to the extreme ice age climate. Gene researchers' theory until 2010 that Neanderthals have completely different DNA from modern people has not been proven valid. Despite the fact that gene analysis is extremely difficult with such ancient bones, analysts in 2010 were able to trace and prove the DNA connection (Pääbo, 2015). Also, see https://en.wikipedia.org/wiki/Svante_P%C3%A4%C3%A4bo.

4   *Arktos* is related to Latin *ursus* and to Old Indic *raksha*. These words go back to the Indo-Germanic root *rksos* or *rktos*, which means "destroyer, demon."

5   Research done by Dr. F. Ed. Koby and H. Schaefer at the Natural Historical Museum in Basel, Switzerland, indicates that it is very unlikely that Neanderthals systematically hunted cave bears. Even if the struggle between early humans and monster bears arouses romantic or Darwinistic notions, the hunting technology of the Neanderthals will have hardly been sophisticated enough to manage such an accomplishment. The Paleolithic bear hunters with their relatively simple weapons only seldom had occasion to kill a bear; most cave bears died of natural causes. For more information, see https://ipna.unibas.ch/archbiol/pdf/1972_Schmid_Knochenatlas.pdf.

CHAPTER 3

1   The word *totem* comes from the Algonquians. *O-t-ote-man* means "relative of one's own brother/sister"; the root word *ote* designates not only relatives within the family but also the animal that is related to the clan (or sometimes also a plant or a dreamtime object).

CHAPTER 4

1   The northern European proverbial expression "an un-licked bear" (German *ein ungeleckter Baer* and French *un ours mal leché*), referring to a coarse,

unrefined person, goes back to a belief, also held by the ancient Romans, that bears are born as formless clumps and licked into the right shape by the mother (Roehrich 2001, 1:145).

2   Black bears gestate for seven months.

CHAPTER 6

1   Professed diseases of civilization, such as diabetes, circulatory diseases, cancer, or tooth decay, were all unknown in tribal times. They became a part of Native American lives only as a result of stress, poverty, and the transition to industrial, refined supermarket foods.

CHAPTER 7

1   Bear milk is indeed rich and full of nourishment. It is ten times as nourishing as cow's milk. With 35 percent milk fat, 11 percent protein, and some 10 percent carbohydrates (Busch 2000, 63).

2   These tasks symbolize the duties of the dead in the otherworld. The ripe apples and the baked loaves of bread stand for the human souls that are ready to be reborn and must be carefully tended by the dead. For more information, see *Witchcraft Medicine* by Mueller-Ebeling, Raetsch, and Storl (2003).

CHAPTER 8

1   Marija Gimbutas, a well-known Lithuanian archeologist, examined hundreds of terracotta figures from the Old Stone Age, which extended from the sixth into the third century BCE in southeastern Europe along the Danube Valley and all the way to the Black Sea. These first farmers etched zigzag lines, which stood for water and also for bear claws, into cultic pots. Gimbutas has found a connection between the water on which all life depends and bears who are guardians of springs and the fertility of the earth: "Toward the end of this time bears partially took on human form. The terracotta figures were now women with a bear's

head. Sometimes she sat on a throne decorated with half-moons and held a bear baby on her lap, like a Madonna, or carried one in a bag on her back. Many of these figures have the left hand on the breast, which suggests an association between bears and water, as water and milk were often connected in ancient mythology" (Sanders 2002, 153). This ancient bear goddess is an early appearance of the great goddess, the foster mother of the gods and the goddess of the cave and rebirth. According to Gimbutas, the cult of Artemis on the Attic Coast developed out of this bear cult. The background of the story of Iphigenia, whom Artemis saved from sacrificial death by putting a small black bear on the altar in her stead, is presumably a remnant of a ritual in which a bear was deified and sacrificed.

2   It wasn't until the prudish, petty-bourgeois Biedermeier times in Europe that the hazelnut rod, this bawdy symbol, was turned into a punishing rod—the fertile rod of the old forest and winter spirit turned into a rod for punishing naughty children.

3   The Church tried to redefine the symbolism. On Fasting Sunday, in 1207, Pope Innocence III had a play put on in which a bear, as a symbol of the devil; young bulls, as a symbol of uninhibited human lust; and a rooster, as a symbol of arousal were all killed (Becker-Huberti 2001, 240).

4   In Berne, a sleeping bear is awakened at the beginning of the carnival time and let out of its cage.

5   In England, "straw-bears" were also known. A man or youth was covered with straw, and on "Plow Monday," the first Monday after the twelve holy nights when regular work could be taken up again, he would go from house to house grumbling like a bear, scaring the women and begging for alms.

CHAPTER 9

1   These cross-quarter days have been disassociated from the moon nowadays and have fixed calendar days, the first or second day of the month.

2   On February 2nd, as an ancient custom in Arles-sur-Tech in the Pyrenees, a young fellow dressed as a bear comes out of a cave, which has been

placed in the middle of the town. He then runs all over the town looking for "Rosetta," his bride-to-be; when he finds her, the two are ritually "married."

3 "The bear is a winter animal. It has grown thick fur and retreats into a cave to avoid masses of snow and icy cold. But, as a polar bear, it can also take the winter on. For that reason, bears love honey, the most wonderful gift of the summer sun, which gives them the strength to resist freezing temperatures" (Koenig 2013, 107).

4 A bear in hibernation uses body fat and carbohydrates in a way that creates water—a method that keeps the body from dehydrating. In a recycling process, urea is taken out of the blood and changed back to protein. Glucose, which is important to keep the brain functioning, is obtained during protein breakdown (Busch 2000, 53ff.). Scientists are trying to understand this process better in the hopes of being able to put astronauts into a similar state of slumber during long flights into outer space. Medical science also hopes to understand coma states better through research of bear hibernation.

CHAPTER 10

1 In France: *Qu'il ne faut jamais, vendre la peau de l'ours qu'on ne l'ait mis par terre.*

2 Also sometimes Jambavat.

CHAPTER 11

1 This story, recorded by the Grimm brothers, is based on an earlier version called "The First Bearskin" (1670) in the book *Simplicissimus*. In this version, a young German lansquenet is the protagonist who becomes Bearskin.

2 This three-fold goddess is also known in Vedic India: white Sarasvathi, red Lakshmi, and black Kali, goddess of destruction. For more information, see my book *Shiva, the Wild God of Power and Ecstasy* (2004), specifically Chapter 10.

CHAPTER 12

1   Ursa Major is called *Rakh,* which can be translated as "brightly shining bear." In its whirling pace, it rules not only over the seasons, rain and drought, and consequently the harvest—it is also the vital spirit of vegetation—but also over all that is whirled into manifestation and whirled back out. For this reason, Hindus paint red whirling patterns on the walls in houses where a birth is about to take place. They want to ensure that the child in the birth canal finds the right direction to come to Earth, that it can orient itself for the birth (Sanders 2002, 262).

2   Alcor, the "little rider," or "Tom Thumb," is "on" the middle star (Mizar) of the three. It can just be seen with the naked eye.

3   See also www.clarkfoundation.org/astro-utah/vondel/songofstars.html.

4   Other Native Americans of the prairie also see this place as sacred and connected to the strength of the bear and where people go to fast and pray. The Crows (Absaroka) call it "Bear's House," the Sioux (Lakota) "Grizzly Bear House," and the Arapaho "Bear's Tipi." The Kiowa, for whom the "Tree Trunk Rock" is also sacred, tell a story of seven small girls who were playing outside their settlement and then were suddenly surrounded by hungry bears. In their distress, they climbed upon a rock and prayed, "Rock, help us!" The rock began to grow taller and taller. The bears that tried to climb up after the girls slid back down to Earth and left deep claw tracks on the rock. One can still see the girls up in the sky today as the seven sisters, the Pleiades.

CHAPTER 13

1   In the Icelandic *Landnámabók* saga, the warrior Ovar Odd held up a bearskin in the middle of battle, and, as soon as the enemies saw it, they lost their courage and retreated.

2   More information on the theme of berserkers and their initiations can be found in my book *Naturrituale* (not yet available in English).

3   As various Native American tribes came ever more under pressure from white settlers and were driven into the areas of other tribes, a similar

development of "professional warriors" took place. The Cheyenne, for example, developed warrior confederacies, such as the "coyote warriors," the "elk warriors," or the famous "dog soldiers."

4   Naturally, bearskin warriors were not just found in northern Europe. The army flag bearers (*signiferi*) in the Roman imperial army received a bearskin placed over their helmet and armor as an award of honor. The Arcadians also fought their battles in bearskins (Roehrich 2001, 1:148).

5   A certificate from 1290 mentions "Chournat, the Sacred Bear" (Baechtold-Staeubli and Hoffmann-Krayer, Vol. 8, 1987).

6   The eagle should be the king of the feathered kingdom because it flies the highest. But the wren claimed it could fly even higher. So they arranged a race; whoever flew highest would become king of the birds. The eagle flew up as high as it could, up to the edge of heaven. The clever wren had hidden on the eagle's back, and, when the eagle got too tired and could not fly higher, the wren flew off and chirped, "I can fly higher than you, so I am the king!" The eagle had to admit defeat, and since then the wren (called "King of the Fence" and, in olden times, also "Snow King," in German) claims the title of king.

7   In mythical, primeval times, the white buffalo woman appeared to the Native Americans of the prairie in the form of a white buffalo calf. She brought them the sacred pipe and led the buffalo, the livelihood of the Native Americans of the prairie, down to Earth. The birth of a white buffalo calf in Wisconsin in August 1994 was, therefore, considered a message from this goddess and a good omen for the rebirth of the western Native American culture.

CHAPTER 14

1   Animism is the belief of many native peoples that everything—including "dead" rocks, plants, mountains, lakes, natural phenomena, etc.—is conscious. Cultural anthropologist Edward Tylor (1832–1917) characterized the "religion of the primitive peoples" with this concept that comprised the opposite of the one-god believers of the progressive, civilized peoples.

2 This nature-alienated delusion still plagues humanity to this day: In the zoo in Kabul, for example, the fundamentalist Taliban hit and agonized the captivated wild boars—one of the sacred animals of the great goddess—"because they are impure animals."

CHAPTER 15

1 The custom of making spring soups and salads out of fresh greens that grow early in the year can still be found in some areas all over Europe. These "nine herbs" refer to any mixture of as many of these fresh green plants one may choose to revive and refresh in the spring.

2 Warning to plant novices: This plant smells strongly of garlic and is hard to miss; however, in Europe, it is often mistaken for lily of the valley or autumn crocus, both highly poisonous plants with leaves similar to those of bear's garlic.

3 Common clubmoss is not to be mistaken for poisonous fir clubmoss (*Hyperzia selago*). Fir clubmoss has no spore spadix, and the leaves do not have hairy tips.

4 Giant hogweed has phototoxic properties due to the furocoumarins that it contains.

CHAPTER 16

1 Medieval magicians apparently did dare consume bear brain, however. Agrippa von Nettesheim writes in his book *Die magischen Werke* (1531, 1:196): "A drink prepared from bear's brain and offered in its skull is said to create a bear-like fury. Whoever drinks it will believe he has been changed into a bear and judge everything from a bear's standpoint. He will remain in this state of semi-madness until the effect of the drink wears off but without any damage otherwise occurring to the person who drank it."

CHAPTER 17

1 The Dolgans of northern Siberia raise reindeer, hunt, and fish. They live in conic leather tents and practice shamanism.

CHAPTER 18

1 The Shinto religion also has a bear *kami*. Incidentally, the name of the sacred mountain, Fujiyama, is also of Ainu language origin and is the name of the goddess (kami) of fire, Huchi, or Fuji, which literally means "grandmother" (Weyer 1958, 202).

2 The arrowhead was prepared with monkshood *(Aconitum)* and other poisonous plants, which lead to an immediate cardiovascular collapse (Raetsch 1991, 28).

CHAPTER 19

1 Hornussen is an indigenous Swiss sport that gets its name from the puck, called a *Hornuss* (hornet). When hit, it can whiz through the air at up to 300 kilometers (approximately 185 miles) per hour and create a buzzing sound.

2 Also known as Swiss wrestling, *Schwingen* somewhat resembles sumo wrestling.

3 Though it may be true that Sigmund Wagner (1759–1835) fabricated the legend of *The Noble Lady Mechthildis,* he, however, must have relied on old prototypes. As far as archetypal structures are concerned, the legend can be taken as "genuine."

4 In Estonia, a "Christ-Bear" Christmas cake is still made at Christmastime, and some of it is given to the animals.

5 Modern studies show that brown bears eat between 80 and 90 percent vegetable foods; the rest of their diet consists of cadavers, insects, fish, rodents, and mushrooms (Busch 2000, 70). It wasn't until the Middle Ages, when humans intruded ever more into the bear's habitat, that bears became evil "predators" that occasionally lashed out at a sheep or another animal on a pasture to still their hunger. They also became increasingly active at night to avoid dangerous humans.

6 Bears disappeared in Germany in the nineteenth century; the last central European bears were slain in 1836 in Bavaria, in 1881 in Tyrol, and in 1921 in the French Alps.

CHAPTER 20

1 See www.goodreads.com/quotes/547623-later-on-when-they-had-all-said
-good-bye-and-thank-you.

CHAPTER 21

1 See www.oxfordshirecotswolds.org/things-to-do/shopping/teddy-bears-of
-witney-p479991.

2 Some travelers to Russia have experienced the good-natured Russian
"heart like a bear." One January, when I flew from New Delhi to Europe,
I had an overnight layover in Moscow. When the porter at my hotel saw
that I only had thin cotton clothes on, he took off his thick fur coat and
gave it to me to wear for as long as I was in the freezing city.

BIBLIOGRAPHY

Ames, Alison. 2002. "Baeren im Zirkus." In *Baeren*, edited by Ian Stirling. Munich: Orbis.

Arens, Werner, and Hans-Martin Braun, eds. 1994. *Der Gesang des schwarzen Baeren*. Munich: C. H. Beck.

Asbjoernson, Peter Christen, and Joergen Moe. 1960. *Norske folke-eventyr*. Oslo: Dreyers Forlag.

Auer, Ludwig. Heiligenlegenden. 1962. Augsburg: Auer/Cassianeum.

Baechtold-Staeubli, Hanns, and Eduard Hoffmann-Krayer. 1987. *Handwoerterbuch des deutschen Aberglauben*. Vols. 1–10, Berlin: Walter de Gruyter.

Bates, Daniel. 2013. "Could Bears Hold the Cure to Obesity? Grizzlies Eat Up to 58,000 Calories a Day Yet Don't Get Fat or Develop Heart Disease." *Daily Mail*, December 16. www.dailymail.co.uk/sciencetech/article-2524726/Could-bears-hold-cure-OBESITY -Grizzlies-eat-58-000-calories-day-dont-fat-develop-heart-disease.html.

Becker-Huberti, Manfred. 2001. *Feiern – Feste – Jahreszeiten*. Freiburg: Herder.

Burri, Margret. 1982. *Germanische Mythologie zwischen Verdraengung und Verfaelschung*. Zurich: Schweizer Spiegel Verlag.

Busch, Robert H. 2000. *The Grizzly Almanac*. New York: Lyons Press.

Campbell, Joseph. 1991. *The Masks of God: Primitive Mythology*. New York: Arkana.

Cockrill, Pauline. 1992. *Das grosse Buch der Teddybaeren*. Munich: Mosaik.

Dehm, Richard. 1976. "Die Erpfinger Hoehle als Baerenhoehle." In *Die Baerenhoehle bei Erpfingen*, edited by Georg Wagner. Sonnenbuehl: Gemeinde Erpfingen.

Densmore, Frances. 1928. "Uses of Plants by the Chippewa Indians." In *Forty-fourth Annual Report of the Bureau of American Ethnology*. Washington, DC: U.S. Government Printing Office.

Devi, Phoolan. 1997. *I, Phoolan Devi: The Autobiography of India's Bandit Queen*. Sphere Publishers.

Duerr, Hans Peter. 1987. *Dreamtime*. Oxford: Blackwell.

Eliade, Mircea. 1981. *History of Religious Ideas*. 4 vols. Chicago: University of Chicago Press. Kindle edition.

Endroes, Hermann, and Alfred Weitnauer. 1990. *Allgaeuer Sagen*. Kempten: Allgaeuer Zeitungsverlag.

Fasching, Gerhard. 1994. *Sternbilder und ihre Mythen*. Vienna: Springer Verlag.

Findeisen, Hans. 1956. *Das Tier als Gott, Daemon und Ahne*. Stuttgart: Kosmos.

Friedrichs, Kurt. 1996. *Das Lexikon des Hinduismus*. Munich: Goldmann.

Garrett, J. T. 2003. *The Cherokee Herbal*. Rochester, VT: Inner Traditions.

Golowin, Sergius. 1986. *Baern im Baerenwald*. Berne: Loeb und der Bund.

Goodman, Felicitas. 2003. *Ecstatic Trance*. Rossdorf, Germany: Binkey Kok.

Grinnell, George Bird. 1923. *The Cheyenne Indians*. Lincoln and London: University of Nebraska Press.

Hauser, Albert. 1973. *Bauernregeln*. Zurich, Muenchen: Artemis.

Honoré, Pierre. 1997. *Das Buch der Altsteinzeit*. Munich: Goldmann.

Koenig, Karl. 2013. *Animals*. Edinburgh: Floris Books.

Kuckenburg, Martin. 1997. *Lag Eden im Neandertal?* Munich: Econ.

Kuenzle, Johann. 1977. *Chrut und Uchrut*. Verlag Kraeuterpfarrer Kuenzle: Minusio (CH).

Lame Deer, John, and Richard Erdoes. 1972. *Lame Deer: Seeker of Visions*. New York: Washington Square Press.

Lissner, Ivar. 1979. *So lebten die Voelker der Urzeit*. Munich: DTV.

Mauer, Kuno. 2002. *Das neue Indiander-Lexikon*. Munich: Langen Mueller.

Mayer, Regula. 2004. *Tierisch gut*. Uhlstaedt-Kirchhasel: Arun.

Meyer, Rudolf. 1988. *The Wisdom of Fairy Tales*. London: Rudolf Steiner Press.

Mills, Judy A. 2002. "Baeren als Haustiere, Nahrungs- und Heilmittel." In *Baeren*, edited by Ian Stirling. Munich: Orbis.

Mooney, James. 2011. "History, Myths, and Sacred Formulas of the Cherokees." In *Nineteenth Annual Report of the Bureau of American Ethnology*. Washington, DC: Smithsonian Institute. Kindle edition.

Mueller-Ebeling, Claudia, Christian Raetsch, and Surendra Bahadur Shahi. 2002. *Shamanism and Tantra in the Himalayas*. Rochester, VT: Inner Traditions.

Mueller-Ebeling, Claudia, Christian Raetsch, and Wolf-Dieter Storl. 2003. *Witchcraft Medicine*. Rochester, VT: Inner Traditions.

Nauwald, Nana. 2002. *Baerenkraft und Jaguarmedizin*. Aarau, Switzerland: AT Verlag.

Paeaebo (Pääbo), Svante. 2015. *Neanderthal Man: In Search of Lost Genomes*. New York: Basic Books.

Raetsch, Christian. 1991. *Von den Wurzeln der Kultur*. Basel: Sphinx.

Roehrich, Lutz. 2001. *Lexikon der sprichwoertichen Redensarten*. Vol 1. Freiburg, Basel, Vienna: Herder.

Sanders, Barry. 2002. "Anthropologie, Geschichte und Kultur." In *Baeren*, edited by Ian Stirling. Munich: Orbis.

Savage, Candice. 1990. *Grizzly Bears*. San Francisco: Sierra Club Books.

Schlesier, Karl H. 2013. *The Wolves of Heaven*. CreateSpace Independent Publishing Platform.

Schmitz, Rudolf. 1998. *Geschichte der Pharmazie*, Vol. I. Eschborn: Govi-Verlag.

Seattle. 1854. "How then can we be brothers?" Speech. http://www.halcyon.com/arborhts /chiefsea.html.

Sède, Gérard de. 1986. *Das Geheimnis der Goten*. Herrsching: Manfred Pawlak Verlagsgesellschaft.

Spence, Lewis. 1994. *North American Indians*. London: George G. Harrap.

Storl, Wolf D. 1974. *Shamanism Among Americans of European Origin*. Inaugural Dissertation, University of Berne, Switzerland.

_____. 2001. *Pflanzendevas*. Aarau, Switzerland: AT Verlag.

_____. 2004. *Shiva: The Wild God of Power and Ecstasy*. Rochester, VA: Inner Traditions.

Treben, Maria. 1982. *Health from God's Garden*. Steyr, Austria: Ennsthaler Publishers.

Vogel, Virgil. 1982. *American Indian Medicine*. Norman, OK: University of Oklahoma Press.

Volmar, Friedrich. 1940. *Das Baerenbuch*. Berne: Paul Haupt.

Weyer Jr., Edward. 1958. *Primitive Peoples Today*. Garden City, NY: Dolphin Books.

Witsen, Nicolaes. 1692. *Noord en Oost Tartarye, Ofte Bondig Ontwerp Van eenig dier Landen en Volken Welke voormaels bekent zijn geweest. Beneffens verscheide tot noch toe onbekende, en meest nooit voorheen beschreve Tartersche en Nabuurige Gewesten, Landstreeken, Steden, Rivieren, en Plaetzen, in de Noorder en Oosterlykste Gedeelten Van Asia En Europa Verdeelt in twee Stukken, Met der zelviger Land-kaerten: mitsgaders, onderscheide Afbeeldingen van Steden, Drachten, enz. Zedert naeuwkeurig onderzoek van veele Jaren, door eigen ondervondinge ontworpen, beschreven, geteekent, en in't licht gegeven*. Amsterdam.

Zerling, Clemens, and Wolfgang Bauer. 2003. *Lexikon der Tiersymbolik*. Munich: Koesel.

INDEX

ABOUT THE AUTHOR

Born in 1942 in Saxony, Germany, with a green thumb and the gift of writing, cultural anthropologist and ethnobotanist Wolf Dieter Storl, who immigrated with his parents to the United States in 1954, has had a special connection to nature since childhood. His specific area of research is shamanism and healing in traditional societies, focusing on the role of plants in all aspects of life, including sacred symbolism, magic, medicine, foods, and poisons. He has pursued this interest in many parts of the world. After finishing his PhD in anthropology on a Fulbright scholarship in 1974 in Berne, Switzerland, he taught anthropology and sociology in Grants Pass, Oregon.

Storl is also an avid traveler and has observed nature around the entire globe, spending time with people who are very connected to the nature that surrounds them. From 1982 to 1983, he spent a year as an official visiting scholar at the Benares Hindu University in Varanasi, India. After returning to the United States in 1984, he spent two years with traditional medicine persons of the Cheyenne and taught courses at Sheridan College in Sheridan, Wyoming. He has traveled and conducted research in South Asia, India, Mexico, the Canary Islands, South Africa, and much of Europe, pursuing ethnobotanical and ethnomedicinal interests. His books and articles have been translated into various languages, including Czech, Danish, Dutch, English, French, Italian, Japanese, Latvian, Polish, Portuguese, Spanish, and Russian. Storl is a frequent guest on German, Swiss, and Austrian television and has also appeared on the BBC. After another visit in India and Nepal in 1986, Storl and his wife moved to Germany, where he is writes and lectures. They live on an old estate with a large garden in the foothills of the Alps.

Storl's books are unique in that he does not treat nature with cold objectivism. He is able to delve into nature's depths and supports his experience with ancient lore from all over the world that has been, for the most part, left on the wayside in the wake of objective science. He theorizes that science is not always as objective as it claims to be and invites his readers on a journey into a world of nature that is completely alive and has its own rhyme and reason. Myths and lore from many cultures also have a prominent place in his writings, as he claims that the images portrayed in this way often tell us more about the true nature of things than dry, scientific facts can do.

ALSO BY WOLF D. STORL

available from North Atlantic Books

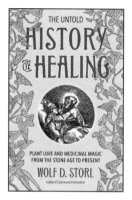

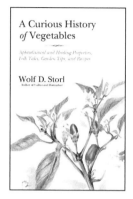

The Untold History
of Healing
978-1-62317-093-6

A Curious History
of Vegetables
978-1-62317-039-4

Culture and Horticulture
978-1-58394-550-6

The Herbal Lore of Wise
Women and Wortcunners
978-1-58394-358-8

Healing Lyme
Disease Naturally
978-1-55643-873-8

North Atlantic Books
www.northatlanticbooks.com

North Atlantic Books is an independent,
nonprofit publisher committed to a bold
exploration of the relationships between
mind, body, spirit, and nature.

About North Atlantic Books

North Atlantic Books (NAB) is an independent, nonprofit publisher committed to a bold exploration of the relationships between mind, body, spirit, and nature. Founded in 1974, NAB aims to nurture a holistic view of the arts, sciences, humanities, and healing. To make a donation or to learn more about our books, authors, events, and newsletter, please visit www.northatlanticbooks.com.

North Atlantic Books is the publishing arm of the Society for the Study of Native Arts and Sciences, a 501(c)(3) nonprofit educational organization that promotes cross-cultural perspectives linking scientific, social, and artistic fields. To learn how you can support us, please visit our website.